Introduction to Community Tourism

A North American Perspective

Samuel V. Lankford

Oksana Grybovych

Jill K. Lankford

SAGAMORE  VENTURE

Publishers: Joseph J. Bannon and Peter L. Bannon
Sales and Marketing Manager: Misti Gilles
Sales and Marketing Assistant: Kimberly Vecchio
Director of Development and Production: Susan M. Davis
Production Coordinator: Amy S. Dagit
Graphic Designer: Marissa Willison

Library of Congress Control Number: 2017947206
ISBN print edition: 978-1-57167-722-8
ISBN ebook: 978-1-57167-723-5

Printed in the United States.

SAGAMORE ◆◆ VENTURE

1807 N. Federal Dr.
Urbana, IL 61801
www.sagamorepublishing.com

This book is dedicated to the heart of community which, when tended,
is the essence of life and provides the vitality we enjoy
and share with others, residents and guests.

———————————————————————

Contents

Acknowledgments

Many people have influenced how we view tourism and the community. The journey to study tourism from a community perspective began with Dr. David Povey, professor emeritus at the University of Oregon. Working with David on community planning projects allowed Jill and Sam to discover the potential and pitfalls of community-based tourism. David, who worked with us on refining our skills and abilities with regard to community planning practice, provided us with a unique graduate education experience through Community Planning Workshop. David's involvement in recreation and tourism planning in Oregon has provided us with a model for teaching and working with students and our communities in which we have lived. A special thank you goes to Dr. Larry Neal, professor emeritus at the University of Oregon for his support over the years. Thanks are also given to Dr. George Ikeda, Dr. Pauline Sheldon, and Dr. Juanita Liu from the University of Hawaii. We would also like to thank Marlowe Campos, Simone Campos, Crystal Espinoza, and Selena Winchell from the Department of Recreation Administration at Fresno State for their assistance with the book. Sophie Karas of Fresno State also provided important library research for the book as well. Thanks also to Richard Harding, Director of Parks, Recreation and Environment, City of Nanaimo, British Columbia, for assistance and insight into community tourism and parks and recreation. Finally, Sam and Jill would like to thank Dr. Ariana Cela, Dr. Oksana Grybovych, Dr. Rodney Dieser, Dr. Chris Kowalski, Dr. Chris Edginton, Dr. Wade Kooiman, and Dr. Anthony Smothers of the University of Northern Iowa for their support over the years. What a great and accomplished group of professionals and visionaries! If only more communities had these leaders, we as a society would be in a better place. We feel blessed to have had the opportunity to work with all of them.

We would also like to recognize Dr. Joseph Bannon Sr. for his support for this book. It has taken longer than anticipated, but we do hope it is useful in teaching. We would also like to thank Susan Davis of Sagamore Publishing. Thank you for your assistance and professionalism! Finally, thank you to the faculty of the Department of Recreation Administration, specifically Dr. Michael Mahoney, Dr. Nancy Nisbett, Dr. Jason Whiting, Dr. L-J Fine, Brandon Taylor, Justin Butchert, Ryan Soares, Alex Clifton, Lerin Winchester, Karen Markland, and our Dean Jody Hironaka-Juteau at Fresno State for their support.

Sam Lankford
Jill Lankford

Above all I want to thank my family for the unconditional love, support, and encouragement, in spite of all the time I took away from you. My husband, Delmar, deserves special praise for spending hours brainstorming, reading, and editing my work. I couldn't have done it without you. A special thank you to Sam and Jill Lankford for your mentorship and support throughout the years. You are such a remarkable family.

Oksana Grybovych

About the Authors

Samuel V. Lankford is professor and chair, Department of Recreation Administration at Fresno State. Formerly he served as a professor, graduate coordinator, and doctoral intensive study area coordinator, and director of the Sustainable Tourism and the Environment Program at the University of Northern Iowa. He taught at the University of Hawaii in the School of Travel Industry Management, and was also the Coordinator of the Recreation and Leisure Science degree program from 1990-2001. He has conducted training workshops in the U.S., Canada, The Netherlands, Japan, and Vietnam. He has a PhD with a focus in community tourism planning and development, and a master of Urban and Regional Planning degree from the University of Oregon. He holds a master of arts in recreation and park planning and a BA in geography from CSU-Chico. Dr. Lankford has been a practicing planner in both staff and consulting roles in California, Oregon, Washington, Iowa, Hawaii, and Canada. He has conducted planning projects, needs assessments, community impact studies, carrying capacity studies, and market research in those states and other countries. He specializes in tourism and recreation development. His research in tourism resulted in the development of a scale titled "Tourism Impact Attitude Scale" (TIAS), which has been used extensively internationally, and was the basis for later research on that topic.

Oksana Grybovych is an associate professor in the Division of Leisure, Youth and Human Services at the University of Northern Iowa. She holds an EdD in Leisure Services from the University of Northern Iowa (USA), MSc in Leisure and Environments from the University of Wageningen (the Netherlands), and a BA in Economics/ Management from the Institute of Economics and Law (Ukraine). Her research interests include civic and community engagement, participatory community tourism planning, economic impacts of tourism, tourism marketing, and sustainable development.

Jill K. Lankford has worked with communities in their planning and design efforts with a particular focus on community character and development. Jill's work with planning and design with small towns has resulted in recognition by the American Planning Association–Oregon Chapter for citizen involvement and economic development. She has provided tourism development training in North America, Bolivia, and Vietnam. She has degrees in landscape architecture (BLA and MLA) from the University of Oregon. She was the coordinator of the Sustainable Tourism and Environment Program at the University of Hawaii and the University of Northern Iowa, where she completed community development projects with students for community and regional agencies and organizations. Jill continues her work in Fresno focusing on community-level park and recreation planning and water-wise design.

Preface

Introduction to Community Tourism: A North American Perspective addresses tourism at the community level within the United States and Canada. The purpose of the book is to illustrate the significance and potential of tourism at the community level. Our examples focus on the small to mid-sized examples. However, on occasion we provide examples of places outside of the U.S. and Canada. Importantly, the book illustrates the ways in which community tourism involves various departments and organizations involved in tourism. For example, numerous examples are given where the parks and recreation department for a community plays a pivotal role in helping to stage tourism events.

Most introductory textbooks on tourism address large scale tourism, often termed "mass tourism." Waikiki Hawaii is an example of this type of tourism. Those books typically focus on world and national organizations, air transportation, rail transportation, distribution process, hospitality, large-scale human-made attractions (e.g., Disneyworld), international travel, and supply and demand. *Introduction to Community Tourism: A North American Perspective* addresses tourism from a slightly different perspective. This perspective is one in which the trend toward understanding community within the context of tourism and the resulting development that occurs. Importantly, we address the organization of tourism within communities that lie outside of the mass tourism markets. There is a focus on main streets, architectural character, destination attributes, and the inventory and management of those attributes. Specific attention is given to sustainability of the community and industry, to include planning, development, and marketing. The book examines the dynamics between social or economic development and the quality of life for residents in those special places blessed with natural, historic, and cultural resources.

The chapters in this book provide learning objectives, examples of tourism in communities, and useful online resources for the reader. Four primary areas of importance to community tourism are covered. The first area addresses the characteristics to community tourism in North America, organizational structures typical to the success of community tourism, and the types of attractions inherent in community tourism. The second area of importance is travel motivation, marketing concepts, and business and entrepreneurship in community tourism. The third section of the book provides the reader with information on the community issues and planning concerns relative to a successful tourism based economy. Community main street strategies are highlighted for readers to appreciate the collaboration and partnerships that exist in successful tourism. This section also addresses special events and community main streets, and concludes with the economic impacts to community tourism. Finally, the fourth area addresses the possible careers for tourism at the community level, many of which are available to students in parks, recreation, and tourism programs. The book concludes with a discussion of tourism futures.

CHAPTER 1

Characteristics of Community-Based Tourism

CHAPTER OBJECTIVES

- To build an awareness and appreciation for community-based tourism
- To understand the factors that influence the development of successful community-based tourism programs
- To gain specific knowledge of the challenges for successful community-based tourism
- To gain knowledge of community tourism and its connections to local government
- To understand contemporary developments in community tourism

Introduction

This book addresses tourism at the community level within the United States and Canada. The purpose of the book is to illustrate the significance and potential of tourism at the community level. Our examples focus on small to mid-sized examples. However, on occasion we provide examples of places outside of the U.S. and Canada. Importantly, the book illustrates the ways in which community tourism involves various departments and organizations involved in tourism. For example, numerous examples are given in which the parks and recreation department for a community plays a pivotal role in helping to stage tourism events.

The travel industry's role in the American and Canadian economy is significant. The U.S. Travel Association (2014) estimates that in 2013, 69.8 billion international travelers visited the U.S., while U.S. residents logged 1.6 billion person trips for leisure, and 452 million person trips for business purposes. These trips were to destinations in all 50 states and Washington, D.C., with spending estimated to be $887.9 billion on goods and services at local businesses, generating 7.9 million jobs. In 2012, overall tourism demand grew 4.2% to $81.9 billion, with domestic demand registering a 4.5% increase to $66.4

billion. Likewise, international demand rose 2.8% to $15.5 billion (Canada Tourism Commission, 2013). Canada received 16 million international overnight visitors in 2012, up 1.7% over 2011. Spending by visitors increased 2.3% to $12.3 billion, as they stayed longer and spent more per trip (Canada Tourism Commission, 2013). A trend in tourism is for travelers to seek experiences in small towns, rural areas, and places that are outside of the mainstream ideas of what tourism is or should be in terms of scale and scope of the development.

Tourism and "the tourism industry" are rather illusive in terms of identification. It is important to understand the definitions in order for one to become aware of the significance and scope of the industry. These definitions also help one to understand the various economic impacts of the industry on local, regional, and national economies. The definition of travel refers to the activity of travelers. A traveler is someone who moves between different geographic locations, for any purpose and any duration (United Nations World Tourism Organization, 2010). These purposes can be for business or leisure. A visitor is a traveler taking a trip to a main destination outside his/her usual environment, for less than a year, for any main purpose (business, leisure, or other personal purpose) other than to be employed by a resident entity in the country or place visited. These trips taken by visitors qualify as tourism trips. Tourism refers to the activity of visitors (United Nations World Tourism Organization, 2010). The Canadian definition of tourism follows that adopted by the World Tourism Organization and the United Nations Statistical Commission: "the activities of persons traveling to and staying in places outside their usual environment for not more than one consecutive year for leisure, business and other purposes" (Canadian Tourism Commission, 2012). Tourism is therefore a subset of travel and visitors are a subset of travelers.

Components of the Tourism Industry

Figure 1.1 provides a simplified view of the necessary components of the tourism industry. There must be a market or attraction that can sustain visitor interest over time. Additionally, the community must be supportive and involved. Resident populations need education about the industry in order to have positive visitor and resident interactions. The government must work with the tourism organizations and supporters to create attractive places for visitors and the resident population. Roads and infrastructure needs to be in place to serve the transportation, water, sewer, and solid waste disposal needs of visitors. Finally, shopping, lodging, restaurants need to be prepared to serve a varying clientele.

Industry Groups in Community Tourism

The Ministry of Tourism and Culture in the Yukon Territory of Canada notes that there are five essential industry groups of the tourism sector (www.tc.gov.yk.ca, 2014). These groups provide community members opportunities for the creation of businesses and employment. These include the following:

1. **Accommodation:** hotels, motels, resorts, cabins, bed and breakfast, campgrounds, lodges, inns, RV parks, hostels, and the accommodation portion of hunting and fishing trips.
2. **Food and beverage services:** restaurants, dining rooms, coffee shops, fast food outlets, pubs, and catering.

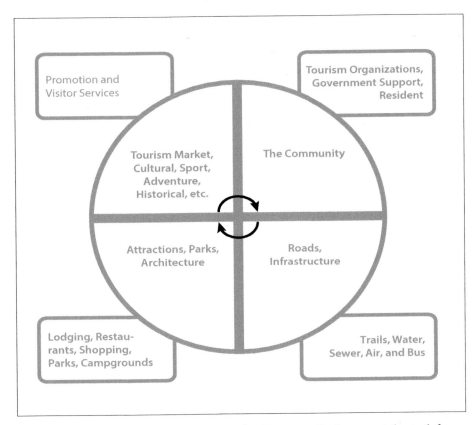

Figure 1.1. Necessary Components of a Tourism Industry. Adapted from University of Missouri, University Extension, (1991). Tourism USA, Guidelines for Tourism Development.

3. **Recreation and entertainment:** ski areas, golf, fishing and hunting, hiking, canoeing, kayaking, rafting and dog-sledding, arts and cultural festivals.
4. **Transportation:** air carriers, motor coaches, railways, cruise lines, car rentals, recreation vehicles, taxis, gas stations.
5. **Travel services:** travel agencies, tour wholesalers, tour operators, tour guides, government tourism departments and information centers, research services, advertising.

It is important to note that while businesses operate separately and competitively, they are dependent on each other for success. For example, the fishing or hunting guide needs the services of the transportation, food, travel, and accommodation sectors. Partnerships may develop between the fishing guide and other complementary companies such as a rafting guide company to enhance the visitor experience.

Community-Based Tourism

Community-based tourism is defined as a tourism or visitor industry organized by the community for its overall benefit. It sounds simple; however, community interests often conflict and the interpretation of overall benefits differ between individuals and groups. Russell (2000) notes that community-based tourism must fulfill three criteria:

It should have the support and participation of local people; as much of its economic benefit as possible should go to people living at or near the destination; and the act of tourism must protect local people's cultural identity and natural environment.

Murphy (1980) notes that community tourism as "an industry which uses the community as a resource, sells it as a product, and in the process, affects the lives of everyone" (p. 1). Murphy and Murphy (2004) later suggest that the community then no longer exists as a home with a communal sense of belonging, but has become an actual or potential profit-making center. This view in fact points out some of the concerns facing community leaders as they move toward tourism as an economic development strategy. Specifically, how does the community help develop a sustainable tourism product, yet keep a communal sense of belonging? We will discuss this in detail in the planning section of the book. In response to the issue, there has been an emergence of organizations and tourism trends such as ecotourism to involve local people in decision-making. The chapter on planning will detail some of these strategies.

Tourism, as the world's largest growing industry, is usually promoted by government for its ability to spread economic development and reduce inequalities in income distribution (Cela, Knowles-Lankford, & Lankford, 2007). Yet tourism is an elusive industry. As quoted by a well-intentioned mayor in a small Midwestern town "we know the tourists are out there, we just have to figure out how to get them into our town." This statement exemplifies what is taking place in communities across North America. When a community or region has resources such as lakes, rivers, oceans, and mountains it becomes an attraction that can be built upon if the community will exists and the investments are made. The town referenced above was some distance to that lake, had a rather odd (or unique depending on your perspective) character in terms of architectural resources, and a rather undeveloped tourist infrastructure. The town's claim to fame was that it was partly destroyed by a tornado decades before. The leaders of the community thought a tornado museum would provide the attraction. A tourism assessment, provided by planners from a regional university to the town, allowed the decision makers a chance to view realistically the chances of developing into a destination. Consequently, when these limitations were identified, the shift to something other than tourism for economic diversification was adopted.

Community leaders sometimes misunderstand the tourism industry and what is required for a destination to be successful. There are very successful tourism-based communities without these natural amenities, but they typically have a strong arts community and are part of a regional tourism framework. Other communities use food-based festivals as a way to enhance visitor spending (Cela et al., 2007; Emmons, 2001). There are many examples such as wine routes in Italy, Spain, Portugal, France, Australia, and California, or beer trails in Canada and Oregon. These are examples of food and beverage tourism. Food has become an increasingly important element in the tourism industry, and up to 25% of total tourist expenditures is accounted for by foods (Quan & Wang, 2004). Tourists are seeking authentic and unique experiences and the consumption of local food and beverages brings the tourist closer to the host culture (Plummer, Telfer, Hashimoto, & Summers 2005). Small festivals in areas with few attractions may be critical in retaining locals' discretionary spending and generating civic pride (Cela et al., 2007; Chhabra, Sills, & Cubbage, 2003; Sanders, 2005).

Tourism is thriving in rural and small towns, primarily due to the relationships the industry has built upon with city, county, and provincial governments. For example, in Cedar Falls, Iowa, the Tourism Office is managed as part of the Department of Leisure and Human Services. The tourism industry in Cedar Falls is reliant on city parks, public bike and walking trails, a public university with sports and art venues, and public camping areas. The responsibility of the Department of Leisure and Human Services is to sponsor and coordinate community events for tourism and to meet the needs of the resident population. However, this relationship is not as direct in places such as Waikiki Hawaii, San Francisco, and New York City. Yes, tourists visit those parks and attend special community events, but the tourism industry is well developed and sophisticated enough to manage those events. Saunders (2005) studied communities and the level of coordination with community organizations for successful festivals. Festival organizers in small, medium, and large communities in the study sample noted they coordinate with (in order of importance) local chambers of commerce, city government (parks, leisure departments), local businesses, nonprofit organizations (churches, schools, youth groups, clubs), and civic organizations.

Rural communities around the nation are facing population and economic decline. Rural populations have declined drastically, resulting in a loss of employment opportunities for younger people. Tourism is viewed as an economic diversification tool in part to stabilize out migration of young people from small towns.

According to a National Association of Governors report (NGA, 2003), rural economic development policies must build upon the strengths of rural America. Two of these strengths are close-knit communities and strong local business networks. Importantly, tourism relies on the close-knit fabric of the community and business networks. The livability and quality of life of rural areas is enhanced when there are numerous and diverse opportunities for participation in leisure and cultural activities, events, and programs. For example, Independence, Iowa utilized recreation development (e.g., public recreation, parks, festivals, trail development, campgrounds, tourism) to stimulate its economy and develop a sense of community. Independence is "... competing [economically] with some of the bigger cities in our state and we're starting with some of the good things we've always had and never thrown away—the beauty of the river, our history—and we are adding in everything from town celebrations to global Internet connections ... [the] kids have got good fun things to do all over town, and they're safe, too, because there's always a neighbor looking out for them" (Witt, 2011, p. 54).

Communities have capitalized on tourism in the following areas (Weaver & Wishard-Lambert, 1996). It is important to note the first three areas are often managed by park and recreation departments on a daily basis:

- Natural features such as open space and parks, lakes, mountains, streams, and caves
- Cultural and ethnic attractions such as antiques, art galleries, ethnic celebrations, and heritage areas
- Created events such as fairs, festivals, rodeos, running events, and tournaments

- Historic attractions such as battlefields, famous buildings, landmarks and sites
- Human-made attractions such as covered bridges, dams, shopping areas, and parks

Obstacles to Tourism Development

Smaller towns and rural areas are unique. They are fragile places, often unprepared for not only the sophisticated development pressure that tourism brings but also naive in terms of their capacity to sustain the industry. Some communities who have transitioned from resource extraction activities such as logging have struggled. One such community (unnamed to protect its identity) in the Pacific Northwest made a swift move to advertise tourism opportunities in a large metropolitan area newspaper. Tourists started coming for camping and vacation. However, the infrastructure was not in place, the training of former mill workers had not yet been implemented, signage for way finding was nonexistent and the story was predictable. People quit coming due to the lack of amenities. This did more long-term damage than the townspeople realized. Table 1.1 illustrates some of the challenges in developing the industry.

Table 1.1
Obstacles to Tourism Development

Obstacles	Descriptions
Underdeveloped Amenities	Limited means (funding, technical support, etc.) to develop and manage amenities like campgrounds, picnic areas, public spaces and gathering places. Tourism plans provide evidence of the opportunity to invest.
Competition	Towns and regions compete for the tourism dollar. In fact most tourists are seeking "thematic" experiences like museums, foods, history, etc. Cooperation is needed for successful development of the industry.
Lack of Understanding of Visitors	Elected officials and civic-minded citizens often lack an appreciation of marketing, research, visitor information systems and visitor motivations. Attractions are not developed to meet needs of visitors. People are not trained to be in a service industry.
Lack of Land Use Plans and Zoning	Urban sprawl, inappropriate architecture for the place, signage that has a "clutter" effect, loss of open space, lack of walking and bicycling services, and loss of the character of the place. This list can be expanded, but the point is without appropriate controls and guidance, a great place becomes a visitor nightmare and the area will decline in visitations. A sense of place is critical to success; we need not destroy what brings them there in the first place.

Table 1 (cont.)

Community Culture	Some places are willing to embrace the tourism industry when it is locally controlled and planned for by citizens. Some places continue to fight even a successful tourism industry due to impacts on quality of life. Additionally, impacts on indigenous peoples are real and must be accounted for in the process.

Importantly, community leaders must understand that tourism is a multidisciplinary industry. Viewpoints of residents, business interests, planners, architects, landscape architects, economists, geographers, and archaeologists to name a few, are needed. This occurs during a planning process. That process consists of assessing resources and amenities, determining market potential, creating business investment opportunities, designing places with the visitor in mind, creating attractive way finding and retail signage. Saunders (2005) identified challenges that small, medium, and large communities in Iowa face with regard to successful tourism events and festivals. These challenges include recruiting and training volunteers, lack of sponsorships and funding, keeping attractions affordable, marketing and promotion, and conducting visitor research.

Often, communities are in transition from resource extraction to service sector economies. However, these communities lack leaders who are attuned to the intricacies and challenges of tourism development. Furthermore, these communities may lack the planning experts who can help guide the development in order to protect the amenities that are attractions.

Process of Tourism Development—How the Industry Develops

Most communities in the United States and Canada are served by some type of tourism organization, such as the Eastern Iowa Tourism Association at a regional level, or Iowa Tourism at the state level. Communities, such as Nanaimo, British Columbia, which is served by the Visitor Centre, a part of the Nanaimo Economic Development Corporation. These organizations can provide assistance to communities and event organizers in terms of coordination, planning, marketing, and other technical assistance. It is also important that communities work together in developing tourism as an industry and not against each other. Later chapters will discuss both the organization of tourism coordination and planning and how a larger regional approach to tourism makes for successful tourism.

The organization of community-based tourism at the onset is often informal until the industry expands. Typically, as tourism activities grow in popularity in a community, the formation of a visitors and convention bureau, tourism office, or arrangements with the chamber of commerce occur. Weaver and Wishard-Lambert (1996) note that the structure is not as critical as its function, which follows a process acceptable to the community and should include developmental, marketing, and community educational strategies. Lewis and deLisle (2004) have provided a model of the way in which tourism develops at the community level (Figure 1.1). This model provides a sense of a timeline in the process. It would be beneficial for tourism supporters to understand the tourism development stage or level of their community tourism at a given moment and reflect upon earlier developmental stages. This allows for the formation of advisory groups, policy support and funding. Figure 1.2 outlines the stages in the tourism development process.

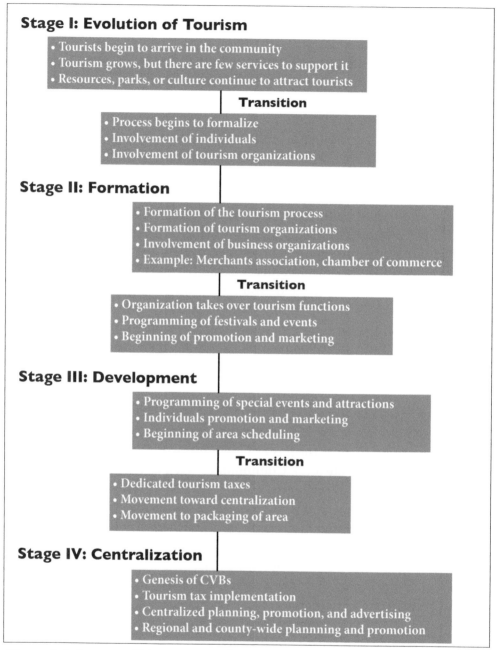

Stage I: Evolution of Tourism
- Tourists begin to arrive in the community
- Tourism grows, but there are few services to support it
- Resources, parks, or culture continue to attract tourists

Transition
- Process begins to formalize
- Involvement of individuals
- Involvement of tourism organizations

Stage II: Formation
- Formation of the tourism process
- Formation of tourism organizations
- Involvement of business organizations
- Example: Merchants association, chamber of commerce

Transition
- Organization takes over tourism functions
- Programming of festivals and events
- Beginning of promotion and marketing

Stage III: Development
- Programming of special events and attractions
- Individuals promotion and marketing
- Beginning of area scheduling

Transition
- Dedicated tourism taxes
- Movement toward centralization
- Movement to packaging of area

Stage IV: Centralization
- Genesis of CVBs
- Tourism tax implementation
- Centralized planning, promotion, and advertising
- Regional and county-wide plannning and promotion

Figure 1.2. Process of Tourism Development in Rural Communities

Factors of Success for Community Tourism

If a community has started the process of tourism development, a number of factors need to be considered. Research in Illinois revealed 10 factors of success for rural community-based tourism (Wilson, Fesenmaier, Fesenmaier, & Van Es, 2001). Table 1.2 presents these factors. In addition, Saunders (2005) tested these same factors and other items in Iowa by examining festivals and events in small, medium, and large communities (27 communities).

Table 1.2
Factors of Success for Rural Community Tourism and Festivals (In Order of Importance)

Wilson et al. (2001) Community Tourism	Saunders (2005) Festivals
A Complete Tourism Package	Widespread Community Support for Tourism and the Festival
Good Leadership	Volunteers
Support and Participation of Local Government	Festival Management
Sufficient Funds for Tourism Development	Coordination and Cooperation With Businesses
Strategic Planning	Sufficient Funding
Coordination and Cooperation between Businesses and Local Leadership	Support and Coordination from Local Government
Coordination and Cooperation between Rural tourism Entrepreneurs	Choice of Festival Activities
Information and Technical Assistance for Development and Promotion	Strategic Planning
Supportive Convention and Visitors Bureau	Supportive Convention and Visitors Bureau
Widespread Community Support for Tourism	Information and Technical Assistance
	Cooperation with Professionals
	Complete Tourism Package

Importantly, one can see that coordination, cooperation, community government, community support are the basis for successful community-based tourism and festivals. This list of factors may be a tool for communities in assessing their current position with regard to developing tourism. Wilson et al. (2001) defined success of community tourism as "a tourism attraction that has established an effective infrastructure to support tourism development." The authors also defined an unsuccessful tourism community as "one with substantial natural/cultural resources, but that has not established the economic, political, and community-based infrastructure necessary to support tourism development."

Stakeholders in Community-Based Tourism

The importance of building and maintaining partnerships in community tourism cannot be overstated. By communicating goals to partners, a community can gather more support (fiscal, technological, human resources) for the local industry. Balancing needs and desires is crucial in community tourism development. The extent to which the community decides to offer various visitor services and what impacts are acceptable requires involvement by the resident population. In community tourism, to the extent possible, policy actions are determined locally and collaboratively. Residents are central to the process. See Figure 1.3 for an example of the types of interests that are represented in community-based tourism.

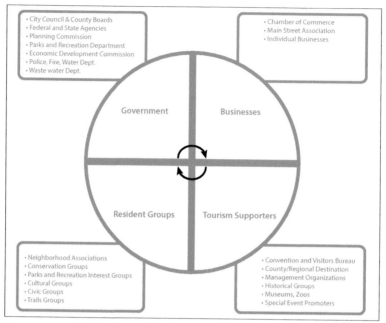

Figure 1.3. Community Stakeholders in Tourism

An example of the complex relationships in community tourism is Gros Morne National Park of Canada. There are eight communities within the park area which creates a need for the park administration to rely on stakeholders for assisting in a collaborative approach to problem solving, decision-making, and planning. The park administration works in collaboration with such groups as the tourism industry, environmental organizations, provincial and municipal governments, Aboriginal groups, and local operators to help improve the ecological integrity of the park and the regional ecosystem (Parks Canada, 2009).

The Gros Morne National Park of Canada Management Plan documents the park involvement in regional programs that take a comprehensive look at issues and involve all levels of the organization from technical staff to senior management. Table 1.3 presents the organizations and their interests and suggests collaboration and partnerships are crucial to community tourism success.

A study of tourism stakeholders representing city administrators, planners, recreation directors, and tourism and convention professionals sought to understand some of the perceptions of community tourism (Nelson, 2014; UNI STEP, 2013). Respondents represented 48 communities that were purposively sampled due to the nature of their tourism industry, which was community-based tourism. As one can see in Table 1.4, when the collective group of respondents were asked to identify benefits of tourism, improvement of the local economy, employment, and increased quality of recreational attractions were the viewed as the primary benefits. This finding further illustrates the importance of working with stakeholders in the establishment of tourism as a community economic strategy. The stakeholders not represented (conservation groups, tourists, residents, etc.) may have alternative but important views and opinions to be considered.

Table 1.3
Stakeholders in Community Tourism

Organization/ Stakeholders	Interests Addressed/Expertise Provided
Gros Morne Co-operating Association:	A nongovernmental, nonprofit association made up of volunteers dedicated to the promotion and interpretation of the values of national parks.
Mayors' Forum:	The intent of the forum is improved mutual understanding of each (the park and the eight adjacent communities) other's needs and constraints, and to support each other in achieving common goals within their respective mandates.
Aboriginal Partners:	Park staff members have developed many initiatives with our Aboriginal partners (Labrador Métis Nation, the Federation of Newfoundland Indians, Mi'kmaq, Innu and Inuit) that focus on the respectful conservation and presentation of their culture.
Sustainable Economic Development Partnerships:	Staff at Gros Morne take an active role in partnering with other agencies and organizations to promote local attractions to visiting tourists. These agencies and organizations include: • Red Ochre Regional Development Board • Hospitality Newfoundland and Labrador • Federal Joint Council • Western Destination Marketing Organization • Atlantic Canada Opportunities Agency
Third Parties:	Heritage preservation staff have worked directly with partners in the shared delivery of interpretive boat tours and sea kayaking excursions and training.
Educational Partners:	Educational partners include the Department of Education, school boards and local schools, Killdevil Camp, the Newfoundland and Labrador Teachers Association, Memorial University of Newfoundland, Sir Wilfred Grenfell College, and the College of the North Atlantic. This group represents an important opportunity to integrate Parks Canada's messages into the classrooms of Newfoundland and Labrador.
Gros Morne Institute for Sustainable Tourism:	Has a mandate to promote and train tourism industry members and other businesses, particularly in Atlantic Canada, toward effective, sustainable tourism practices. Its vision includes being recognized internationally as an innovator and leader in developing capacity for sustainable tourism; reaching a national audience, attracting participants from Atlantic Canada and Canada; and having Gros Morne and Atlantic Canada recognized as destinations committed to the improvement of sustainable tourism practices.

Table 1.4

Perceived Importance of Benefits of Tourism to Community

How important are the following tourism benefits to your community?	Very Important	Important	Not Important
Improvement of local economy	84.9%	15.1%	
Increased employment opportunities	66%	32.1%	1.9%
Improvement of quality of life	49.1%	50.9%	
Development of community pride	37.7%	60.4%	1.9%
Promotion of cultural exchange	30.2%	52.8%	17%
Preservation of cultural identity of host population	28.3%	50.9%	20.8%
Increased quality of attractions/recreational opportunities	56.6%	43.4%	

Source: UNI-STEP; 2012-2013 Community-Based Tourism Survey

Furthermore, the same study (see Table 1.5) found that various stakeholders collaborate to make a successful tourism industry. Not surprisingly, the visitor convention bureau always collaborates followed by the chamber of commerce. Of particular interest is that the parks and recreation department always or sometimes (97.3%) collaborates for community tourism. This finding suggests that the role of the local government is particularly important to support tourism efforts.

Table 1.5

Stakeholder Collaboration

Which stakeholders collaborate toward a successful visitor industry in your community?	Always Collaborate	Sometimes	Never
Parks and recreation	67.3%	30.8%	1.9%
Visitor convention bureau/visitor center/ tourism office	90.2%	7.8%	2%
Chamber of commerce	58.5%	34%	7.5%
Economic development authority	50%	37.5%	12.5%
Main street organization	42.2%	31.1%	26.7%
Community festival group	48%	38%	14%

Source: UNI-STEP; 2012-2013 Community-Based Tourism Survey

Summary

In this chapter we have examined tourism from a community approach. The size and breadth of the industry is vast. Research with regard to community tourism has grown over the last 25 years and covers a broad spectrum of topics. These include economic impacts, travel motivations, festival and event management, marketing, planning, and social and environmental impacts.

Tourism is thriving in rural and small towns. This is primarily due to the relationships the industry has built upon with city, county, and provincial governments. Obstacles to successful tourism development include lack of planning for the industry and community. Not knowing the visitor profile results in ill-timed messages or misguided marketing campaigns. Finally, community culture plays a role in acceptance of the tourism industry.

However, there are some success factors that we may be able to model tourism development after. These include packaging visitor experiences, having adequate and meaningful partnerships in place, and having widespread community support. The issue of widespread community support can be an obstacle as noted previously, but a thoughtful and balanced process of involvement will alleviate some or most of the concerns.

The process in which tourism grows in a rural and small town environment allows for stakeholders and authorities to slowly engage the industry. These phases include the evolution of the industry from first arrivals to the community to awareness of the community about the industry and the formation of organizations and processes. Tourism organizations emerge in leadership roles, with development of marketing programs and taxation programs following. Finally, a centralized tourism bureau or visitor bureau emerges.

Community-based tourism differs from other forms of tourism. Community-based tourism infers planning, coordination, and management of a visitor industry in a community by diverse stakeholders. These include government, associations, resident groups, businesses, and entrepreneurs.

Key Concepts

- Community-based tourism
- Obstacles to tourism development
- Process of tourism development
- Success factors for tourism and festivals
- Tourism
- Tourist
- Travel

Useful Internet Sites, Exercises, and Resources

Exercise 1

Visit the following website and examine the tools to develop and promote tourism. Then watch the Youtube segment on Gros Morne National Park and how the community works with the National Park Service of Canada. Then visit the Gros Morne Sustainable Tourism Institute for more details. Compare and contrast the U.S. Travel website toolkits for tourism development.

http://en-corporate.canada.travel/resources-industry/tools
http://www.youtube.com/watch?v=tERWqD7e-dU
http://www.gmist.ca/tools-resources/
http://www.ustravel.org/news/toolkits

Exercise 2

Visit the Canada Travel website and the U.S. Travel website to examine the research publications.

http://en-corporate.canada.travel/about-ctc
http://www.ustravel.org/

Questions for Review and Case Problems

1. Identify the obstacles of tourism development in your home town or area.
2. What factors of success for tourism are prevalent in your home town or area?
3. Can you identify the process/phases of tourism development in your home town or area?
4. What makes community-based tourism unique?
5. Find a community in which tourism is coordinated by or supported by the leisure services, parks and recreation department. What functions does the department fill, and what other organizations are active in tourism development and management?

References

Canadian Tourism Commission. (2011). Destination Canada welcomes eight new directors. Retrieved from http://en-corporate.canada.travel/sites/default/files/pdf/Research/Stats-figures/Year-in-review-facts-figures/Tourism%20Snapshot%20-%20Year%20in%20review/2011_year-in-review_en.pdf

Canadian Tourism Commission. (2012). Tourism in Canada. Retrieved from http://en-corporate.canada.travel/research/glossary

Canadian Tourism Commission. (2013). Tourism snapshot 2012 year-in-review. Retrieved from http://en-corporate.canada.travel/sites/default/files/pdf/Research/Stats-figures/Year-in-review-facts-figures/Tourism%20Snapshot%20-%20Year%20in%20review/2012_year-in-review_en.pdf

Cela, A., Knowles-Lankford, J., & Lankford, S. (2007). Local food festivals in Northeast Iowa communities: A visitor and economic impact study. *Managing Leisure, 12*(2 & 3), 171–186.

Chhabra, D., Sills, E., & Cubbage, F. W. (2003). The significance of festivals to rural economies: Estimating the economic impacts of Scottish Highland games in North Carolina. *Journal of Travel Research, 41*(May), 421–427.

Ministry of Tourism and Culture, Yukon Territory, Canada. (2014). The big picture. Retrieved from www.tc.gov.yk.ca

Murphy, P. (1980). Tourism management in host communities. *The Canadian Geographer, 24*(1), 1–2.

Murphy, P. E., & Murphy, A. E. (2004). *Strategic management for tourism communities: Bridging gaps.* Buffalo, NY: Channel View Publications.

Nelson, M. (2014). *Characteristics of community-based tourism practices: A stakeholder perspective.* MA Research Paper. University of Northern Iowa.

Parks Canada. (2009). Gros Morne National Park of Canada Management Plan. Retrieved from http://www.pc.gc.ca/pn-np/nl/grosmorne/plan.aspx

Quan, S., & Wang, R. (2004). Towards a structural model of the tourist Experience: An illustration from food experiences in food tourism. *Tourism Management, 25*(3), 297–305.

Russell, P. (2000). Community-based tourism: Institutional and organizational challenges. Unpublished report prepared for the Land and Agriculture Policy Centre, Johannesburg.

Saunders, K. (2005). Factors of success in Northeast Iowa community festivals. MA Thesis, University of Northern Iowa, pp. 64.

United Nations World Tourism Organization. (2010). Tourism statistics. Retrieved from http://unstats.un.org/unsd/tradeserv/Workshops/Chisinau/docs/05%20a%20 -%20UNWTO-Basis%20concepts.pdf

UNI STEP. (2013). Community-based tourism study. Retrieved from www.uni.edu/step

U.S. Travel Association. (2014). U.S. travel answer sheet. Retrieved from https://www. ustravel.org/sites/default/files/page/2009/09/US_Travel_AnswerSheet_June_2014. pdf, June 7, 2015.

Weaver, G., & Wishard-Lambert, V. (1996). Community tourism development: An opportunity for park and recreation departments. *Parks & Recreation, 31*(9), 81–107.

Wilson, S., Fesenmaier, D. R., Fesenmaier, J., & Van Es, J. C. (2001). Factors for success in rural tourism development. *Journal of Travel Research, 40*, 132–138.

CHAPTER 2

Organization of Community-Based Tourism

CHAPTER OBJECTIVES

- To build an awareness and appreciation for the organization of community-based tourism
- To understand the factors that influence organizing community-based tourism offices
- To gain specific knowledge of the challenges for developing organizations for community-based tourism
- To gain knowledge of international, national, state and provincial tourism authorities and its connections to local government efforts to promote tourism
- To understand contemporary examples of community-based tourism organizational models currently in practice

Introduction

This chapter presents various models currently used in community-based tourism. While some information is presented on the numerous national and international organizations, the main focus of this chapter is on community. Therefore, some examples of provincial, territorial, state, and regional tourism organizations are discussed. Although many organizations could be presented in this chapter, only a select few are outlined, based on their importance and influence.

International Organizations

World Tourism Organization

The World Tourism Organization (UNWTO) is the United Nations agency responsible for the promotion of responsible, sustainable, and universally accessible tourism. The UNWTO promotes tourism as a driver of economic growth, inclusive development, and environmental sustainability and offers leadership and support to the sector in advancing knowledge and tourism policies worldwide. The UNWTO encourages the implementation of the Global Code of Ethics for Tourism, to maximize tourism's socioeconomic contribution while minimizing its possible negative impacts, and is committed to promoting tourism as an instrument in achieving the United Nations Millennium Development Goals (MDGs), geared toward reducing poverty and fostering sustainable development. Research is also produced regarding markets, competition, education, and training, and technical assistance to countries. There are 155 member countries.

World Travel and Tourism Council (WTTC)

The WTTC believes in the right of people to cross international borders efficiently for leisure or business travel purposes without compromising national security. Despite an increasing number of visa waiver programs around the world, many individuals still find it too difficult to enter certain countries as international travelers. WTTC's ongoing focus is visa facilitation, convincing governments of the huge economic advantages generated by visa policies that encourage inbound visitors.

The WTTC also campaigns for governments to implement policies that ensure the business environment is conducive to the growth of travel and tourism. This means planning and investing in appropriate infrastructure and creating a tax system that allows the private sector to be competitive. The WTTC has a priority to raise awareness of the negative impact punitive taxation has—particularly aviation tax—on inbound and outbound tourism. Specifically, the WTTC promotes sustainable tourism through an awards and recognition program.

Global Travel Association Coalition (GTAC)

The Global Travel Association Coalition (GTAC) exists to promote a better understanding of travel and tourism's role as a driver of economic growth and employment. It encourages governments to develop policies that contribute to the profitable, sustainable, and long-term growth of the industry. The GTAC is comprised of the Airports Council International (ACI), the Cruise Line International Association (CLIA), the International Air Transport Association (IATA), the International Civil Aviation Organization (ICAO), the Pacific Asia Travel Association (PATA), the World Economic Forum (WEF), the World Tourism Organization (UNWTO), and the World Travel and Tourism Council (WTTC).

National Organizations

United States National Organizations

In the United States, there are numerous departments at the federal level that in some part address and impact tourism policy. The range of organizations does, in fact, cause some confusion for the local community supporters of tourism. In fact, many argue there is no coherent policy or structure in the United States at the federal level. Later in this chapter, the Canadian system will be presented for comparative purposes.

Table 2.1

Lead Tourism Agencies within the U.S. Federal System

GOALS AND STRATEGIES WITH LEAD AGENCIES	
Increase U.S. travel and tourism exports and encourage Americans to travel within the United States and its territories.	
Provide a Welcoming Entry Experience to Foreign Visitors	Department of State
	Department of Homeland Security
	Department of Commerce
Coordinate with Brand USA and Leverage Partnerships	Department of Commerce
Enhance Federal Promotional Efforts	Department of Commerce
	Department of the Interior
Provide User-Friendly Planning Tools and Resources	Department of the Agriculture
	Department of the Interior
Reduce barriers to trade and make it safer and more efficient for visitors to enter and travel within the United States and its territories.	
Lower Barriers to Trade in Travel Services and Increase Travel Flows	Department of Commerce
	The Office of the U.S. Trade Representative
Streamline the Visa Application Process	The Department of State
	The Department of Homeland Security
Expand the Visa Application Process	The Department of State
	The Department of Homeland Security
Improve Customer Service at Ports of Entry	Department of Homeland Security
Enhance Airport Screening	Department of Homeland Security
Maintain and Improve Transportation Infrastructure	Department of Transportation
Provide a high-quality visitor experience for U.S. and international visitors to achieve high customer satisfaction and inspire repeat visits.	
Improve Visitor Services at Federally Managed Sites	The Department of Interior
	Department of Agriculture
	Department of Defense/ Army Corps of Engineers
	The Department of Commerce/ National Oceanic and Atmospheric Administration
Foster a Skilled Hospitality and Tourism Industry Workforce	The Department of Labor
Support Small Business in Travel and Tourism	Small Business Administration

Table 2.1 (cont.)

Prioritize and coordinate support for travel and tourism across the federal government.	
Emphasize Travel and Tourism as a U.S. Government Priority	The Department of Commerce
	Department of Interior
Support Tourism Development	Department of Transportation
	Department of the Interior
Collect and analyze data to support decision-making in the public and private sectors and allow the Federal government to better measure the effectiveness of its efforts to increase travel and tourism.	
Conduct Research	The Department of Commerce
Monitor and Evaluate Results	The Department of Commerce

Source: Office of Travel and Tourism Industries. (2012). National Travel and Tourism Strategy: Task Force on Travel and Competitiveness, U.S. Department of Commerce. Retrieved from http://tinet.ita.doc.gov/pdf/national-travel-and-tourism-strategy.pdf

The Office of Travel and Tourism Industries

Under the U.S. Department of Commerce, within the International Trade Administration for Manufacturing and Services, the Office of Travel and Tourism Industries (OTTI) is located. The goal of the OTTI is to enhance the international competitiveness of the U.S. travel and tourism industry and increase its exports, thereby creating U.S. employment and economic growth. The primary functions of the OTTI are as follows (National Travel and Tourism Office, n.d.):

- Management of the travel and tourism statistical system for assessing the economic contribution of the industry and providing the sole source for characteristic statistics on international travel to and from the United States
- Design and administration of export expansion activities
- Development and management of tourism policy, strategy and advocacy
- Technical assistance for expanding this key export (international tourism) and assisting in domestic economic development

The OTTI plays an active role in domestic and international policy issues related to the U.S. travel and tourism industry. The OTTI fosters the development of policies that encourage the growth of travel and tourism to the United States as follows (OTTI, n.d.):

- Promotes the growth of U.S. travel exports through bilateral agreements with countries of strategic importance, including the Memorandum of Understanding with China on group leisure travel
- Represents U.S. tourism interests in intergovernmental organizations to lead the global efforts for travel and tourism policy concerns and issues, including chairing the Tourism Committee for the Organization for Economic Cooperation and Development (www.oecd.org)
- Serves as the Secretariat for the interagency Tourism Policy Council, ensuring that the nation's travel and tourism interests are considered in federal decision-

making. More than 18 agencies and offices of the government participate in this Council

- Serves as the USG official head delegate to the Asia Pacific Economic Cooperation (APEC) Tourism Working Group (www.apec.org)
- Serves as the official U.S. government observer and participant on committees and activities of the United Nations World Tourism Organization

United States Travel and Tourism Advisory Board

There is also an advisory board within the U.S. Department of Commerce titled United States Travel and Tourism Advisory Board. The authority for the board comes from the Secretary of Commerce, which renews the United States Travel and Tourism Advisory Board (Board), pursuant to Commerce's authority under 15 U.S.C. 1512, established under the Federal Advisory Committee Act (FACA), as amended, 5 U.S.C. App. and with the concurrence of the General Services Administration. The objectives and scope of the board's activities primarily provide advice for the secretary on matters relating to the U.S. travel and tourism industry. The board acts as a liaison among the stakeholders represented by the membership and provides a forum for those stakeholders on current and emerging issues in the travel and tourism industry, ensuring regular contact between the government and the U.S. travel and tourism industry. The International Trade Administration of the U.S. Department of Commerce provides administrative and staff services, support, and facilities for the board, which has an annual operating cost for the board at about $160,000, which includes 1.3 person years of staff support. Members of the board are not be compensated for their services or reimbursed for their travel expenses.

The board consists of no more than 32 members appointed by the secretary. Members represent companies and organizations in the travel and tourism sector from a broad range of products and services, company sizes, and geographic locations and are drawn from large, medium, and small travel and tourism companies, private-sector organizations involved in the export of travel and tourism-related products and services, and other tourism-related entities. Members of the board are selected, in accordance with applicable Department of Commerce guidelines, based on their ability to carry out the objectives of the board as set forth above and in a manner that ensures that the board is balanced in terms of points of view, industry subsector, demographics, geography, and company size. Importantly, members serve in a representative capacity, representing the views and interests of their particular business sector, and not as Special Government employees. The secretaries of Homeland Security, the Interior, State and Transportation (or their designees) serve on the board as ex officio, nonvoting members. Other than these ex officio members, the board members are not full-time federal officers or employees (Department of Commerce, n.d.).

U.S. Travel Association (USTA)

The U.S. Travel Association (USTA) is the national, nonprofit organization representing all components of the travel industry. The USTA notes tourism in the U.S. generates $2.1 trillion in economic output and supports 14.9 million jobs (United States Travel Association, 2017).

The USTA's mission is to increase travel to and within the United States. The vision statement notes that "U.S. Travel is the leading force that grows and sustains travel and protects the freedom to travel. Efforts are focused on achieving a shared vision for the industry. Travel is understood as essential to the economy, American jobs, security, image and well-being of the U.S. and travelers." Priorities include conducting research and communicating the impact of travel; enhancing and leveraging influence in the policy arenas, engaging and informing the industry and removing barriers to the travel industry. There are more than 1,300 member organizations with membership representing travel service providers, destinations, allied and affiliate organizations and travel associations (https://www.ustravel.org/answersheet).

Canadian National Organizations

Destination Canada

Destination Canada is Canada's national tourism marketing organization. A federal Crown corporation of the Government of Canada, Destination Canada markets Canada as a four-season tourism destination. They provide a consistent voice for Canada in the international tourism marketplace. They work in collaboration with the Canadian private sector, international travel trade, meeting professionals, and the governments of Canada, the provinces and the territories to position Canada as a destination. The marketing focuses on selected countries: Australia, Brazil, China, France, Germany, India, Japan, Mexico, South Korea, the UK, and the United States. Market research is also provided through their offices. Assistance is provided to Canada's small and medium-sized tourism enterprises (SMEs) to deliver tourism experiences.

Canadian Tourism Commission

The Canadian Tourism Commission has considerable influence and independence in the promotion and management of tourism from a federal perspective. A Crown corporation that is wholly owned by the Government of Canada, the Commission reports to Parliament through the Minister of Industry. The legislated mandate is to do the following:

- Sustain a vibrant and profitable Canadian tourism industry
- Market Canada as a desirable tourism destination
- Support a cooperative relationship between the private sector and the governments of Canada, the provinces, and the territories with respect to Canadian tourism
- Provide information about Canadian tourism to the private sector and to the governments of Canada, the provinces and the territories

The mission, according to the Commission, is to "harness Canada's collective voice to grow tourism export revenues." Among the primary activities of the Commission is to provide advertising to influence demand for Canada as a vacation destination. Utilizing an integrated advertising campaign using broadcast, social media, newspapers, magazines, and out of home, which includes billboards, e-marketing, and database marketing. Advertising and marketing campaigns are run in partnership with key private and public sector tourism partners.

In addition, the Commission provides public relations activities aimed to develop key relationships with international media to influence a high level of positive coverage about Canada. Key activities, such as organized experiential travel for international media, plus access to broadcast quality video, images, and information, are used to highlight positive stories about Canada. The engagement with international journalists is facilitated through the CTC Media Centre (Destination Canada, 2015).

The Commission actively engages international travel agents and tour operators regarding Canadian products. The goal is to influence tour operators to include Canada in their sales offerings in competition with other destinations around the world. In addition, there is a focus on meetings, conventions and incentive travel through the "Business Events Canada" program. The aim is to generate positive economic impact at the local level and increase international tourism revenue. Furthermore, the Commission is heavily invested in social media, with photos, stories, and videos on Facebook, Twitter, YouTube, and Flickr.

Finally, the research program provides relevant and practice-based studies to assist communities and businesses strategically place their tourism development programs. The range of research products can be viewed at http://en-corporate.canada.travel/research.

Tourism Industry Association of Canada (TIAC)

The Tourism Industry Association of Canada (TIAC) parallels the United States Office of Travel and Tourism Industries. Founded in 1930, the TIAC is the only national organization representing the full cross-section of Canada's $78.8 billion tourism industry. TIAC's members include air and passenger rail services, airport authorities, local and provincial destination authorities, hotels, attractions, and tour operators. TIAC is responsible for representing tourism interests at the national level, and its advocacy work involves promoting and supporting policies, programs and activities that will benefit the sector's growth and development. TIAC's membership reflects partnerships among all sectors of the industry, enabling the association to address the full range of issues facing Canadian tourism. TIAC's membership is diverse (Tourism Industry Association of Canada, n.d.):

- Over 300 members and thousands of affiliate members from coast to coast to coast
- Over 1.6 million Canadians whose jobs depend on the economic activity generated by travel and tourism
- Large national and multinational companies as well as small and medium-sized enterprises
- Airports, attractions, concert halls, convention centers, duty-free shops, festivals and events, restaurants and food services, arenas, transportation, travel services, travel trades, destination and provincial/territorial marketing organizations, suppliers, travel media, and educational institutions.

Other Tourism Associations in Canada

Canadian Association of Tour Operators (CATO)

The Canadian Association of Tour Operators (CATO) represents respected companies with offices in Canada, operating tour programs and packages from Canada to international destinations, trans-border, as well as overseas. The association is composed of outbound tour companies, represented by their owners and senior executives who speak not only for their respective companies, but for the industry. Associate (nonvoting) membership is also offered to smaller Canadian tour operators. In addition, Travel Service Suppliers and Destination Tourism Authorities or other interested organizations may apply to join CATO as supporting members. In addition, the association co-operates and maintains relations with other similar associations or organizations in Canada and other countries.

The mandate of the association is as follows (Canadian Association of Tour Operators, 2017):

1. To consider and act on behalf of tour operators with offices in Canada on all matters which the Association considers to be of mutual interest to or affect the trade of tour operators conducting business in Canada.
2. To provide a voice on behalf of all tour operators in dealing with all levels of government in Canada and abroad, in all destination markets.
3. To work within the tour operator industry and with governments at all levels in Canada to provide the travelling public with the greatest practicable financial protection at the lowest cost, against the financial failure of any travel service supplier organization which has received funds from the travelling public for services that have not yet been rendered.
4. To provide tour operator input to regulatory bodies in all provinces and at the federal level, to encourage and promote inter-provincial and national harmonization of travel industry regulations and legislation.
5. To establish a communications network for members to convey information valuable to the members and the industry.

Canadian Tourism Human Resource Council (CTHRC)

Established in 1993 as a national nonprofit organization, the Canadian Tourism Human Resource Council (CTHRC) addresses labor market issues and promotes professionalism in the Canadian tourism sector. Collectively, council members work on behalf of 174,000 businesses that make up the sector. The CTHRC brings together tourism businesses, labor unions, associations, educators, and governments to coordinate human resource development activities in support of a globally competitive and sustainable Canadian tourism sector.

The council undertakes various initiatives to capture, document and disseminate Labor Market Information (LMI) and other research to the tourism sector. The CTHRC conducts research to assist employers, educators, researchers, and job seekers in understanding the workforce dynamics operating in the tourism sector. Research includes the demographics of the tourism workforce, compensation, and benefits practices of businesses, projected labor supply and demand requirements.

Skills training, upgrading and certification are a part of the Council's mission. They are addressed through the emerit Tourism Training brand. With more than 50 National Occupational Standards, occupation-specific training in paper-based and online versions, human resources tools for employers, and professional certification, emerit is a comprehensive industry developed training program. Constituencies include business, workers, national industry associations, education, national and provincial tourism authorities, government, and one organization in each province or territory concerned with tourism labor market issues (Tourism HR Canada, n.d.).

Hotel Association of Canada (HAC)

The Hotel Association of Canada (HAC) advocates on behalf of the lodging industry to build a favorable business climate and influence policies. They offer member engagements, government advocacy, and the provision of value-added programs and services. The HAC network is over 8,000 strong and encompasses hotel companies, hotels, resorts, provincial and international lodging associations, industry suppliers, educators and students (Hotel Association of Canada, n.d.).

Parks Canada

Parks Canada holdings provide significant tourism resources and tourist opportunities for the promotion of tourism in Canada. Parks Canada's mandate is to "protect and present nationally significant examples of Canada's natural and cultural heritage and foster public understanding, appreciation, and enjoyment in ways that ensure their ecological and commemorative integrity for present and future generations." Parks Canada also provides tourism guides and information (Parks Canada, 2017).

State, Province, and Regional Organizations and Associations

In the United States, all states have a tourism department, office, or bureau. Typically, these entities provide or pay for research on the visitor market for the state. Ad campaigns are central to these entities as well. Travel and tourism state and territory office listings are provided at a federal website (http://www.usa.gov/Citizen/Topics/Travel-Tourism/State-Tourism.shtml). The following table provides the state and the title of the entity. Note the variations in the names of the tourism offices for both the U.S. (Table 2.2) and Canada (Table 2.3).

Table 2.2
U.S. State and Travel Office Name(s)

State	Title of Tourism Office
Alabama	Bureau of Tourism and Travel
Alaska	Department of Commerce, Community & Economic Development Division of Economic Development: Tourism Development and Marketing

Table 2.2 (cont.)

Arizona	Arizona Highways Online Office of Tourism: Arizona Guide
Arkansas	Department of Parks and Tourism
California	Division of Tourism: California Travel and Tourism
Colorado	Colorado Tourism Office
Connecticut	Department of Economic and Community Development Offices of Culture and Tourism
Delaware	Tourism Office: Visit Delaware
Florida	Florida Commission on Tourism
Hawaii	Department of Business, Economic Development, and Tourism
Idaho	Idaho Travel and Tourism Guide
Illinois	Illinois Bureau of Tourism
Indiana	Office of Tourism Development
Iowa	Iowa Travel/Tourism
Kansas	Department of Travel and Tourism
Kentucky	Kentucky Travel and Tourism
Louisiana	Department of Culture, Recreation, and Tourism
Maine	Office of Tourism
Maryland	Office of Tourism Development
Massachusetts	Office of Travel and Tourism
Minnesota	Department of Trade and Economic Development: Office of Tourism
Mississippi	Mississippi Division of Tourism
Missouri	Division of Tourism
Montana	Travel Montana
Nebraska	Nebraska Tourism Office
Nevada	Nevada Commission on Tourism
New Hampshire	Division of Travel and Tourism Development
New Jersey	Travel and Tourism
New Mexico	New Mexico Tourism Department
New York	Department of Economic Development: Tourism
North Carolina	Tourism Department of Commerce
North Dakota	Department of Tourism
Ohio	Division of Travel and Tourism
Oklahoma	Oklahoma Tourism and Recreation Department
Oregon	Oregon Tourism Commissions office

Table 2.2 (cont.)

Pennsylvania	Department of Community and Economic Development Tourism
Rhode Island	Rhode Island Travel Guide
South Carolina	Department of Parks, Recreation, and Tourism
South Dakota	Department of Tourism
Tennessee	Department of Tourist Development
Texas	Texas Tourism
Utah	Utah Office of Tourism
Vermont	Department of Tourism and Marketing Department of Tourism and Marketing: *Vermont Life* Magazine
Virginia	Virginia Tourism Corporation
Washington	Washington State Tourism
West Virginia	Division of Tourism
Wisconsin	Wisconsin Department of Tourism
Wyoming	Wyoming Tourism

Table 2.3
Canadian Provincial and Territorial Tourism Offices

Province/Territory	Title of Tourism Office
Alberta	Travel Alberta
British Columbia	Tourism British Columbia
Manitoba	Travel Manitoba
New Brunswick	Tourism, Heritage, and Culture
Newfoundland and Labrador	Newfoundland and Labrador Tourism
Southwest Territories	Tourism Northwest Territories
Nova Scotia	Nova Scotia Tourism Agency
Nunavut	Tourism
Ontario	Marketing Partnership Corporation
Prince Edward Island	Department of Economic Development and Tourism
Québec	Tourisme Quebec
Saskatchewan	Tourism Saskatchewan
Yukon	Department of Tourism and Culture

Source: Visit Canada (2017)

Example organizational charts for the Northwest Territory and the Province of Manitoba are found in Figure 2.1 and Figure 2.2. It is interesting to note the unique emphasis, yet both use culture in the approach to developing tourism and tourism markets.

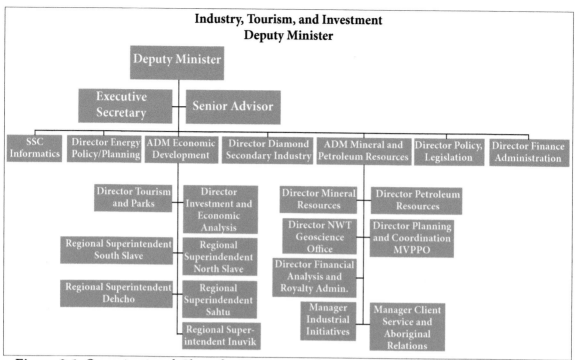

Figure 2.1. Organizational Chart for Tourism in the Northwest Territories, Canada.

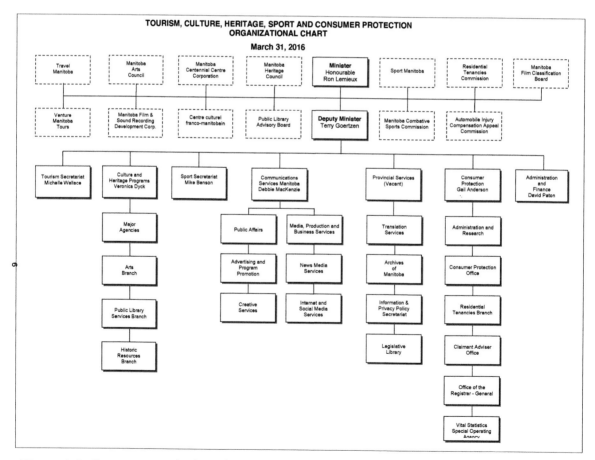

Figure 2.2. Organizational Chart for Tourism in Manitoba, Canada.

Case in POINT

The Travel Industry Council of Ontario (TICO) is a self-managed, nonprofit corporation, responsible for administration and enforcement of the Ontario *Travel Industry Act, 2002* and Ontario Regulation 26/05 on behalf of the Ontario government. The legislation governs all of the approximately 2,500 travel retailers and travel wholesalers registered in Ontario. In addition, TICO administers an industry-financed Travel Compensation Fund.

TICO was established in 1997 as a delegated administrative authority under the *Safety and Consumer Statutes Administration Act*, as a result of the mutual desire of the government and the travel industry to enhance professionalism, increase consumer protection and provide an effective and efficient regulatory body. The Ministry of Consumer Services continues to be responsible for the *Ontario Travel Industry Act, 2002* and Ontario Regulation 26/05 as well as general oversight of TICO.

TICO is a wholly financed by registration fees paid by Ontario travel agencies and travel wholesalers. The Travel Industry Compensation Fund is financed entirely by Ontario travel industry registrants through contributions based on their sales revenues.

TICO has its own board of directors and chief executive officer and manages its own financial and operational affairs. The CEO is also registrar of the *Travel Industry Act, 2002*. TICO's 15-member board of directors consists of 10 industry representatives and five ministerial appointees.

The Travel Industry Council of Ontario's mission is to promote a fair and informed marketplace where consumers can be confident in their travel purchases. They support the mission of the Ontario Ministry of Consumer Services to maintain a fair, safe, and informed marketplace as it relates to Ontario's *Travel Industry Act, 2002*. They accomplish this through developing high standards and efficient, effective, and relevant regulatory mechanisms in areas such as the following:

- Consumer protection
- Consumer education and awareness
- Registration, inspection, supervision and discipline of registrants
- Investigating and mediating disputes between consumers and registrants

TICO has set up programs to support its mandate that aims to promote fair and ethical competition in the industry, support a code of ethics, maintain and enforce programs that provide for consumer compensation in specific circumstances, promote an expected level of education as a criterion for registration, and encourage legislative and regulatory amendments aimed at industry professionalism and consumer confidence. In carrying out its mandate and initiatives, TICO works with stakeholder groups, including the following:

- **Consumers**—to increase awareness of their rights and responsibilities under the Ontario *Travel Industry Act, 2002*
- **Registrants and industry associations**—to harness their knowledge and commitment to ethical and open competition

Community-Based Tourism Organizations

This section presents selected examples of the organization of tourism at the community level. To provide a framework, and as presented in Chapter 1, Figure 2.3 displays a simplified model of the various components of the tourism industry. As one can appreciate, there are interconnected and separate organizations that work to provide a coordinated set of tourist experiences. The items listed within the circle are the main components of what a community needs to have a vibrant tourism economy. The items listed in the rectangles provide examples of the organizational components of the industry. This section of the chapter aims to highlight some of the models used to deliver tourism experiences for visitors.

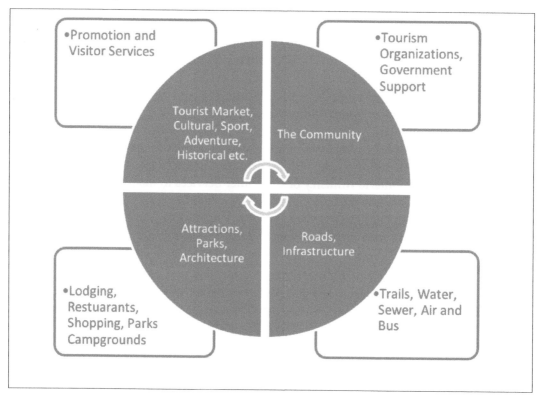

Figure 2.3. Necessary Components of a Tourism Industry

A simplified community based organizational structure might look like Figure 2.4. Three primary components exist, local government and its committees and commissions, a primary tourism authority (bureau, office etc.), and affiliated stakeholders representing businesses, community and civic organizations and resident associations.

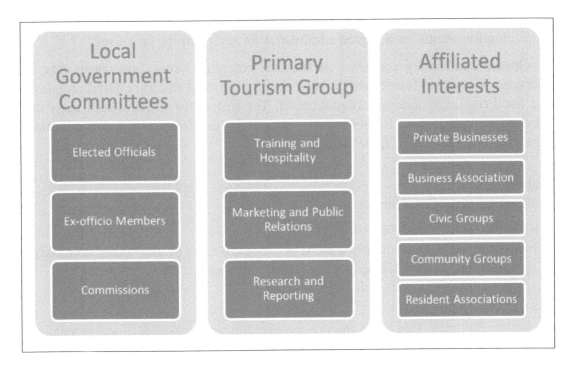

Figure 2.4. Simplified Community-Based Tourism Organizational Structure

Organizational Structure for Community-Based Tourism

When establishing a tourism organizational structure, a number of considerations come into question. The community has options to affiliate with a county or regional authority, partner with another community, or establish an independent effort. In any case, the following considerations (modified from Alexander, 1987; Richardson, 1991; and University of Minnesota Extension Service 2001) must be addressed in a public manner to develop a sustainable tourism industry.

- Determine the most appropriate organization and affiliation. Is the organization a bureau with nonprofit status, or is it a department within a city or part of a department such as parks and recreation? Ensure that the organizational structure adopted does not overlap with other existing organizations. In that situation, a partnership, not an independent organization is needed.
- Identify stakeholders and work toward an understanding in writing of each other's roles, responsibilities, collaborations, and partnership opportunities.
- Be open to the resident groups, take an educational viewpoint to help all community stakeholders understand the industry and how it can enhance livability and quality of life. Be honest about the potential negative impacts of tourism and how they will be monitored, reported, acted upon, and by whom.
- Secure appropriate official designations by local government for the tourism organization, its scope of responsibilities, its name, any oversight and coordinating requirements, and funding.
- Use appropriate planning and administrative processes to develop by laws, goals, objectives, and standard operating procedures.

- Identify financing of operations, revenue streams, promotion, and capital improvements via accepted administration and planning processes.

Once a community considers its tourism potential, issues, and constraints, an effort can be made to investigate the type of organizational structure based on human and fiscal resources and legal requirements. The University of Minnesota Extension Service (2001) provides a framework in which to discuss the pros and cons of various organizational structures (Table 2.4).

Table 2.4
Tourism Organizational Structures

Structure	Characteristics
Chamber of Commerce and pertinent committees	Commonly used, C of C already exists in most cases, members often interested in tourism, as tourism grows a separate organization can evolve
Volunteer Tourism Groups	Can begin the process of planning, but paid staff will be needed in the future as conditions change, may encompass a number of communities, can be effective means of influencing policy and marketing, membership can represent all stakeholders in the community, some formal processes need to be used to develop the group
Local Government Departments	Provides official recognition of tourism, provides staffing for coordination and management, may support growth of industry, may also limit involvement of some stakeholder groups (citizens and businesses)
Tourism Federation	Umbrella organization of trade groups (restaurant, lodging, attractions, museums, entertainment etc.), can coordinate interests of stakeholders, can lobby, effectiveness varies based on membership and leadership, can be dominated by one sector of a trade group
Lodging/Room Tax Organizations	Used to provide oversight of revenues and expenditures from this common funding method, locality dictates how system legally works, consists of a board representing segments of the industry, some localities restrict how the funds can be spent (marketing, infrastructure etc.), portion of revenues used to staff organization

The community would decide on the organizational model that works best given existing local conditions. Once that decision is made, the community then would consider components of a tourism organization that is suitable and beneficial to the community. Table 2.5 provides a description of the components and the role of each. Local circumstances dictate staffing needs and types of committees.

Table 2.5
Components of Tourism Organizations

Position	Responsibility
Board of Directors	Volunteer board members representing the industry set policy, strategies and goals
Director	Paid role to coordinate marketing and operations
Staff	Paid staff in the area of marketing, group tours, meetings and conventions, festivals and events, visitor center and information
Office Staff	Administration, accounting, secretarial
Standing and Ad Hoc Committees	Volunteers work on marketing, special events, membership, government relations, public relations, budget/finance etc.
Stakeholder Organizations	Representatives from historical society, industry-specific (lodging, restaurants, attractions), sporting organizations, government, economic development corporations, regional tourism groups, festival groups, federal and state land management agencies

Examples of organizational models in practice. The following example (Figure 2.5) of a community-based tourism organization is the City of Cedar Falls, Iowa. Unique to this example is that the tourism initiative is administratively housed within the Department of Human and Leisure Services within the city. The City of Cedar Falls and its Tourism and Visitors Bureau have a visitor center located at one of the entrances to the city. There is a strong link to the Main Street organization for events and promotion. The city has a population of 35,000, with a comprehensive state university (13,000 students). The City of Cedar Falls and its Tourism and Visitors Bureau offers grant monies to be used to attract, develop, or market an event, meeting, or convention, sporting competition, or attraction, that will bring visitors to Cedar Falls, thereby increasing overnight stays and/or tourism spending. Applications can be submitted to the Cedar Falls Tourism and Visitors Bureau at any time throughout the year and funds will be awarded until they are depleted. Projects eligible to receive funding are limited to events, attractions, and projects that will potentially create overnight tourism and/or encourage tourism-related economic activity in Cedar Falls (Cedar Falls Tourism and Visitors Bureau, 2015).

Examples of successful projects have included the following:

- Design and/or production and mailing of brochures, postcards, fliers, and posters
- Advertising design and placement in media outlets that reach outside of the county
- Website development, bid fees, venue rental, travel show materials and booth fees, and travel expenses

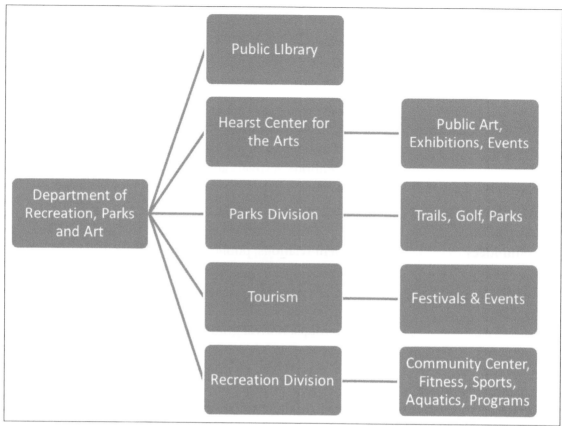

Figure 2.5. Organization of Cedar Falls Human and Leisure Services: A Community-Based Tourism Model

Adjacent to Cedar Falls is the City of Waterloo, Iowa, with a population of 100,000, which has a visitor and convention bureau, an independent organization. There is a metropolitan tourism committee that represents both Waterloo and Cedar Falls. The Waterloo Convention and Visitors Bureau is a nonprofit organization that promotes the region as a premier destination, welcoming visitors with a personal touch, in order to generate jobs, tax revenues, and, thus, an exceptional quality of life for area residents. The Bureau coordinates with the City of Cedar Falls, the Parks and Recreation Department for Waterloo, and the Cedar Valley Sports Commission (created to attract and grow youth and amateur sporting events in the Cedar Valley area. The Commission markets venues and the entire area as a premier destination for these events). Both tourism organizations work closely with the Eastern Iowa Tourism Association and the Iowa Economic Development Authority–Iowa Tourism Office.

The Waterloo Convention and Visitors Bureau (CVB) provides another example of the use of the hotel-motel tax and how it can be used to develop the local industry. The Waterloo Convention and Visitors Bureau offers grant monies for events and projects that will have a positive impact on the tourism industry in Waterloo, both in the short- and long-term. Grants are available to organizations whose events are held in Waterloo, regardless of where the organization itself is based. Three kinds of proposals or projects are eligible for funding:

- Visitor Events (draw **greater than 50%** of attendance from outside Black Hawk County)
- Community Events (draw **less than 50%** of attendance from outside Black Hawk County)
- Capital Projects

The grants have been established to do the following:

- Drive overnight stays in Waterloo
- Support active partners who serve and drive visitors to Waterloo
- Support organizations and activities that have a positive impact on Waterloo
- Provide seed money for new or innovative ideas/projects
- Provide assistance in marketing outside of Black Hawk County

Grant funds may support the following:

- Marketing and advertising
- Capital improvements
- Honorariums and entertainment
- Prize funds
- Basic facility rental costs
- Event-related safety and security
- Transportation
- Other similar projects that help promote visitation to Waterloo

Collaboration and partnerships. Not all tourism organizations are independently operated as a stand-alone organizational unit. The following example highlights the various ways in which tourism promotion can be organized and how the flow of hotel use tax money can be organized.

In Nanaimo, British Columbia, The Nanaimo Hospitality Association is a nonprofit society registered with the BC Corporate Registry. It was established on June 1, 2011, and has an eight-person board of directors comprised of a president, secretary, treasurer, and five directors at large. All 24 tourism lodging accommodators located within the boundaries of the City of Nanaimo are members of the NHA. The key purposes of the NHA, as set out in its constitution, are to do the following:

- Promote economic development for the City of Nanaimo
- Promote the City of Nanaimo as a tourism and business destination and support activities that also promote the Nanaimo Region
- Promote goodwill amongst members, the public, government agencies and the media
- Represent its members in matters of public importance, including any proposed legislation or regulations affecting the hospitality industry
- Advance and promote learning, education, training and professionalism in the hospitality industry

The Nanaimo Economic Development Corporation has been created to promote tourism for the City. Historically, responsibility for tourism in the City of Nanaimo fell to Tourism Nanaimo (Destination Marketing Organization for the City). However, in 2011, Tourism Nanaimo was disbanded, and on June 23, 2011, the Nanaimo Economic Development Corporation was established by the City of Nanaimo as an arm's-length corporation. According to th Articles of Incorporation (Section 1.3): With the establishment of the NEDC, the City of Nanaimo effectively removed itself from any direct role in tourism, and city funds previously allocated to Tourism Nanaimo for tourism marketing are now being allocated to the NEDC. This streamlined organizational structure reflects the synergies between economic development and tourism and aims to ensure a coordinated approach to related planning and marketing activities.

Tourism activities of the NEDC are guided by the NEDC Tourism Leadership Committee (TLC), which is comprised of 14 individuals who were selected through a formal process based on consideration of their relevant skills and tourism experience. According to the TLC's Terms of Reference, their mandate is to provide strategic recommendations to the NEDC's board of directors regarding tourism strategy and marketing. In addition the TLC provides input/insight to the NEDC board regarding infrastructure gaps, product development, and regulatory issues with a tourism impact. Prior to the establishment of the NEDC, economic development was a city department. The functions of both Tourism Nanaimo (previously a stand-alone tourism destination marketing organization) and Destination Nanaimo (previously the marketing arm of the city's economic development office), are now the responsibility of the tourism division of NEDC which has kept the name Tourism Nanaimo. Tourism Nanaimo is the tourism destination marketing organization for the City and region of Nanaimo and is a member of the B.C. Visitor Centre Network administered by Tourism B.C. (City of Nanaimo, B.C., 2014) Figure 2.6 depicts the organizational structure of the City of Nanaimo with regard to parks, recreation, culture, and tourism. Figure 2.7 demonstrates the flow of hotel tax monies through the various entities.

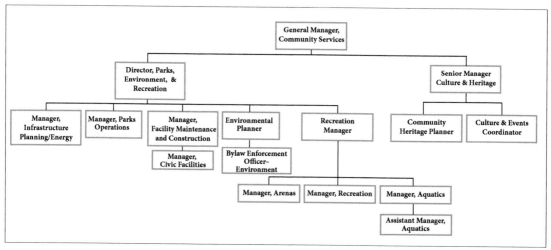

Figure 2.6. Organizational structure of the City of Nanaimo

Summary

In this chapter we have examined tourism from an organizational design approach. We have reviewed the primary organizations at the international level, U.S. and Canada federal and state level and local level. Tourism organizations are, for the most part, sophisticated in their research, target marketing, planning events, and coordination.

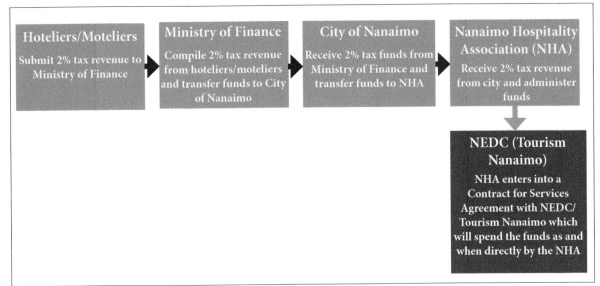

Figure 2.7. Flow of City of Nanaimo Tax Money

International, federal, and state and provincial level organizations have paid professional staff. Local organizations have paid staff, but also rely heavily on volunteers and community groups to facilitate a strong vibrant tourism program.

Tourism works where strong relationships in the industry are built with city, county, and provincial governments. Recognizing the local context, limitations, and opportunities of tourism should dictate the design and management of the local tourism organization. Tourism associations and industry groups play important roles in developing a sustainable product.

Key Concepts

- Community-based tourism
- International tourism organizations
- U.S. national tourism organizations
- Canadian national, provincial, and territorial tourism organizations
- Local tourism organizations
- Components of tourism organizations
- Hotel motel use tax

Useful Internet Sites, Exercises, and Resources

Canada
Canada Travel, http://us.canada.travel/
Canada Tourist Board Information, http://www.tripadvisor.com/Travel-g153339-s207/
    Canada:Tourist.Board.Info.html
Destination Canada: http://en-corporate.canada.travel/about-ctc
Parks Canada, http://www.pc.gc.ca/eng/index.aspx.
Niagara Falls: http://www.niagarasrto.com/about
Travel Alberta: http://industry.travelalberta.com/About%20Us.aspx

British Columbia: http://www.hellobc.com/british-columbia/about-bc/tourism-bc-information.aspx

Travel Manitoba: http://media.travelmanitoba.com/

New Brunswick: http://www.media.tourismnewbrunswick.ca/

Newfoundland and Labrador: http://www.newfoundlandlabrador.com/travelmedia

Northwest Territories: http://www.spectacularnwt.com/nwttmedia

Nova Scotia: http://www.novascotia.com/travelmedia

Nunavut: http://www.nunavuttourism.com/media/default.aspx

Ontario Tourism Marketing Partnership Corporation: www.ontariotravel.net. and http://www.tico.ca/about-tico/who-we-are.html

Prince Edward Island: http://www.tourismpei.com/pei-media-stories

Quebec: http://www.bonjourquebec.com/medias/index.php?Langue=en

Saskatchewan: http://media.sasktourism.com/

Yukon: http://www.travelyukon.com/media

International

United Nations World Tourism Organization: http://www2.unwto.org/

Visit Canada: http://www.visit-canada.com/

World Travel and Tourism Council: http://www.wttc.org/about/

World Tourism Organization, http://www2.unwto.org/

United States

50 States Travel Information, http://www.50states.com/tools/moreinfo.htm#.UQhAZ_KjJFd

Office of Travel Tourism Industries, U.S. Department of Commerce, http://tinet.ita.doc.gov/

State Travel and Tourism Office links, http://www.sirlinksalot.net/travel.html

Tourism Office Directory – Canada, http://www.towd.com/search.php?country=Canada

U.S. Chamber of Commerce, with links to tourism, http://www.uschamber.com/

U.S. State Tourism Websites: http://www.statelocalgov.net/50states-tourism.cfm

U.S. Travel Association: https://www.ustravel.org/about-us-travel

U.S. Travel Association and National Council of State Tourism Directors, http://www.ustravel.org/member-services/national-council-of-state-tourism-directors

Exercise 1

Visit the following websites and examine the partnerships and nature of the tourism product by region of Oregon. Can you determine the emphasis and niche marketing approach to all for communities. Comment on the Travel Oregon site and how it is coordinated with each of the communities.

Ashland Oregon (2015) http://www.ashlandchamber.com/Splash.asp

Bend Oregon (2013-2014) http://www.visitbend.com/Visit-Bend-Business-Plan-2013-small.pdf

Government Camp (2015) http://mounthoodinfo.com/

Hood River Oregon (2015) http://hoodriver.org/

Travel Oregon (2015) http://traveloregon.com/cities-regions/

Exercise 2

Visit the Canada Travel website and the U.S. Travel website to examine the activities and programs as they pertain to local communities. Is it evident that they are connected and supportive of smaller communities?

http://en-corporate.canada.travel/about-ctc

http://www.ustravel.org/

Questions for Review and Case Problems

Identify the obstacles of tourism development in your home town or area.

1. What ways can the United Nations World Tourism Organization influence, assist, and enhance local community-based tourism?
2. Identify the impact that the U.S. and Canadian national-level organizations have on local community-based tourism. Which country seems to be more supportive of smaller communities?
3. Why do you think states, provinces, and territories have different names for their offices of tourism?
4. Discuss the similarities, differences, and partnership that exists between Cedar Falls, Iowa tourism and Waterloo, Iowa tourism programs. What are the strengths and weaknesses of each reflecting on the section about developing a tourism organization?

References

Canadian Association of Tour Operators. (2017). About CATO. Retrieved from http://www.cato.ca/cato.php

Cedar Falls Tourism and Visitors Bureau. (2015). About us. Retrieved from http://www.cedarfallstourism.org/about-us/partner-info.aspx

City of Cedar Falls, IA. (2015). Tourism and Visitors Bureau. Retrieved from http://www.cedarfallstourism.org/about-us/partner-info.aspx.

City of Nanaimo, BC. (2014). City of Nanaimo business plan and application for the municipal and regional district hotel room tax. Retrieved from http://www.nanaimo.ca/assets/Departments/Legislative~Services/Background/AccommodationTax-Background.pdf?utm_source=goto&utm_campaign=goto&utm_term=Accommodation TaxBackground&utm_medium=goto

City of Waterloo, IA. (2015) Waterloo Convention and Visitors Bureau. Retrieved from http://www.travelwaterloo.com/

Department of Commerce. (n.d.). Travel and tourism advisory board charter. Retrieved from http://trade.gov/ttab/charter.asp

Destination Canada. (2015). For media. Retrieved from http://en-corporate.canada.travel/media-centre).

Hotel Association of Canada. (n.d.). The voice of the Canadian hotel and lodging industry. Retrieved from http://www.hotelassociation.ca

National Travel and Tourism Office. (n.d.). Oveview. Retrieved from http://tinet.ita.doc.gov/about/overview.html

Office of Travel and Tourism Industries (OTTI). (n.d.). Tourism policy. Retrieved from http://tinet.ita.doc.gov/about/tourism_policy.html

Parks Canada. (2017). Research in national parks. Retrieved from http://www.pc.gc.ca/en/nature/recherche-research

Travel Industry Council of Ontario. (n.d.). Who we are. Retrieved from http://www.tico.ca/about-tico/who-we-are.html

Tourism HR Canada. (n.d.). About us. Retrieved from http://cthrc.ca/

Tourism Industry Association of Canada. (n.d.). About TIAC. Retrieved from http://tiac.travel/cgi/page.cgi/_zine.html/TopStories/trending

UNWTO (2011). Policy and practice for global tourism. Retrieved from http://www2.unwto.org/publication/policy-and-practice-global-tourism

United States Travel Association (USTA). (2017). Travel facts and figures. Retrieved from https://www.ustravel.org/research/travel-facts-and-figures

University of Minnesota Extension Service. (2001). Community tourism development, MI-07650-S. Retrieved from https://www.extension.umn.edu/community/tourism-development/

Visit Canada. (2017). Planning to visit Canada? Retrieved from http://www.visit-canada.com/#canada-provinces-territories

CHAPTER 3

Attractions and Amenities in Community-Based Tourism

"In hundreds of regions, the heritage area idea is the unifying force that is strengthening communities and helping them successfully plan for their environmental, cultural, and economic future."
— J. Glenn Eugster (2003)

CHAPTER OBJECTIVES

- To build an awareness and appreciation for the types of attractions used in community based tourism
- To understand the different attractions that communities use to develop tourism
- To gain specific knowledge of the types of amenities that can be promoted in a community
- To gain knowledge of issues related to attraction management
- To understand contemporary examples of attractions and amenities currently being promoted in a variety of communities

Introduction

The tourism product consists of goods and services (attractions, accommodations, transportation, etc.). The attraction of a community can be seen as a function of supply (all natural and retail services produced for the traveler), and demand (motivations of travelers). Choi (2012), Morachat (2003), Formica (2000), Leiper (1995), Smith (1994), and Lew (1987) provided research on the push (sociopsychological motivations that increase desire to travel), and pull (attractions) factors of tourism, and the relationship between supply (this is the pull factor) and demand (this is the push factor) for tourism. Figure 3.1 provides a conceptual framework of this relationship.

Figure 3.1. Framework for Community-Based Tourism System and Attractions

Based on the list by Weaver and Lawton (2006) and modified to reflect a North American perspective, the following attractions are considered part of the community-based tourism inventory. Note that not all communities have all of many of these; in fact, some successful communities may only have one or two of these types of attractions.

Natural Sites: Natural sites subdivided into topographic (physical areas such as the Grand Canyon), climate (arctic and desert regions), hydrology (Great Lakes, oceans, rivers), wildlife, and vegetation.

Iconic Attractions: An attraction such as the Statue of Liberty, Mt. Shasta California, Mt. Rushmore.

Temporary Seasonal Attractions: Wildflower displays, fall season displays in the Northeastern U.S., migration of birds and butterflies.

Cultural Sites: Prehistorical, historical, and popular culture

Dark Tourism: Sites associated with death, supernatural, battlefields (Civil War).

Food Tourism: Locally produced drink and food.

Winescapes, Hard Liquorscapes, Beerscapes: Regions known for beverages and the trails that link these sites and communities (Oregon Beer Trails, NE Iowa Wine Trail, Kentucky Bourbon Trail).

Recreationscapes: Places that provide whitewater rafting, skiing, backpacking etc.

Cultural Events: Attractions that occur regularly over a period of time, historical recreations, state and county fairs, sporting events (Iowa RAGBRAI), festivals (Mardi Gras).

Gateway Communities: Places adjacent to national parks and other venues often thrive due to the location of a natural attraction.

Attractions and Amenities

Some of the positioning of a tourism product is geographically focused. Wang and Pfister (2008) observed that the cultural heritage theme has long been the strength of the east and south due to early settlement history, nation-building, and battlefields. Restoring heritage resources and historic districts presents opportunities to host visitors and to organize festival and the re-enactment of historical events. In the Midwest and West, the tourism products are more likely to favor agritourism, dude ranches, outdoor adventure, and nature-based experiences associated with public lands and frontier assets of the region.

Importantly, visitors find interest in various attractions. A study by Choi (2012) addressed the attractiveness (attractions) of the 37 county area of the Silos and

Smokestacks National Heritage Area (SSNHA). This region is in the northeast corner of Iowa, consisting of mainly rural areas, small towns, and some medium-sized communities. A report of travel to the region suggests an economic impact of $64 million per year in visitor spending (UNI STEP, 2004). Choi studied visitors to the 37-county area. The SSNHA manages its attractions around the themes of scenic routes, historical sites, museums and galleries, and parks and nature centers. The findings are quite interesting in light of the discussion on attractions and amenities. Table 3.1 presents the findings, which compared 18 attributes of destination attractiveness in rank order of importance. The rankings were derived by the average attractiveness score multiplied by the average importance of the attraction score. A 5-point rating scale was used to measure responses to the items. The rankings of visitors to a heritage area and its communities provide some food for thought. Specifically, shopping is ranked low, along with nighttime recreation and climate (note that the area is in Iowa, which has a cold winter and hot summer). One might think that shopping and nighttime entertainment are crucial to successful tourism. These findings suggest that place (landscape and the people), interpretive opportunities (museums, historical attractions, and educational opportunities), and recreation play more important roles. Our preconceived notions of successful tourism programs need to be balanced by research within our own communities. Importantly, each community lends itself to a different market based on its attractions (pull factors) and traveler motivation (push factors) as noted earlier.

Table 3.1
Visitors' Rankings of the Attractions of the SSNHA

Attribute/Attraction	Rank
Attitudes Toward Tourists	1
Landscape	2
Educational Facilities/Programs	3
Museums and Cultural Attractions	4
Recreational Facilities	5
Historical Prominence	6
Prices and Cost to Visit	7
Accessibility to the Attractions	8
Architectural Features	9
Adequate Food and Lodging	10
Adequate Infrastructure	11
Festivals, Fairs and Exhibits	12
Distinctive Local Features	13
Historical Ruins	14
Shopping Facilities	15
Climate	16
Nighttime Recreation	17
Religious Significance	18

A study by the Sustainable Tourism and Environment Program (STEP) at the University of Northern Iowa of small, medium, and large tourism-based communities notes a variety of reasons that visitors come to the communities. Communities were purposely selected based on their dependence on tourism as an economic strategy. It is interesting to note the various reasons for visiting in relation to amenities and attractions. Scenery, parks, gardens, outdoor recreation, and recreation top the list. Although sports, museums, shopping, and food are listed, they are not the main attractions in the selected communities (See Figure 3.2).

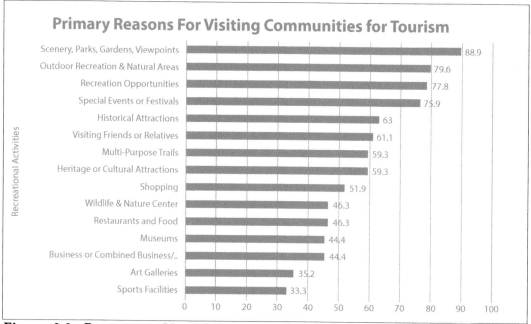

Figure 3.2. Reasons to Visit Community (Nelson, 2014; UNI-STEP; 2012-2013 Community-Based Tourism Survey)

Comparison of Attractions and Amenities

Another study by Betz and Perdue (1993) showed a significant correlation between tourist visits and community amenities. Outdoor areas such as scenic trails and beaches, as well as activities such as fishing and camping, create a large amount of interest. Historic and heritage sites are also popular with both resident and nonresident visitors. Along with outdoor recreation resources, amenities include shopping, museums, festivals, food-based events, and other attractions. Table 3.2 compares popular community-based tourism destinations and their amenities. Interestingly, a review of the table suggests that each community has identified primary and secondary amenity attractions. For example, the primary attractions in Hot Springs, Arkansas, are the hot springs and bathhouses, which now comprise a national park. Built around and to support the primary attraction are festivals (including food and beverage-based events) and events, historical sites, and water-based attractions. Of particular interest is the interdependency among the tourism industry, community, businesses, and environmentalists who work to ensure an improved quality of life for area residents (Hawkins & Cunningham 1996), while enhancing the tourism product. As one can see, the success of a community tourism program is a result of public and private partnerships.

Table 3.2

Comparison of Amenities by Community and Type

State	City	Amenities	Website
AR	Hot Springs	Outdoors: Ouachita Mountains, Hot Springs Country Club, bathing rituals in the hot springs (world famous mineral baths), national parks, baseball trail, gardens, lakes, biking trails Festivals: Hot Springs Music Festival, Hot Springs Fishing Challenge Shopping: galleries, antiques Attractions: Bathhouse, The Gangster Museum of America, Hot Springs Mountain Tower, Magic Springs Water and Theme Park, Hot Springs Convention Center, aquarium, arenas, amphitheaters, concert series, historic downtown	http://www.hotsprings.org
AZ	Flagstaff	Outdoors: Riodan Mansion State Park, horseback riding, fishing, hiking, camping, disc golf, golf, bowling, recreation and fitness centers, biking, indoor climbing, county parks Shopping: Flagstaff Mall and Market Place (over 80 stores) Attractions: Route 66, The Grand Canyon Railway, Flagstaff Symphony Orchestra, Museum of Northern Arizona, Pioneer Museum, The Meteor Crater, ropes course and zip lines, pub crawls, observatory, theaters, art centers, amphitheaters, auditoriums, ski resorts	http://www.flagstaff.az.gov http://www.flagstaffarizona.org

Table 3.2 (cont.)

CO	Aspen	<u>Outdoors</u>: Maroon Bells ("one of the state's most iconic mountain views"), paragliding, white water rafting, skiing, snowboarding, zip lining, Rio Grande Park, running marathons <u>Festivals</u>: Winter X Games, JAS Aspen June Snowmass Experience, tribal dances, food and wine festivals, writing festivals <u>Shopping</u>: fur shops, florists, leather goods, antiques, farmer's market <u>Attractions</u>: Aspen Snowmass: Snowmass, Aspen Mountain, Aspen Highlands, & Buttermilk (X Games for 14 years), Wheeler Opera House, Aspen Santa Fe Ballet, Aspen Art Museum, art studios, Adventures Out West (tour of wildlife and scenic area), Aspen Brewing Company, Aspen Culinary Tour, Aspen Art Museum, Daydream Destination (self discovery program through adventure), Woody Creek Cellars, Aspen Golf Club	http://www.colorado.com/cities-and-towns/aspen http://www.aspenchamber.org/explore-aspen/shopping
CO	Glenwood Springs	<u>Outdoors</u>: Iron Mountain Springs, Hanging Lake, The Glenwood Hot Springs Pool (largest in the world), Glenwood Caverns Adventure Park, Glenwood Canyon, White River National Forest, watchable wildlife, cavern tours, skydiving, ropes course, biking, rafting, fishing, whitewater activity, kayaking, paddle boarding, rock and ice climbing outside, canoeing, hiking, horseback riding, ATV, Jeep and Hummer Tours, Segway Tours, zip lining, paragliding, golf course, disc golf, mini golf, skiing, snowboarding, snowmobiling, snowshoeing, hunting, ice skating, spas <u>Festivals</u>: Strawberry Days Festival, ghost walk event <u>Shopping</u>: market street shops, malls, farmer's markets, downtown <u>Attractions</u>: Hot Springs pool, ghost walks, vaudeville, Frontier Historical Museum, resorts, spas	http://www.visitglenwood.com

Table 3.2 (cont.)

IA	Amana Colonies	Outdoors: Amana Colonies Trails, tipi camping Festivals: Culinary, Car Clubs, Oktoberfest, Maipole dancers for Maifest (German heritage celebration) Shopping: Amana Furniture & Clock Shop, Broom & Basket Shop, Custom Cutlery & Iron Works, Fern Hill Gifts and Quilts, meat shop & smokehouse Attractions: woodworking, willow basketry, needlework, art galleries, Amana Heritage Museum, arts guild, Iowa's largest walnut rocker (rocking chair), water parks, wineries, theaters, art studios	http://www.amanacolonies.com
IA	Decorah	Outdoors: Malanphy Springs, Twin Springs Park, Ice Cave State Preserve, city parks, eagle watching, apple picking, fishing, hiking Festivals: Oneota Film Festival, Tractor Days, Nordic Fest, Lawn Chair Nights for concerts, Rendezvous Days Shopping: Farmer's Market, boutiques, gift shops, home goods Attractions: Artist Studio Tours, theater performances, Laura Ingalls Wilder Museum, Heritage Center, wineries, crafts	http://www.visitdecorah.com
IL	Galena	Outdoors: Apple River Canyon State Park, hiking, kayaking, skiing, snowboarding, boating, fishing Festivals: hot air balloon race, art festivals, vintage orchestra, Oktoberfest, county fair, pub crawls, parades, pottery tours, ice sculpting festivals, dance festivals, 50's themed festivals, wine lovers Shopping: art galleries, studios, antique, collectibles, home and garden, apparel, accessories, food products, boutiques Attractions: spa treatments, water parks, ghost tours, art centers, hypnosis shows, theaters, gardens, trolleys, lounges, museums, wineries and tasting rooms, breweries, wedding venues	http://www.visitgalena.org/index.cfm

Table 3.2 (cont.)

IL	Springfield	<u>Outdoors</u>: theater in the park, skate parks, city parks, hiking, wildlife sanctuary, golfing, aquatic centers, bowling, canoeing, biking <u>Festivals</u>: Historic events, Abraham Lincoln tributes <u>Shopping</u>: antiques, collectibles, fashion, thrift stores, art galleries <u>Attractions</u>: Abraham Lincoln's Tomb, Springfield Semi-Pro Football, Springfield Jr. Blues Hockey Team, Springfield Sliders Baseball Team, saloons, convention center, auditorium, movie theaters, comedy clubs, roller derby, fairgrounds, Ferris Wheel, aquarium, art galleries, museums, ballet performances, theatres, opera performances, Broadway shows, wineries, breweries	http://www.visitspringfieldillinois.com
MI	Traverse City	<u>Outdoors</u>: dunes, beaches, ship sailing, water sports (canoeing, paddling, parasailing), hiking, cycling, four wheelers, hot air balloons, skiing, snowboarding, horseback riding, bird watching, fishing, zip-lines, marathons <u>Festivals</u>: music festivals, film festivals, microbrew festivals, wine and art festivals <u>Shopping</u>: boutiques, specialty shops, candy stores, antiques, sports stores <u>Attractions</u>: casinos, Traverse Symphony Orchestra, water parks, lighthouse tours, spas, beer and wine tours, art galleries, motorcycle tours, downtown Traverse, farmers markets, amphitheatres, museums, gardens, festival grounds	http://www.traversecity.com/summer/things-to-do/events/festivals/

Table 3.2 (cont.)

MN	Wabasha	<u>Outdoors</u>: sailing, kayak tours, paddle boats, golf, disc golf, skiing, snowboarding, carriage rides, riverboat cruises, camping, state and city parks <u>Festivals</u>: SeptOberFest, Riverboat Days, Grumpy Old Men Festival, Watermelon Festival <u>Shopping</u>: seasonal boutiques, gift shops, markets <u>Attractions</u>: Wabasha Bridge, Mississippi River, Antique Toy Museum, Historical Society Museum, "music under the bridge," Eagle Center, Wabasha nutcrackers, breweries, galleries, spas	http://www.exploremississippibluffs.com/wabasha/
OR	Ashland	<u>Outdoors</u>: city parks, park trails, golf course, nature centers, river rafting, tubing, picnics, pavilions, gardens, recreation programs, sport fields, camping windsurfing, rowing, tennis, Shakespeare festival, Crab Fest, holiday festivals, honey festival, multicultural festivals, film, food, wine and brew festivals, walkathons, running relays <u>Shopping</u>: home chef cookware, boutiques, crafts, organic product shops <u>Attractions</u>: wedding venues, museums, theaters, artisan emporium, wineries, concerts, bird observatory, conventions, breweries, historic downtown	http://www.ashland.or.us https://www.osfashland.org http://www.ashlandchamber.com/Page.asp?NavID=893
WA	Leavenworth	<u>Outdoors</u>: dog sledding, birding, sleigh rides, ice climbing, snow tubing, snowshoeing, river tubing, fishing, snowmobiling, kayaking, rafting, wagon rides, horseback riding, outdoor theatre, whale watching <u>Festivals</u>: International celebrations, music festivals, Kinder Fest (Bavarian Village Celebration, River Salmon Festival, Autumn Leaf Festival, Quilt Festival, Rockfest (climbing) <u>Shopping</u>: handcrafted gift shops, specialty food shops, imported goods from Bavarian villages, boutiques <u>Attractions</u>: agritourism, culinary, gardens, breweries, wineries, flight tours, fish hatchery, museums	http://www.leavenworth.org

Table 3.2 (cont.)

WA	Walla Walla	<u>Outdoors</u>: BMX track, cycling tourism, Walla Walla Sweets collegiate baseball team, fishing and hunting, birding, night skiing, snowboarding, public parks <u>Festivals</u>: Sweet Onion Festival, Stopover music festival <u>Shopping</u>: antiques malls and collectibles, boutiques <u>Attractions</u>: over 27 wineries, wine tours, agriculture, bronze sculptures, Main Street, Downtown, pet friendly areas, worship services, public art walk tour, Walla Walla Symphony, Blue Mountains, Bennington Lake, musicals, plays, comedies, museums	http://www.wallawalla.org
WI	Mineral Point	<u>Outdoors</u>: bike tours, snowmobiles, golfing, swimming, trails, state and city parks, lakes, mountain biking, campsites, skiing <u>Festivals</u>: Cornish Festival, Book Festival, film festivals, county fair, "city-wide garage sales" <u>Shopping</u>: family owned businesses, antiques and collectibles, local art, farm equipment, fabric shops, specialty stores <u>Attractions</u>: Mineral Point's dog statue, Cave tours, Wisconsin River, House on the Rock Resort, golf course, artist's studios, art classes, railroad and art museums, aquarium, professional theater, opera house, farmer's market, gardens	http://mineralpoint.com

Now celebrating its 37th anniversary, the College Hill Arts Festival was conceived in 1979 and came alive with 30 or so local and northeast Iowa artists showcasing their original artwork. Today this top-ranked national arts festival features 75 talented artists who turn the corner of West 23rd & College Street on the campus of the University of Northern Iowa into a living museum. These artists have come to Cedar Falls from all over the United States to give festival patrons the very best art experience possible. These juried artists exhibit and sell their original artwork in categories including ceramics, fiber, wood, jewelry, metal sculpture, painting, photography, and glass. The festival, staffed entirely by volunteers, has become a very unique opportunity to connect nationally known artists and the Cedar Valley community in an effort to create a top-quality juried art festival and to make fine art easily accessible to the public.

Nationally recognized artist Gary Kelley became a festival supporter in 1985 by creating his first College Hill Arts Festival poster. Kelley's annual creations have become "must haves" for festival supporters, and he has won numerous national awards for his festival designs.

Complementing the artists' exhibits are a variety of musical groups performing on stage, hands-on creative activities for children sponsored by the Hearst Center for the Arts, plus balloon sculptures and face painting—all free—and a variety of food vendors to entice festival attendees. And, unique to festivals, the College Hill Arts Festival features a Young Art Collectors Gallery, with original artwork created by the exhibiting artists with prices of $10 or less, which encourages youth aged 14 and under to make independent decisions about art based on their own feelings.

The 2014 festival was ranked in the top 300 events nationwide by *Art Fair Source Book*. In addition, for nine out of the last 10 years, the College Hill Arts Festival has been named by *Sunshine Artist* magazine to their list of 100 Best Fine Art & Design Shows in the United States (Mary-Sue Bartlett, University of Northern Iowa. Personal Communication, July 10, 2015).

Assessment of Attractions and Amenities

Importantly, communities must identify their unique attraction and then build and expand upon that attraction base to support tourism. Amenities and attractions can be any combination of physical, social, historic, or cultural qualities that are valued by the community. Assets can be event based or place based. The Strawberry Days Festival in Strawberry Point, Iowa, a community located near a spring that was once abundant with wild strawberries, is an example of combining event and place. Community assets are not limited to the size of community nor are communities limited to a particular number of assets. Often community assets are defined through a community process.

Community leadership and participation are essential to community-based tourism since the local people are one of the tourism assets along with natural environment, infrastructure, facilities and special events or festivals. A matrix may be used (see Table 3.3, adapted from Yukon Tourism and Culture, 2014, www.tc.gov.yk.ca) to assess the tourism attractions as a starting point. Market research into the motivations and expectations of travelers is also warranted.

Table 3.3

Assessing the Tourism Attractions

Attraction/ Resource	Number	Quality	Potential for Tourism	Description/ Issues	Public/ Private
Natural Scenic Attractions Recreation Resources Native Americans					
Historic Museums Sites					
Cultural Festivals Events People					
Accommodations Camping Lodging B & B					
Restaurants Fine Dining Fast Food Local Foods					
Interpretive Services Guides Brochures Tours					
Human Resources Guides and Leaders Safety Personnel					
Infrastructure Medical Transportation Communications Water and Sewer					

After assessing attraction potential, the community must begin a process of development (addressed later in the book). However, there are identified success factors which must be present in any tourism development effort. Carlsen and others (2008) identified success factors for thematic heritage tourism (Table 3.4). Most small communities have identified some form of heritage tourism, with a theme, thus the term thematic tourism. The following have been identified for the successful development and management of thematic heritage tourism. Importantly, these success factors can be considered for any type of tourism development program. The local tourism committee or board must ensure the presence of these factors in the planning process.

Table 3.4
Criteria for Successful Thematic Heritage Tourism

Agreement on objectives and concepts
Financial planning for budgeting, capital raising, and price setting
Effective marketing strategies based on sound market research
Destination and proximity to major markets and visitor flows
Human resource management, including paid staff and volunteers
Planning for product differentiation, life cycles, and value adding
Quality and authenticity of products and experiences
Engage cultural heritage and tourism expertise in conservation and promotion
Design interpretation as an integral part of the heritage tourism experience

As an example, the Silos and Smokestacks National Heritage Area (SSNHA) (see http://www.silosandsmokestacks.org/) in northeast Iowa has incorporated these elements in their long-range, short-range and interpretation plans. For communities and businesses to partner with the SSNHA, they must address the items in Table 3.4 in some fashion.

Thematic tourism: Some examples of amenities. The following section provides a brief review of natural, human made, festivals, heritage, shopping, and trails as attractions in community tourism. Tabata and Kuehn (2000) noted that throughout the United States, scenic byways and heritage corridors and areas are being developed to 1) preserve and interpret natural and cultural resources unique to an area; 2) coordinate efforts of public, private, and nonprofit interests; and 3) market the thematic itineraries. The authors note that with the growing interest in nature, culture, and historical tourism, thematic itinerary tourism provides an excellent opportunity to integrate community -based tourism development with enhanced interpretation and visitor information services. While reviewing the following material, keep in mind the ways in which the communities mentioned earlier in the chapter have created or tried to create thematic community-based tourism.

Natural attractions. Hood River, Oregon is said to be the "outdoor recreation capital of Oregon" (Hood River County Chamber of Commerce, 2013). The county is known for its natural attractions such as: rivers, waterfalls, and mountain ranges. These natural attractions allow tourists and natives of the county to experience various recreational activities. The Hood River County Chamber of Commerce encourages visitors to take the "35-mile scenic drive" where they can see wildlife and an array of greenery (Hood River County Chamber of Commerce, 2013). Some of the outdoor activities that visitors can enjoy at Hood River include hiking, backpacking, bike riding, windsurfing, kayaking, and much more (Hood River County Chamber of Commerce, (2013).

Springdale, Utah has a "small-town feel" and is known as "the gateway to Zion National Park" (Springdale Town, n.d.). Springdale serves as the hospitality spot for tourists visiting Zion National Park. This town not only provides lodging and dining to national park visitors, but it also offers entertainment such as festivals and events (Springdale Town, n.d.). The town is surrounded by the scenery of Zion National Park's great canyons, which adds to the overall atmosphere of the town.

Human-made attractions as amenities. The Grotto of Redemption is a tourist attraction located in West Bend, Iowa. The building is a human-made attraction, made up of minerals, stones, rocks, and jewels. Father Dobberstein, a pastor from the early 1900s created the Grotto of Redemption as a repayment of gratitude to the Virgin Mary for answering his prayers to save his life while suffering from pneumonia (West Bend Grotto, n.d.). The ornate detail and construction of the building has attracted visitors for hundreds of years. It is also referred to as "the eighth wonder of the world," and "the largest known accomplishment of its kind anywhere in the world" (West Bend Grotto, n.d.).

The Hot Springs National Park Bathhouses are located in Hot Springs, Arkansas (National Park Service U.S. Department of the Interior, 2015). The bathhouses are a historical landmark of Hot Springs, and have evolved into a modern-day attraction (National Park Service U.S. Department of the Interior, 2015). Tourists are drawn to the bathhouses because they offer "thermal waters" that can help people heal as well as relax (National Park Service U.S. Department of the Interior, 2015).

Festivals and events as amenities. Ashland, Oregon focuses on creating a strong community. They bring the community together by hosting seasonal and annual events such as 4th of July parades, Halloween celebrations, and culinary festivals (Ashland, Oregon Chamber of Commerce, 2015). The events that are offered can appeal to many different personal interests and cultures. Ashland's most successful annual festival is the Shakespeare Festival, which attracts tourists from all over the United States. The Shakespeare Festival integrates Shakespeare's traditional plays as well as new plays created by the Oregon Shakespeare Festival Organization, making it enjoyable for all theater and art fans (Oregon Shakespeare Festival, n.d.).

Cedar Falls, Iowa has a distinct mission "to foster, promote, market, and service our community as a quality destination for visitors" (Cedar Falls Tourism Convention & Visitors Bureau, 2015). One of the ways that Cedar Falls keeps a rich community is by hosting annual events that promote community engagement and attract tourists. Some of the events that Cedar Falls is known for are farmers markets, exhibitions, and festivals (Cedar Falls Tourism Convention & Visitors Bureau, 2015). Their events range from themes such as sports, music, art, food, holidays, and many others (Cedar Falls Tourism Convention & Visitors Bureau, 2015). Some of the more unique events include gun shows, ghost tours, and bingo nights (Cedar Falls Tourism Convention & Visitors Bureau, 2015).

In 2013, Iowa was ranked as the second highest agricultural producing state in the U.S. (United States Department of Agriculture Economic Research, 2015). Iowa has a rich agricultural community, which is demonstrated in events year round. Some of the types of events that are hosted include apple fests, farmers markets, corn harvests, and wine festivals (Travel Iowa, 2015). The events and festivals attract all groups of people locally and nationally.

Heritage and culture as amenities. Canada is a heavily diverse country. The prominent language spoken in Canada is English, but there are also many French-speaking citizens as well (Every Culture, 2015). Canadians are understood to be accepting of people from other cultures (Every Culture, 2015). Canadian society holds general expectations of how people should behave in public (Every Culture, 2015). They are generalized as being "soft spoken, patient, and somewhat apologetic in their public behavior" (Every Culture, 2015). An exception to this would be during celebrations, such as Canada Day, which is the country's day of independence (Every Culture, 2015).

Nova Scotia, one of Canada's provinces, celebrates something similar to Canada Day, known as Natal Day where citizens celebrate the independence day of their province (Time and Date, 2015). Nova Scotia's heritage is formed by the many nationalities and cultures of their first settlers. Some of the cultures include Acadian, African, Celtic, Gaelic, and Mi'kmaq (Nova Scotia, 2015). Nova Scotia's unique culture is brought out through its "art, music, language, and spirituality" (Nova Scotia, 2015).

Amana Colonies, located in the state of Iowa is known as "the handcrafted escape" (Amana Colonies, 2015). This communal town is a National Historic Landmark that has continued to express its value of history and hospitality (Amana Colonies, 2015). As a society, they value all forms of art and handcrafted items. These items can range from homemade candy, clocks, quilts, pottery, and much more (Amana Colonies, 2015). The town mainly consists of small businesses, which adds to the unique and original culture of Amana Colonies.

Mineral Point, Wisconsin is a small town with a strong historical and artistic culture (Mineral Point Chamber of Commerce, n.d.). Mineral Point's architecture still portrays the town's history as an old mining town. Areas such as underground living shelters have been preserved to show how settlers lived in the town during the early 1800s (Mineral Point Chamber of Commerce, n.d.). The history of Mineral Point is also revealed through local art. Mineral Point's community takes great pride in handcrafted works of art ranging from pottery, paintings, woodworking, and many others (Mineral Point Chamber of Commerce, n.d.).

Shopping as amenities. One of the many tourist attractions to communities such as Mineral Point, Wisconsin, or Cannon Beach, Oregon, is shopping. While both towns offer a variety of shops to browse, they differ in content. Mineral Point and Cannon Beach support their small business shop owners, which tend to be the most cherished by tourists. These small businesses contribute to the town's culture and provide customers with unique goods that represent the authenticity of the town.

While visiting Mineral Point you can expect to find family-owned shops and handcrafted items. The shopping experience is truly original, because Mineral Point does not have malls or big name-brand stores; instead you will find antiques and vintage items (Mineral Point Chamber of Commerce, n.d.). Shopping in Cannon Beach is similar, but the environment is more modern. Cannon Beach is a small beach community and the shops in the area show their culture. It is more typical to find farmers markets, sporting goods, and pet shops in this town (Cannon Beach Chamber of Commerce, 2015).

Trails as amenities. Park organizations strive to create opportunities for community members and tourists that promote well-being. In places such as Red Wing and Lanesboro, Minnesota, you can enjoy the outdoors and explore nature trails. Lanesboro, Minnesota's most used trail is the Root River Bike Trail, which is a 60-mile bike route (Lanesboro Chamber of Commerce, 2015). The trail is in a valley along the Root River that goes over hills and through an abundance of greenery (Lanesboro Chamber of Commerce, 2015). Red Wing, Minnesota also has bike trails and multiple nature trails that are ideal for hiking (Live Healthy Red Wing, n.d.). Some of these trails are located within the city's 38 parks (City of Red Wing MN, 2015).

Other types of outside trails that are appealing to some audiences are beer and wine trails. These types of trails can be found in various locations across the United States. Kalamazoo, Michigan, is an example of one city that has a prominent beer community (Pure Michigan, 2013). The city has over 12 breweries, and most of them offer beer trails throughout the year as a local and tourist attraction (Pure Michigan, 2013). The trails allow people to taste various types of beers from the local breweries on a fun and unique tour.

Wildlife as amenities. Wildlife tourism brings millions of dollars to what are called gateway communities to national parks. For example, each spring in the Greater Yellowstone Ecosystem (GYE), thousands of elk migrate from winter ranges in Wyoming, Montana, and Idaho, to high-elevation summer ranges nearer to the core of Yellowstone National Park (YNP). These migratory elk link the ecosystem's outermost foothills to its deepest mountain wilderness. Their abundance sustains diverse carnivores and scavengers, attracts tens of millions of dollars to gateway communities, and inspires national and global conceptions of the beloved YNP wilderness (Wyoming Migration Initiative, 2015).

Wildlife tourism is increasingly becoming a popular recreational pursuit, while also causing concerns because of its impact on wild species and their habitats. Of concern is wildlife-dependent recreation, which is generally more disruptive since visitor's satisfaction relies on the presence of wild species (Sinha, 2001). These activities include leisure tracking of wildlife for fun or adventure, photographing, and hunting and fishing. Often, wildlife organizations and government agencies are at odds with wildlife tourism due to potential and real impacts on wildlife. While acknowledging the economic benefits of this type of tourism, these concerned agencies still have to manage the increasing number of tourists impacting preserves. Wildlife tourism can involve attractions, tours, experiences available in association with tourist accommodation, or it can occur as unguided encounters by independent travelers (Higginbottom, 2004). Classification of wildlife tourism includes the following:

- Wildlife-watching tourism (viewing or otherwise interacting with free-ranging animals)

- Captive-wildlife tourism (viewing animals in man-made confinement; principally zoos, wildlife parks, animal sanctuaries and aquariums; also includes circuses and shows by mobile wildlife exhibitors)
- Hunting and fishing tourism

The Texas Parks and Wildlife Department actively promotes nature-based tourism, and conserving habitat by working with landowners, communities, and businesses. The department notes "by empowering people at the local level, we hope to build and provide guidance to a growing industry that holds great promise for sustainable economic development and conservation of wildlife habitat" (Texas Parks and Wildlife 2015).

Attraction Management

A number of models and methodologies exist to manage communities and their attractions. The most noteworthy is the Butler (1980) Tourism Area Lifecycle (TALC) model (Figure 3.3). Communities can be at any one of the states from exploration to stagnation. While tourism has long been considered as a viable alternative to stimulating dwindling rural economies that previously depended on resource extractive enterprises such as mining, manufacturing and farming, lack of adequate prior planning and evaluation of current efforts and resources have yielded mixed results (West Virginia University Extension, 2015). The initial stages are when a community is attempting to develop tourism, with a lack of resources, marketing etc. Subsequent stages indicate the growth of tourism and larger business chains move in and take over. At some point, destinations may experience a leveling off of visitors or a decline. In part this decline can be explained by mismanagement of the resources, poor maintenance, overcrowding, and/or lack of planning.

Tourism Lifecycle

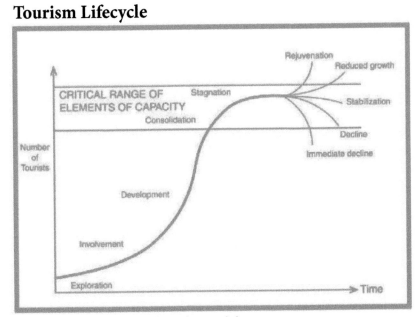

Figure 3.3. Tourism Lifecycle Model

From a management point of view, Weaver and Lawton (2006) note that two scenarios can come into play to manage the decline or stagnation of tourism; both address carrying capacity. One way is through various regulatory and economic methods the number of visitor arrivals prior to the decline. Another way is to increase the infrastructure to allow more visitors, thereby increasing carrying capacity. Table 3.5 displays the lifecycle model and how the West Virginia University Extension Service addresses each phase for community-based tourism (Arbogast, Deng, & Maumbe, 2017). The important lesson here is that a model can be translated into action to assist community-based tourism developers manage attractions through community input and planning.

Table 3.5
Tourism Lifecycle and Collaborative Support by West Virginia University Extension

Stage	Community Response	WVU Tourism Collaborative Support
Exploration/ Introduction	• Community is trying to diversify its economy • Community tries to mobilize residents in support of tourism development • Community members have feelings of euphoria and also uncertainty • Community members try to identify their tourism assets	• Engage community members of all types to participate in discussions about tourism development • Conduct tourism resource inventory • Identify the community's tourism weaknesses and strengths • Assist with tourism planning, including identifying community-based tourism development goals and objectives • Conduct research on residents' attitudes toward tourism development and visitor preferences
Involvement	• Community starts to get involved • Community members seek entrepreneurship opportunities • Some community members may start businesses targeted at visitors • Outsiders may move into the community and start businesses targeted at visitors • Some feelings of apathy may develop	• Skills development/education and training in customer service • Business-related training for those who need help • Research on adoption and acceptance rates by community • Establish carrying capacities • Establish visitor needs, demands, and satisfaction • Destination/community branding/ positioning, and marketing, etc.
Development /Growth	• Community tourism is well defined and growing • Some annoyance among residents noticed from growth issues (traffic, crowding, rapid development, etc.) • Community needs/seeks help to manage growth • Community needs to have mechanisms in place to prevent uncontrolled or unplanned growth • Responsible for resource stewardship and sustainability • Many and rapid changes may occur in community • Community may start to lose its authenticity or sense of place	• Training and skills building continues with growing needs/demand • Help community manage and control resource stewardship/ sustainability • Routine research to establish and manage impacts of tourism and manage carrying capacities • More destination marketing and management support to sustain growth • Research on visitor patterns • Research on community responses/ coping mechanisms/changes • Research on community participation and benefit from tourism

Table 3.5 (cont.)

Stage	Community Response	WVU Tourism Collaborative Support
Consolidation/ Maturity	• Annoyance grows as small community businesses get swallowed by large conglomerates • Community may feel powerless and loss of control • Some continue to benefit from growing tourism	• Skills development and training continue to adapt to changing needs • Assist with more effective and sustainable destination marketing and management practices • Tourism is still growing but at decreasing rates • Research on alternative niches to prepare for stagnation and decline stages • Research on impacts, visitor patterns, etc. continues
Stagnation	• Peak is reached and community has to be innovative to keep visitors coming • Community members may become antagonistic to more tourism-related projects	• Skills development and training to adapt to new ventures that may be required to avoid decline • Help with identification of alternative, more lucrative, or emerging aspects of tourism • All other tourism-related research continues
Decline or Rejuvenation	• Tourism either declines or gets rejuvenated depending on actions from previous stages • Community seeks help with alternatives for new direction	• Assist community in avoiding decline by implementing alternative measures identified in preceding phases • Identify and adopt emerging trends in tourism • Training and skills development for new ventures • Help identify diversification opportunities to broaden community economic base, etc.

Adapted from Maumbe, Deng, & Arbogast (2013)

Ward-Perkins and Dimanche (2012) provide a monitoring example for managing tourism flows and managing impacts. The measurement system they argue for can be used to monitor the TALC if certain steps are followed. They note that there is a "paucity of visitor management tools that help managers make decisions (Ward-Perkins & Dimanche, 2012, p. 1) for cultural tourism (to include heritage, museums, wildlife reserves, and parks). They argue that 1) any framework should be based on elements that apply universally to all cultural sites and that are undisputedly measurable, 2) visitor flow offers such an assurance, 3) such a framework must be able to encompass and address all aspects of management of a visitor destination, and 4) visitor flow comes closer to any other type of measurement to providing this kind of universality. Importantly, a standardized measurement system it warranted in order to establish benchmarks. The movements that compose visitor flows can be determined and measured as follows:

• Average distance travelled to a destination
• Proportions of visitors arriving from specific regions

- Length of time spent at the destination
- Popularity of specific attractions within a destination.

One can thereby establish models showing patterns of visitor flow, initially against objective criteria: seasonality, time of day, weather patterns, pricing, etc.

Role of Planning

Planning as an ongoing process is necessary to manage attractions. Potential overuse of natural resources or impacts upon wildlife and natural areas within a community and regionally is a common concern with regard to tourism and tourists. Therefore, communities need to conduct planning and assessment studies to ensure a sustainable industry. As resources can be impacted by overuse, it is important for both resource managers and community leaders to plan, monitor and assess the sustainability of the travel program (Texas Parks and Wildlife, 2015). The purpose of planning is to develop a vision and strategy by identifying nature-based and cultural tourism opportunities, infrastructure assets and needs, and developing an action plan to achieve the desired goals of the community. Importantly, a basic understanding is needed of the kinds and intensity of activities the resources can accommodate. The areas to be considered should include the following (Texas Parks and Wildlife, 2015):

- **Assessing the impact of nature-based tourism on the resource, the land owners and managers, the community and the tourism industry.**
  - How many visitors and use types can a resource accommodate without adverse impact? How will that impact be measured?
  - How will conflicting uses of resources be planned for and managed?
  - How can managers encourage and secure community involvement?
  - How do resource managers bring resource users (individuals, user groups and tourism businesses) into the planning and management process?
- **Assessing the current tourism situation and potential.**
  - What is the current level of visitation?
  - Is that level causing an adverse impact on the resource?
  - What is the attitude of the surrounding community toward the resource/ visitation?
  - Are there problems associated with the current level of resource use?
  - What are the physical assets and liabilities of the resource?

To moderate the impacts of visitors and manage destination attractions, Middleton and Hawkins (1998) suggest the following:
- Making judgements on carrying capacity
- Selecting and targeting market segments
- Partnering with organizations for planning and marketing
- Developing a variety of attraction management practices for each target market
- Monitoring the results and making required changes

Pearce (1989), Middleton (1994), and Mason (2003) provide a framework that community leaders can consider for the management of attractions (See Table 3.6).

Table 3.6
Resource Constraints and Market Forces

Resource Constraints (supply side) Mainly Public Sector	Market Forces (demand side) Mainly Commercial Sector
Regulation of land use	Knowledge of visitor profiles, behavior, needs and travel trends
Regulation of buildings	Design of visitor experiences (quality and satisfaction)
Region of environmental impacts	Capacity (number and intensity of visitor experiences marketed)
Provision of infrastructure	Promotion (image of attractions and amenities; positioning in market place)
Control by licensing businesses	Distribution of products and access for visitors
Provision of information about community	Provision of information about tourism
Fiscal controls, incentives and funding	Prices

Essentially, planning is critically important and it is imperative to establish benchmarks, adapt a model to monitor the tourism performance of the community, conduct research and make necessary management decisions. The sustainability of community-based tourism may be at risk without leaders aware of the problems, such as overcrowding, resident concerns, waste and litter, tourist dissatisfaction, etc. Importantly, the stakeholders in the community must agree upon a management scheme for the sustainability of the tourism product being offered in the community.

Summary

This chapter identified the types of attractions used in community-based tourism. Importantly, the framework for attraction and importance of attractions were identified. Various amenities were identified by different communities as part of their tourism package. Issues related to attraction management were identified and models proposed to manage those attractions.

The tourism product consists of goods and services (attractions, accommodations, transportation, etc.). The attraction of a community can be seen as a function of supply (all natural and retail services produced for the traveler), and demand (motivations of travelers).

Key Concepts

- Amenities
- Assessing Attractions
- Attraction Management
- Community Tourism System and Attractions
- Demand

- Natural Attractions
- Pull Factors
- Push Factors
- Recreational Impacts
- Success Factors in Heritage Thematic Tourism
- Supply
- Tourism Lifecycle

Useful Internet Sites, Exercises and Resources

Butlers Tourism Area Lifecycle model, http://www.coolgeography.co.uk/GCSE/AQA/Tourism/Life%20cycle%20model/Tourism%20Model.htm

Silos and Smokestacks National Heritage Area, http://www.silosandsmokestacks.org/

Smithsonian Magazine 20 Best Small Towns to Visit, http://www.smithsonianmag.com/travel/20-best-small-towns-to-visit-in-2014-180950173/

Texas Parks and Wildlife, https://tpwd.texas.gov/

U.S. Fish and Wildlife Service Historic Preservation, http://www.fws.gov/historicpreservation/crp/

U.S. Forest Service, Travel and Tourism Goals, http://www.fs.fed.us/recreation/programs/tourism/

West Virginia University Extension Services, http://cred.ext.wvu.edu/tourism/tourism-lifecycle.

World Wildlife Fund, http://gifts.worldwildlife.org/gift-center/gifts/Species-Adoptions.aspx?sc=AWY1200WCGA1&gclid=CMOQ_MekrMYCFVKEfgodcK8H1Q

Questions for Review and Case Problems

1. What is meant by push and pull factors?
2. What are the main or usual attractions for community-based tourism?
3. Discuss food based tourism. Identify communities near where you live that have community-based food tourism events. How have these events changed the community?
4. What is attraction management?
5. What is the product lifecycle?
6. What ways can we manage attractions?

Case Problem

1. Identify a community that is successful with tourism. Try to identify the thematic attractions. How are they marketed? How is the attraction managed in a sustainable way? Can you apply the Butler TALC to the community? If so how, if not why?
2. Write a 500-word report comparing two communities list in Table 3.1. How do they differ? Why do they differ? What makes them unique? What challenges do they have in managing their attractions?

3. Research the Silos and Smokestacks National Heritage Area. Identify its market, review its website. Review the rank-ordered list of attractions in this chapter. Discuss and write a 250-word reason why these are in the order that they are.

References

Amana Colonies. (2015). History of Amana. Retrieved from http://www.amanacolonies.com.

Arbogast, D., Deng, J., & Maumbe, K. (2017). TALC: A Tourism Management Planning and Decision Making Model for Rural Communities. West Virginia University. Personal Communication, June 27, 2017.

Ashland, Oregon Chamber of Commerce. (2015). Our seasonal events in Ashland, Oregon. Retrieved from http://www.ashlandchamber.com/SectionIndex.asp?Section-ID=115.

Betz, C. J., & Perdue, R. R. (1993). The role of amenity resources in rural recreation and tourism development. *Journal of Park and Recreation Administration, 11*(4), 15–24.

Butler, R. W. (1980). The concept of a tourist area cycle of evolution: Implications for management of resources. *The Canadian Geographer/Le Géographe Canadien, 24*(1), 5–12.

Cannon Beach Chamber of Commerce. (2015). Shops. Oregon's Cannon Beach. Retrieved from http://www.cannonbeach.org/businesses/Shop

Carlsen, J., Huges, M., Frost, W., Pocock, C., & Peel, V. (2008). *Success factors in cultural heritage tourism enterprise management.* Queensland: CRC for Sustainable Tourism Pty Ltd.

Cedar Falls Tourism Convention & Visitors Bureau. (2015). Events. Retrieved from http://www.cedarfallstourism.org/events/annual-events.aspx

Choi, P. (2012). Destination attractiveness of the Silos Smokestacks National Heritage Area (Unpublished doctoral dissertation). University of Northern Iowa, Cedar Falls, IA.

City of Red Wing, MN. (2015). Parks around Red Wing. Retrieved from http://www.red-wing.org/redwingparks.html

Eugster, J. G. (2003). Evolution of the heritage movement. *Forum Journal, 17*(3), 13–21.

Every Culture. (2015). Canada. Retrieved from http://www.everyculture.com/Bo-Co/Canada.html

Formica, S. (2000). Destination attractiveness as a function of supply and demand interaction (Unpublished doctoral dissertation). Blacksburg, VA: Virginia Polytechnic Institute and State University.

Hawkins, D., & Cunningham, J. (1996). It is "never-never land" when interest groups prevail: Disney's America project, Prince William County, Virginia, USA. In L. C. Harrison & W. Husbands (Eds.), *Practicing responsible tourism* (pp. 350–365). New York, NY: John Wiley.

Hetherington, A. (1991). *Rural tourism: Marketing small communities.* Bainbridge Island, WA: Meta-Link.

Higginbottom, K. (2004). *Wildlife tourism impacts, management, and planning.* Altona Victoria, Australia: Common Ground Publishing Pty Ltd. Retrieved from http://www.crctourism.com.au/wms/upload/resources/wildlifetourism-impacts.pdf.

Hood River County Chamber of Commerce. (2013). Ten "must do activities when visiting Hood River County. Retrieved from http://hoodriver.org/travelers-guide/ten-must-do-activities

Lanesboro Chamber of Commerce. (2015). Root River bike trail. Retrieved from http://www.lanesboro.com

Leiper, N. (1995). Tourism attraction systems. *Annals of Tourism Research, 17*(3), 367.

Lew, A. (1987). A model of tourist attraction research. *Annals of Tourism Research, 14,* 553–575.

Live Healthy Red Wing. (n.d.) Walking maps. Retrieved from http://www.livehealthyredwing.org/maps.htm

Mason, P. (2003). *Tourism impacts, planning, and management.* Oxford, UK: Butterworth Heinemann.

Maumbe, K., Deng., J., & Arbogast, D. (2013). Application of tourism area lifecyle (TALC) model to tourism development in WV. Unpublished report. Morgantown, WV: West Virginia University.

Middleton, V. (1994). *Marketing in travel and tourism.* London, UK: Routledge.

Mineral Point Chamber of Commerce. (n.d.) History and art. Retrieved from http://mineralpoint.com

Morachat, C. (2003). A study of destination attractiveness through tourists' perspectives: A focus on Chaing Mai, Thailand (Unpublished doctoral dissertation). Perth, Western Australia: Edith Cowan University.

National Park Service U.S. Department of the Interior. (2015). Hot springs in the middle of town. Retrieved from http://www.nps.gov/hosp/index.htm

Nelson, M. (2014). Characteristics of community-based tourism practices: A stakeholder analysis (Unpublished MA research paper). Cedar Falls, IA: University of Northern Iowa.

Nova Scotia. (2015). Nova Scotia's culture. Retrieved from http://www.novascotia.com/explore/culture .

Oregon Shakespeare Festival. (n.d.) What is OSF? Retrieved from https://www.osfashland.org/en/about/what-is-osf.aspx .

Pearce, D. (1989). *Tourism development* (2nd ed.). New York, NY: Longman Scientific and Technical.

Pearce, P. L. (1994). Tourist-resident impact: Examples and emerging solutions. In W. F. Theobald (Ed.), *Global tourism: The next decade* (pp. 103–123). Oxford, UK: Butterworth-Heinemann.

Pure Michigan. (2013). Give a craft beer trail. http://www.discoverkalamazoo.com/give-a-craft™-beer-trail-192/#/gallery/recent

Salazar, N. B. (2012). Community-based cultural tourism: Issues, threats, and opportunities. *Journal of Sustainable Tourism, 20*(1), 9–22.

Sinha, C. C. (2001). *Wildlife tourism: A geographical perspective.* Paper presented during the Geography Curriculum In-service Conference, Tourism Geography: Issues, Challenges and the Changing Nature of Contemporary Tourism, University of Western Sydney, Hawkesbury Campus, 27 July 2001.

Smith, S. L. J. (1994). Regional analysis of tourism resources. *Annals of Tourism Research, 14,* 253–273.

Springdale Town. (n.d.). Springdale: The gateway to Zion National Park. Retrieved from http://www.springdaletown.com/community/zion-national-park/

Tabata, R., & Kuehn, D. (2000). Thematic itineraries. *Legacy, 11*(5), 15–22.

Texas Parks and Wildlife. (2015). Community planning for nature tourism. Retrieved from http://tpwd.texas.gov/landwater/land/programs/tourism/your_business/guidance/

Time and Date. (2015). Natal Day in Canada. Retrieved from http://www.timeanddate.com/holidays/canada/natal-day

Travel Iowa. (2015). Calendar of events. Retrieved from http://www.traveliowa.com/aspx/calendar.aspx?dfrom=&dto=&k=&clist=&catid=15&catlist=23

UNI STEP. (2004). Economic impact of the Silos and Smokestacks National Heritage Area. Retrieved from http://www.uni.edu/step/reports/silos_final.pdf

United States Department of Agriculture Economic Research. (2015). FAQs: What are the top 10 agricultural producing states? Retrieved from http://www.ers.usda.gov/faqs.aspx#10

Ward-Perkins, D., & Dimanche, F. (2012). *From measuring visitor flows to tourism attraction management: A new managerial approach.* Paper published in the Proceedings of the 2012 TTRA Europe conference. Retrieved from https://www.academia.edu/1518513/From_Measuring_Visitor_Flows_to_Tourism_Attraction_Management.

Wang, Y., & Pfister, R. (2008). Residents' attitudes toward tourism and perceived personal benefits in a rural community. *Journal of Travel Research.* January 14, 2008.

Weaver, D., & Lawton, L. (2006). *Tourism management.* Australia: John Wiley.

West Bend Grotto. (n.d.). History. Retrieved from http://www.westbendgrotto.com/history.

Whyte, B., Hood, T., & White, B. (2012). *Cultural and heritage tourism: A handbook for community champions.* Canada's Federal, Provincial, and Territorial Minister of Culture and Heritage.

Wyoming Migration Initiative. (2015). Elk migrations of the Greater Yellowstone. Retrieved from http://migrationinitiative.org/content/elk-migrations-greater-yellowstone

Yukon Tourism and Culture. (2014). Developing your product 3.11. www.tc.gov.yk.ca.

CHAPTER 4

Travel Motivations and Understanding Thematic Tourism

"It has been suggested that it is possible to describe the 'who,' 'when,' 'where' and 'how' of tourism, together with the economic and social characteristics of tourists, but not to answer the question 'why.'"

–John Crompton (1979)

CHAPTER OBJECTIVES

- Define and discuss the concept of thematic tourism
- Briefly discuss various types of thematic tourism
- Outline and discuss the main travel motivation theories
- Discuss the typical process for conducting visitor motivation studies
- Review a case study examining motivations of wine travelers in rural Northeast Iowa.

Introduction

A common definition of motivation is something that stimulates interest or causes a person to act in a certain way. The wants and needs of tourists are often regarded as travel motivations. While many tourist destinations and sites gather visitor data, tourist behavior characteristics, as well as the wants and needs of tourists, are frequently left unexplored. At the same time, knowing why tourists travel is the most fundamental question in the study of visitor behavior; in fact, motivations are believed to be fundamental reasons for human behavior (Pearce, 1991b). Understanding travel motivations is critical to understanding vacation decision making (Dann, 1977) and determining visitor satisfaction (Yoon & Uysal, 2005). In addition, travel motivations data can be extremely useful for marketing purposes, as understanding of tourist needs, wants, expectations, and behaviors can enable communities to design smart and sound long-term marketing strategies, and provide their customers experiences they want and expect, and not products and services they are assumed to desire (Marzo-Navarro & Pedraja-Iglesias, 2009).

Travelers with similar motivations create a demand for specialized tourism products. As the demand increases, niche tourism emerges as a means by which destinations can differentiate their tourism products and compete in an increasingly cluttered tourism environment (Sharpley & Telfer, 2002). To successfully operate in a chosen market segment, destinations therefore must have a good grasp of understanding the motivations and needs of tourists who seek these specialized products and services.

Understanding Thematic Tourism

The concepts of thematic tourism, special interest tourism, and niche tourism all refer to the same basic concept of tailoring a specific tourism product to meet the needs of a particular audience or a market segment (Novelli, 2005). *Thematic tourism* typically refers to a broad range of offerings including theme parks, health tourism, sport tourism, religious tourism etc.; each of these categories of thematic tourism has its own set of subcategories; for example, there are theme parks that focus on history (Camelot in the United Kingdom), a particular product (Legoland in Denmark), or movie themes and characters (Disney World in Florida) (examples from Lubbe, 2003). Similarly, *special interest travel (SIT)* is usually defined as travel taking place when the "traveler's motivation and decision-making are primarily determined by a particular special interest with a focus either on activities and/or destinations and settings" (Hall & Weiler, 1992, p. 5). A slightly different definition positions special interest travel as "the provision of customized leisure and recreational experiences driven by the specific expressed interest of individuals and groups" (Derrett, 2001, p. xvii). Finally, the term *niche tourism* is largely borrowed from the term *niche marketing* (concentrating all marketing efforts on a small but specific and well-defined segment of the population).

While tourism denotes mass participation, thematic (special interest, or niche) tourism suggests noncommercialized individual travel. Arguably, this type of travel is the opposite of mass tourism and is often sustainable in nature. Some of the growing thematic tourism markets are outlined below:

- **Theme trails**–themed routes and roads; includes pilgrimages, fairytale trails, nature trails, educational trails, heritage trails, wine trails and routes, etc.
- **Nature-based tourism**–travel to natural places; tourism based on the natural attractions of an area (birdwatching, photography, stargazing, camping, hiking, hunting, fishing, visiting parks, etc.)
- **Coastal and marine tourism**–travel for recreational activities in the marine or coastal environment; includes beach-based tourism and recreation activities (coastal tourism), as well as sailing, nautical sports, and cruising (marine tourism)
- **Ecotourism**–responsible travel to natural areas that conserves the environment and improves the well-being of local people (low-impact, small-scale, educational travel)
- **Educational tourism**–travel for educational and learning purposes; includes career enhancement, job development, self-actualization experiences, student exchanges, etc.

- **Culinary tourism**–travel to learn about, appreciate, consume, or indulge in food and drink that reflects the local cuisine, heritage, or culture of a place; includes food tourism, beer tourism, wine tourism, chocolate tourism, tea tourism, farmhouse cooking vacations, etc.
- **Cultural and heritage tourism**–travel directed toward experiencing the arts, heritage, and special character of a place; includes travel to museums, historic sites, dance, music, theater, book and other festivals, historic buildings, arts and crafts fairs, neighborhoods, and landscapes
- **Religious tourism (faith tourism)**–travel individually or in groups for pilgrimage, missionary, or leisure (fellowship) purposes
- **Health tourism**–comprises of *medical tourism* (travel to treat/cure a medical condition) and *wellness tourism* (travel to maintain or improve one's health, lose weight, slow the effects of aging, relieve pain or discomfort, manage stress, or to partake in the use of natural supplement)
- **Adventure tourism**–exploration or travel with perceived (and possibly actual) risk involved, potentially requiring specialized skills and physical exertion; it must include two of the following three components: a physical activity, a cultural exchange or interaction, and engagement with nature
- **Sport tourism**–travel to observe or participating in sport-related activities; includes sport event tourism, active sport tourism, and nostalgia sport tourism
- **Rural tourism**–any form of tourism that showcases the rural life, art, culture and heritage at rural locations; an activity that takes place in the countryside. Includes farm/agricultural tourism, cultural tourism, nature tourism, adventure tourism, and ecotourism

What makes one a wellness tourist? A culinary (wine) tourist? An ecotourist? The answer is primary travel motivations. For example, those traveling specifically to unwind and enjoy reflexology and massages could be classified as wellness tourists; those visiting wine-growing regions and wine routes, vineyards, wineries (cellar tours and tasting rooms), and wine festivals with the purpose of consuming or purchasing wine, are wine tourists; and those going on birdwatching tours are most likely ecotourists or avitourists (birdwatching tourists).

The purpose of this chapter is to help the reader understand the complexity of visitor motivations. We do not provide a simple recipe for answering the question "why do people travel?" as it is, in fact, quite difficult, especially taking into consideration an observation made by Lundberg (1972) that "what the traveler says are his motivations for travelling may only be reflections of deeper needs, needs which he himself does not understand nor wish to articulate" (p.107). Having said that, there are many theories that can be used as a starting point in approaching the subject; the following section reviews some of these theories and outlines their application in the field of tourism.

Travel Motivation Theories

As stated earlier, motivation can be described as the driving force within individuals that impels them to action (Shiffman & Kanuk, 2000). This driving force emerges from a state of tension that exists as the result of an unfulfilled need (need being the difference between a person's actual and desired state) (Dunne, 2009). Since it is needs that arouse motivated behavior, understanding visitors' needs is necessary for understanding visitor's motivation.

Over the years, a number of theories and frameworks have been developed to explain tourist motivations for traveling. The most common theories and models are reviewed below. None of them are without criticism, and many have been revised and modified. Each of the models, however elegant and simple, should be considered and applied only within their limitations. We leave the in-depth discussion of each of the models to the other authors, and instead provide a general overview in hope to draw a complex picture of tourist needs, wants, and expectations.

Maslow's Hierarchy of Needs

In *A Theory of Human Motivation* (1943), Abraham Maslow argued that human actions are directed toward goal attainment and humans are motivated to achieve certain needs. As basic needs are met, people seek to satisfy successively higher needs that occupy a set of hierarchy:

> It is quite true that man lives by bread alone—when there is no bread. But what happens to man's desires when there is plenty of bread and when his belly is chronically filled? At once other (and 'higher') needs emerge, and these, rather than physiological hungers, dominate the organism. And when these in turn are satisfied, again new (and still 'higher') needs emerge, and so on. This is what we mean by saying that the basic human needs are organized into a hierarchy of relative prepotency. (Maslow, 1943, p. 375)

Maslow illustrated this hierarchy of needs with a pyramid, where the first four levels (lower-order needs, also known as deficiency, or deprivation needs) are considered physiological needs, and the fifth (top level) is considered growth needs. The lower level needs need to be satisfied before higher-order needs can influence behavior. The highest level is self-actualization, or self-fulfillment, which refers "to the person's desire for self-fulfillment, namely, to the tendency for him to become actualized in what he is potentially" (Maslow, 1943, pp. 382–383). At this stage, human behavior is no longer driven or motivated by deficiencies, but rather by one's desire for personal growth and the need to become all the things that a person is capable of becoming (Maslow, 1970).

While every person is capable and has the desire to move up the hierarchy toward a level of self-actualization, Maslow believed that only one in a hundred people actually become fully self-actualized, for a number of reasons. Mainly it is because our society rewards motivation primarily based on esteem, love, and other social needs; in addition, the progress up the hierarchy can also be disrupted by failure to meet lower level needs.

The original hierarchy of needs included five stages; in his later works, *Motivation and Personality* (1970) and *Religions, Values, and Peak experiences* (1970), Maslow expanded his original model to include cognitive, aesthetic, and transcendence needs. The revised model thus comprises of the following eight levels (see Figure 4.1):

- **Biological and physiological needs:** air, food, drink, shelter, warmth, sex, sleep, etc.
- **Safety needs:** protection from elements, security, order, law, limits, stability, etc.

- **Belongingness and love needs:** work group, family, affection, relationships, etc.
- **Esteem needs:** self-esteem, achievement, mastery, independence, status, dominance, prestige, managerial responsibility, etc.
- **Cognitive needs:** knowledge, meaning, etc.
- **Aesthetic needs:** appreciation and search for beauty, balance, form, etc.
- **Self-actualization needs:** realizing personal potential, self-fulfillment, seeking personal growth and peak experiences
- **Transcendence needs:** helping others to achieve self-actualization

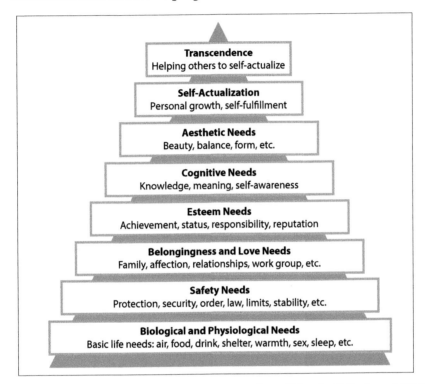

Figure 4.1. Maslow's Eight-Stage Hierarchy of Needs (Maslow, 1970)

Maslow's hierarchy of needs has been used in the tourism industry in several ways: (1) to understand changes in travelers' needs that come with age/gender/social status/etc.; for example, tourist behavior research shows that while older tourists are more oriented toward relationships and self-actualization needs, younger tourists are more oriented toward physiological needs; (2) the level of needs can provide tourism businesses with a better understanding of their travel market and can help improve effectiveness of promotional communication; for example, knowing that one of the reasons people join a cruise is because of their need for friendships, cruise lines may emphasize opportunities for meeting new people in their advertising; (3) destinations can take specific steps to address each of the identified needs; for example, by offering frequent rest stops and ensuring food outlets are easily accessible (physiological needs), providing tour guides and guaranteeing medical services (safety needs), organizing trips to explore one's roots or thematic group tours (belonging needs), offering elite status in frequent user programs and guest recognition (esteem needs), and designing educational tours and cruises or culture/language immersion courses (self-actualization needs).

Travel Career Ladder (TCL) and Travel Career Pattern (TCP)

Based on Maslow's hierarchy of needs, Pearce and Caltabiano (1983) designed a similar framework specifically for tourism. They put forward the notion of a motivational career in travel (also known as the Travel Career Ladder, see Figure 4.2), whereas more experienced tourists display higher lever needs than less experienced travelers:

> The five motivational levels described in the scheme are: a concern with biological needs (including relaxation), safety and security needs (or levels of stimulation), relationship development and extension needs, special interest and self-development needs, and fulfillment or deep involvement needs (formally defined as self-actualization) (Pearce, 1996, p.13).

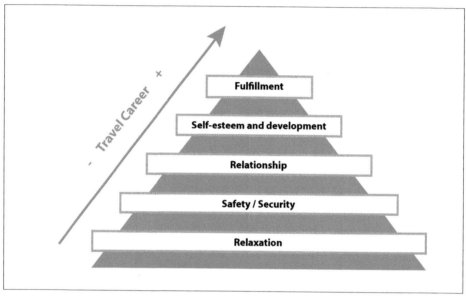

Figure 4.2. Travel Career Ladder (Pearce,1988)

Like with any career, tourists can start at different levels and will likely change levels (ascending or descending the ladder) during their life cycle either on one or on both sides of the model. However, as they become more experienced, people will increasingly seek satisfaction of higher needs (Pearce, 1991a). In other words, holiday experiences arguably enable people to psychologically mature.

The core of the model is its developmental and dynamic nature, for as people travel and acquire experiences (develop a travel "career"), their motivations change. Ryan (1998) illustrates this with an example of those traveling abroad; while those going abroad for the first time may prefer the security of a package tour, over time they will most likely opt for a more independent travel itinerary.

Just as in Maslow's hierarchy of needs, the model assumes that tourists ascend to higher needs once lower needs for a tourism experience are fulfilled. The main steps of the ladder are as follows:

- **Relaxation and bodily needs:** need for basic services and restoration
- **Stimulation:** need for excitement and safety (thrills of the amusement park, experiences of different foods and people)

- **Relationship:** need to build and extend personal relationships
- **Self-esteem and development:** need to develop skills, knowledge and abilities
- **Fulfillment:** need to feel peaceful and profoundly happy (totally engaged in the tourist setting)

In 2005, Pearce and his colleagues revised the original TCL and proposed instead a *Travel Career Pattern (TCP)* model (Pearce, 2005; Pearce and Lee, 2005). Unlike Travel Career Ladder, Travel Career Pattern emphasizes the pattern of motivations rather than the hierarchy of needs and motives (Teichmann & Zins, 2009). The model includes 14 motivational factors, and can be depicted using three layers of travel motivation, where each layer consists of different travel motives (see Figure 3). The core layer includes the most important common motives (such as novelty, escape/relax), the surrounding layer includes moderately important travel motives (such as self actualization, nature, and host-site involvement), and the outer layer consists of common, less important travel motives (such as nostalgia, social status, isolation).

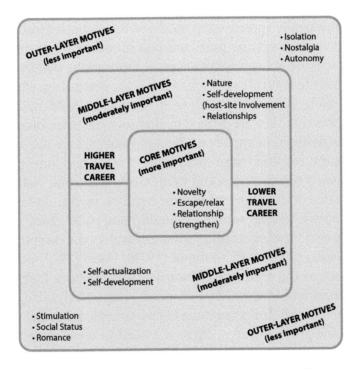

Figure 4.3. Travel Career Pattern (Pearce, 2005)

Having examined the relationship between travel motivation and travel experience level, Pearce and Lee (2005) concluded:

Within the identified 14 travel motivational factors, people with high-travel-experience levels gave more emphasis to motivations regarding self-development through host-site involvement and nature seeking. Low-travel-experience-level people stressed more on other motivation factors such as stimulation, personal development, self-actualization, security, nostalgia, romance, and recognition... Furthermore, travel motives related to novelty, escape/relax, and relationship, and self-development [can be described] as a foundation regardless of one's travel experience. Therefore, these four central motivation factors could be understood as the "backbone" or "skeleton" of all travel motivation and travel career patterns (pp.235–236).

Compared to the Travel Career Ladder, Travel Career Pattern model reveals more meaningful information and does a better job explaining travel motivations. It supports the notion that travel motivation a multidimensional concept, yet several of its assumptions require further clarification. For example, age can be a misleading indicator of travel experience (advanced age does not mean extensive travel experience), the actual concept of travel experience is a bit vague (whether it is the number of times a person has travelled, the number of different destinations a person has travelled to, or the amount of time a person has spent travelling), and finally it is unclear whether travel experience is treated as a component of broader human experiences (Filep & Greenacre, 2007).

Push and Pull Factors

Even though a universally agreed-upon model of travel motivations does not exist, most tourism researchers accept the push and pull model of travel decision making. *Push factors* in this scheme are sociopsychological motivations that predispose, while the *pull factors* are those that attract a person to a specific destination when the decision to travel has been made (adapted from Bogari, Crowther, & Marr, 2004). In other words, people travel because they are pushed by their own internal forces and pulled by external forces of the destination attributes. Most push factors are intrinsic motivators, such as desire for escape, rest and relaxation, prestige, health and fitness, adventure and social interaction, family togetherness, and excitement, while pull factors emerge due to the attractiveness of a destination and include beaches, recreation facilities, cultural attractions, entertainment, natural scenery, shopping, and parks (Yoon & Uysal, 2005).

The two most known travel motivation models developed to support the push and pull theory are of Dann (1977) and Crompton (1979). Dann (1977) proposed anomie and ego enhancement as the main travel motives (some believe that these reinforce Maslow's belongingness and love and esteem needs, respectively). He argued that we live in an anomic society and this generates a need in people for social interaction that is missing in the home place, therefore there is a need to travel away from the home environment (Dann, 1977). Ego enhancement, on the other hand, derives from the need for recognition, which is obtained through the status conferred by travel (Dunne, 2009).

In a later study, Crompton (1979) identified nine travel motives and grouped them in two clusters of seven sociopsychological and two cultural motives, implicitly arguing that these categories represented push and pull factors, respectively. The sociopsychological (push) motives identified by Crompton (1979) were escape from a perceived mundane environment, exploration and evaluation of self, relaxation, prestige, regression, enhancement of kinship relationships, and facilitation of social interaction. The cultural (pull) motives identified were novelty and education (some question, however, whether the cultural motives could indeed be considered a pull factor).

The push and pull dichotomy has been widely used in tourism research. While most of the studies employed the concept to identify or classify travel motives, some examined interrelationship between push and pull factors, suggesting that both factors respond to and reinforce each other in a complex manner (Mehmetoglu, 2011). A noted interpretation was given by Lundberg (1971), who illustrated the model with an advertisement directed toward potential tourists showing sunny beaches with sunbathers. This strategy, he argued, not only promoted a specific location, but also generated a push force to pry potential tourists out of their homes.

Despite its common application in tourism, researchers tend to disagree on the interpretation of the push and pull concept. While most assume that both push and pull factors are motivational factors, others argue that only push factors can serve as motivational forces, while pull factors represent destination attributes. Finally, there are also those who believe that push and pull factors correspond to separate stages in travel decision making (Hsu & Huang, 2008).

Plog's Model of Allocentricity and Psychocentricity

In *Why Destination Areas Rise and Fall in Popularity* (1974), Stanley Plog outlined a model of allocentricity and psychocentricity for the tourism industry. He presented these two personality traits at the opposite ends of a continuum that approximated a normally distributed curve. On one end of continuum were *psychocentric* travelers, described as nervous, not adventurous, and self-inhibited—thus preferring familiarity in their choice of travel destinations. On the other end were *allocentric* travelers, described as outgoing, curious, and self-confident explorers. In between were the majority of travelers, classified by Plog as *mid-centric*, along with *near-psychocentric* and *near-allocentric* travelers (see Figure 4.4). As Litvin (2006) explains, those with near-allocentric tendencies are among the first major wave of adopters (after a destination has been found by the allocentrics), while the near-psychocentrics are most likely to consider a destination after it has been well traveled.

In 2001, Plog updated his model and renamed psychocentrics as *dependables* and allocentric as *venturers*. He further argued that about 2.5% of the U.S. population can be classified as dependables, and slightly over 4% as venturers, with the remainder being *near-dependables*, *near-venturers,* and *centrics* (centrics being the largest group of travelers) (Figure 4.4).

According to Plog (1974), destinations, like people, can also be plotted along a psychocentric-allocentric continuum. The original model, for example, listed Myrtle Beach (South Carolina) and Coney Island (New York) as psychocentric destinations, and Japan, Asia, and South Pacific as allocentric destinations – classification that is no longer valid for North American travelers, and is clearly not applicable for travelers from other regions and countries.

While examining the underlying causes for why destinations rise and fall in popularity, Plog (2001) concluded:

Destinations appeal to specific types of people and typically follow a relatively predictable pattern of growth and decline in popularity over time. The reasons lie in the fact that the character of most destinations changes as a result of growth and development of tourist-oriented facilities. As destinations change, they lose the audience or market segments that made them popular and appeal instead to an ever shrinking group of travelers. (p. 13)

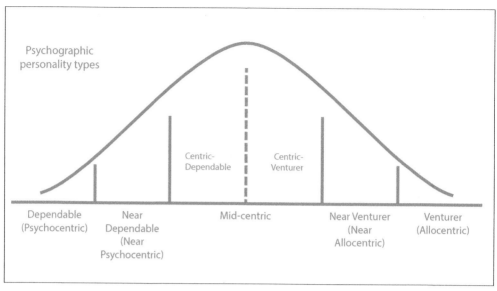

Figure 4.4. Plog's Model of Allocentricity and Psychocentricity (Plog, 2001)

This elegant yet simple statement has important practical implication for destinations. When a destination first develops tourism, few support services exist (hotels, restaurants), and a few visitors that do arrive are mostly venturers. As these visitors return home and spread the word, near-venturers begin to visit the place, and as the number of tourists increases, more facilities and support services are developed and provided. Over time, demand increases, destinations take on a more touristy look, and thus become unattractive to venturers (hence the normal rise of the curve gradually declines). It is therefore a good strategy for most destinations to position themselves in the middle of the near-venturer segment, while carefully planning and controlling their tourism development to maintain an ideal market position (Plog, 2001).

Cohen's (1972) Tourist Typologies

Cohen's (1972) model could be related to Plog's (1974, 2001) model, wherein psychocentrics are further divided into *organized* and *individualized* and allocentrics into *explorers* and *drifters*:

- **Organized mass tourists:** value familiarity in a destination, do not seek novelty. Prefer package tour fixed itineraries, planned stops, and guided organizers making the decisions.
- **Individual mass tourists:** have some control over their itineraries but make major arrangements through travel intermediaries. Typically prefer traveling in their own country and remain largely within their personal bubble.
- **Explorers:** tourists usually planning their own trips and trying to avoid developed tourist attractions. Enjoy mixing with locals but still remain in their personal bubble.
- **Drifters:** plan their trips alone, prefer tourist destinations, live with the locals. Enjoy being immersed in the host culture, value novelty.

Seeking and Escaping Dimensions, and Optimal Arousal

The development of this framework started with Dann (1981), who grouped tourist motivations into seven categories:

1. Travel as a response to what is lacking yet desired (typically the need for getting away)
2. Destination "pull" in response to motivational "push"
3. Motivation as fantasy (tourism being liberating experience)
4. Motivation as a classified purpose (viewing motivation according to the purpose of visit, such as study, pilgrimage, health, etc.)
5. Motivational typologies (this approach is concerned with tourist roles or types)
6. Motivation and tourist experiences (focuses on the actual experiences tourists go through)
7. Motivation as auto-definition and meaning (how tourists define situations provides a greater understanding of their action than a mere examination of their behavior).

In a rejoinder to Dann (1981), Iso-Ahola (1982) proposed a different take on leisure motivations, putting forth the concepts of *seeking* (intrinsic rewards) and *escaping* (routine environments) dimensions. The framework constructed a desired state of stimulation for travelers, and was initially referred to as the *intrinsic optimal arousal*. Leisure behavior, Iso-Ahola (1980, 1982) argued, takes place in a context that allows individuals to find a comfortable space between overstimulation (too much arousal) and understimulation (boredom). Thus, when setting goals for traveling, tourists tend to optimize (or compensate) their levels of arousal. For example, if a person's life is too quiet, the person may seek out stimulation through activity; whereas if there is too much happening in a person's life, then the person will seek to cut off stimulation and find a quieter environment. While dichotomous, these two motives, however, are not mutually exclusive, since it is possible for an individual to be engaged in both motives simultaneously. As Iso-Ahola (1982) concluded, "tourism is a dialectical process because it provides an outlet for avoiding something and for simultaneously seeking something" (p. 261).

In 1987, Mannell and Iso-Ahola revisited the framework and added that both seeking and escaping dimensions have a *personal (psychological)* and *interpersonal (social)* component. As a result, the revised framework included four motives (also considered push factors): personal seeking, personal escape, interpersonal seeking, and interpersonal escape. It also implied that there was an optimal level of arousal for travelers (see Figure 4.5).

Some researchers argue that tourism provides an excellent means of accommodating a person's need for an optimal level of stimulation. Even though the seeking and escaping framework was developed for leisure, examining the arousal level of people's daily life and work may yield valuable insights as to their travel motivations (Hsu & Huang, 2008). Someone whose daily life is overbearing may choose to visit a remote, peaceful setting to counter the pressures of home and work, and someone whose work and life are boring may want a vacation that supplies adventure and excitement.

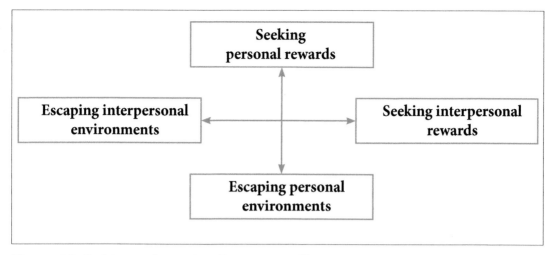

Figure 4.5. Seeking and escaping dimensions of leisure motivation
(Mannell & Iso-Ahola, 1987)

Other Travel Motivation Theories

Indeed, an examination of the many studies on tourist motivation reveals a core of similar motives appearing again and again under different names. Following is a brief overview of a few more travel motivation theories:

- **Lundberg's (1971) 18 motivational factors**
  - Educational motives (attending special events, visiting historical sites)
  - Relaxation and pleasure seeking motives (having a good time, or a romantic experience)
  - Ethnic motives (visiting places of family origin)
  - Sundry motives (sports, conformity with neighbors/relatives)
- **Schmoll's (1977) motivational groupings**
  - Educational and cultural
  - Relaxation
  - Adventure and pleasure
  - Health and recreation
  - Ethnic and family
  - Social and competitive (including status and prestige)
- **Beard and Ragheb's (1983) four motivational needs**
  - The intellectual component (motivation to engage in learning, exploring, discovering, thought, or imagining)
  - The social component (the need for friendship and interpersonal relationships, as well as the need for the esteem of others)
  - The competence-mastery component (motivation to achieve, master, challenge and compete in physical activities)

- The stimulus-avoidance component (the drive to escape and get away from over-stimulating life situations; the need to avoid social contacts, to seek solitude and calm conditions)
- **Krippendorf's (1987) eight travel motivations**
  - Recuperation and regeneration
  - Compensation and social integration
  - Escape
  - Communication
  - Broadening of the mind
  - Freedom and self determination
  - Self-realization
  - Happiness
- **Smith's (1977) interactional tourist typologies**
  - Explore
  - Elite
  - Off-beat
  - Unusual
  - Incipient mass
  - Mass
  - Charter
- **Shoemaker's (1994) tourism market segments**
  - Get away/family travelers
  - Adventurous travelers
  - Gambler/fun travelers
- **McIntosh, Goeldner, and Ritchie's (1995) travel motivations categories**
  - Physical motivators (refreshment of body and mind, health purposes, sport and pleasure; they seem to be linked to tension reducing activities)
  - Cultural motivators (include the desire for knowledge of other countries and place—their music, art, folklore, dances, paintings, and religion)
  - Interpersonal motivators (involve a desire to meet new people, to visit friends or relatives, to escape from routine, family or neighbors, or to make new friendships)
  - Status and prestige motivators (include desire for recognition, attention, appreciation, and a good reputation)

Having examined a number of travel motivation theories, the next step is to discuss how these can be applied in practice.

Practical Application: Travel Motivation Research

A number of studies have generated evidence that tourist behavior is influenced by culture, nationality, age, gender, class, previous travel experience, type of travel, benefits sought, attitudes, and other situational and environmental factors. Yet extrapolating and generalizing findings needs to be done with a great caution as motivational studies are highly contextual.

Examination of Motivations of Wine Travelers in Rural Northeast Iowa

Purpose of the study: To assist wineries on the Iowa Wine Trail in understanding behavioral characteristics and motivations of their visitors.

Methodology: A questionnaire survey was administered in 2005 at three participating wineries. In addition to gathering data on visitors' demographic characteristics and spending patterns, the survey also examined motivations. Visitors were asked to indicate their agreement with several motives for visiting the wineries/wine trail on a 5-point Likert-type scale (5=*strongly agree*, 4=*agree*, 3=*neither agree nor disagree*, 2=*disagree*, 1=*strongly disagree*). The list of motivation questions was drawn from the literature, discussed with the wineries, and modified to suit the local context.

Results: Survey results indicated that the main motives for visiting the wineries were (in order by mean scores): "to taste wine," "to enjoy the scenery," "to have a good time with friends and family," "to relax," "to support local wine producers," and "to taste locally produced foods." Factor analysis (principal components analysis with varimax rotation) was used to understand the variance among the thirteen items. Results revealed three main groups of motives: "to learn about the wine and winemaking process" (Factor 1), "to gain an authentic Northeast Iowa experience" (Factor 2), and "to enjoy having a good time" (Factor 3).

Conclusions: Results of the study suggested a more efficient marketing strategy for the wineries. While wine tasting appeared to be the main motive of those visiting the wineries, scenery and landscape of the Upper Mississippi River, along with the opportunity to enjoy time with friends and family and taste local foods, scored similarly high. In other words, visitors were drawn to the area not only by wine cellar-type experiences, but also by the scenery and the wider appeal of the area. Effective marketing regional wineries and a trail itself would therefore include not only wine-related experiences, but also rural features and attractions.

Destination-specific consumer behavior research could provide numerous benefits to communities embarking on a tourism development path. To effectively attract new and generate repeat visitors, communities need to correctly segment their markets based on the nature of tourists, their intentions, motivations, and preferences. As tourists traveling for adventure or cultural reasons greatly differ from backpackers or wine connoisseurs, it is increasingly important to analyze travel motivations in their respective contexts.

For destinations considering travel motivation research, a number of options are available. Typically, motivational studies rely on quantitative methods and follow a well-established process of developing a list of motivational items→designing questionnaire surveys that include motivational statements with a (5-point) Likert-type scale to measure the importance of each item →surveying a random sample of visitors to the area→analyzing the data using factor analysis and ANOVA to identify relationships between motivational dimensions and selected sociodemographic variables. When primary research involving data collection is not feasible, destinations can purchase travel market research data collected by state and national organizations.

While the above-mentioned process remains prevalent in travel motivation research, many argue that given the nature of tourist motivations, qualitative approaches may in fact be preferred (e.g., focus groups, interviews, observations, etc.) because of their ability to generate more complete unbiased motivational information (Dann & Phillips, 2000). Overall, we would argue that combining quantitative and qualitative methods is most helpful: quantitative methods can provide hard data, while qualitative methods can support and improve interpretation of the data that was collected.

To illustrate travel motivation research in practice, we share a study that was conducted in rural Northeastern Iowa in order to understand travel motivations of visitors to the wineries on the Iowa Wine Trail.

Summary

This chapter sought to examine travel motivations and thematic tourism. Thematic tourism (also known as special interest tourism or niche tourism) refers to tailoring a specific tourism product to meet the needs of a particular audience or a market segment. As the definition implies, the needs of the visitors arouse motivated behavior, and impel them to action. Knowing (and understanding) why tourists travel is therefore the most fundamental question communities need to answer.

This chapter does not provide a simple recipe for explaining tourist motivations for traveling. Instead, it outlines a number of motivation theories and approaches, and discusses how they can be applied in practice. It is up to communities to choose the approach that works for them—keeping in mind that there is no right or wrong way to do this. Ultimately, any attempt to systematically understand the visitors is better than doing nothing at all.

Key Concepts

- Thematic tourism (special interest tourism, niche tourism)
- Maslow's hierarchy of needs
- Travel Career Ladder (TCL) and Travel Career Pattern (TCP)
- Push and pull factors
- Plog's model of allocentricity and psychocentricity
- Seeking and escaping dimensions, and optimal arousal
- Travel motivation research

Useful Sites, Exercises, and Resources

1. Visit European Travel Commission website at http://www.etc-corporate.org. Search for "travel motivation," review research undertaken by the agency to understand motivations of travelers to Europe.
2. Visit Destination British Columbia website at http://www.destinationbc.ca. Go to "Research" tab, then select "Travel motivations." Review research on motivations of North American travelers, compare motivations of do¬mestic (Canadian) travelers with those from the United States of America.

Questions for Review and Case Problems

1. Explain the concept of thematic tourism. What are the different types of thematic tourism you have experienced?
2. Discuss the main travel motivation theories.
2. What is the purpose of visitor motivation studies? Briefly discuss how are these studies typically conducted.

References

Bogari, N. B., Crowther, G., & Marr, N. (2004). Motivation for domestic tourism: A case study of the Kingdom of Saudi Arabia. In G. I. Crouch, R. R. Perdue, H. J. P. Timmermans, & M. Uysal (Eds.), *Consumer psychology of tourism, hospitality and leisure* (Vol. 3, pp. 51–64). Cambridge, UK: CABI.

Crompton, J. (1979). Motivation for pleasure vacation. *Annals of Tourism Research, 6,* 408–424.

Dann, G. M. S. (1977). Anomie, ego-enhancement, and tourism. *Annals of Tourism Research, 4,* 184–194.

Dann, G. M. S. (1981). Tourism motivation: An appraisal. *Annals of Tourism Research, 8,* 187–219.

Dann, G. M. S., & Phillips, J. (2001). Qualitative tourism research in the late twentieth century and beyond. In B. Faulkner, G. Moscardo, & E. Laws (Eds.), *Tourism in the twenty-first century* (pp. 247–265). London, UK: Continuum.

Derrett, R. (2001). Special interest tourism: starting with the individual. In N. Douglas, N. Douglas, & R. Derret (Eds.), *Special interest tourism* (pp. 1–28). Brisbane, AU: Wiley.

Dunne, G. (2009). *Motivation and decision making in city break travel: The case of Dublin.* Saarbrucken, Germany: VDM Publishing.

Filep, S., & Greenacre, L. (2007). Evaluating and extending the travel career patterns model. *TOURISM, An International Interdisciplinary Journal, 55*(1), 23–38.

Hall, M., & Weiler, B. (1992). Introduction. What's special about special interest tourism? In B. Weiler & C. M. Hall (Eds.), *Special interest tourism* (pp. 1–14). London: Bellhaven Press.

Hsu, C. H. C., & Huang, S. (2008). Travel motivation: A critical review of the concept's development. In A. G. Woodside & D. Martin (Eds.), *Tourism management: Analysis, behavior, and strategy* (pp. 14–27). Cambridge, UK: CABI.

Iso-Ahola, S. E. (1980). *The social psychology of leisure and recreation*. Dubuque, IA: Brown.

Iso-Ahola, S. E. (1982). Toward a social psychological theory of tourism motivation: a rejoinder. *Annals of Tourism Research, 9*, 256–262.

Iso-Ahola, S. E. (1983). Toward a social psychology of recreational travel. *Leisure Studies, 2*, 45–56.

Iso-Ahola, S. E. (1990). Motivation for leisure. In E. L. Jackson & T. L. Burton (Eds.), Understanding leisure and recreation: Mapping the past, charting the future (pp. 247–279). State College, PA: Venture Publishing.

Litvin, S. W. (2006). Revisiting Plog's model of allocentricity and psychocentricity… one more time. *Cornell Hotel and Restaurant Administration Quarterly, 47*(3), 245–253.

Lubbe, B. A. (2003). Tourism management in Southern Africa. Cape Town, South Africa: Pearson Education.

Lundberg, D. E. (1971). Why people travel. *Cornell Hotel and Restaurant Administration Quarterly, 11*, 75–81.

Mannell, R. C., & Iso-Ahola, S. E. (1987). Psychological nature of leisure and tourism experience. *Annals of Tourism Research, 14*, 314–331.

Maslow, A. H. (1943). A theory of human motivation. *Psychological Review, 50*(4): 370–96.

Maslow, A. H. (1970a). *Motivation and personality*. New York, NY: Harper & Row.

Maslow, A. H. (1970b). *Religions, values, and peak experiences*. New York, NY: Penguin. (Original work published 1964)

McLeod, S. A. (2007). Maslow's hierarchy of needs. Retrieved from http://www. simplypsychology.org

Pearce, P. L. (1988). *The Ulysses factor: Evaluating visitors in tourist settings*. New York, NY: Springer-Verlag.

Pearce, P. L. (1991a). Analysing tourist attractions. *Journal of Tourism Studies, 2*(1), 46–55.

Pearce, P. L. (1991b). Fundamentals of tourist motivation. In D. G. Pearce, & R.W. Butler (Eds.), Fundamentals of tourism motivation (pp. 113–134). London, UK: Routledge.

Pearce, P. L. (1996). Recent research in tourist behavior. *AsiaPacific Journal of Tourism Research, 1*(1), 7–17.

Pearce, P. L. (2005). Tourism behavior: Themes and conceptual schemes. Clevedon, UK: Channel View.

Pearce, P. L., & Caltabiano, M. (1983). Inferring travel motivation from travelers' experiences. *Journal of Travel Research, 12*(2), 16–20.

Pearce, P. L., & Lee, U. (2005). Developing the travel career approach to tourist motivation. *Journal of Travel Research, 43*(3), 226–237.

Plog, S. C. (1974). Why destination areas rise and fall in popularity. *Cornell Hotel and Restaurant Administration Quarterly, 14*(4), 55–58.

Plog, S. C. (2001). Why destination areas rise and fall in popularity: An update of a Cornell Quarterly classic. *Cornell Hotel and Restaurant Administration Quarterly, 42*(3), 13–24.

Ryan, C. (1998). The travel career ladder: An appraisal. *Annals of Tourism Research, 25*(4), 936–957.

Sharpley, R., & Tefler, D. J. (2002). *Tourism and development: Concepts and issues.* Buffalo, NY:Channel View Publications.

Shiffman, L. G., & Kanuk, L. (2000). *Consumer behavior* (7th ed.) Upper Saddle River, NJ: Prentice Hall.

Teichmann, K., & Zins, A. H. (2009). *Travel career pattern and travel horizon: Some common ground?* Paper presented at the Australian and New Zealand Marketing Academy (ANZMAC) Conference, Melbourne, Australia.

Yoon, Y., & M. Uysal. (2005). An examination of the effects of motivation and satisfaction on destination loyalty: A structural model. *Tourism Management, 26*, 45–56.

CHAPTER 5

Marketing the Community

"Because the purpose of business is to create a customer, the business enterprise has two—and only two—basic functions: marketing and innovation. Marketing and innovation produce results; all the rest are costs. Marketing is the distinguishing, unique function of the business."

–Peter Drucker (1954)

CHAPTER OBJECTIVES

- Outline the core marketing concepts, including SWOT analysis, destination mapping, destination branding and positioning, market segmentation, target marketing, and marketing mix
- Outline differences between commodity, product, services, and experience economy, and introduce the concept of experiential marketing
- Introduce and outline the concepts of relationship marketing and sustainable marketing
- Discuss practical application of marketing principles in the travel and tourism industry
- Outline the most useful strategies for destination/community marketing
- Discuss destination marketing challenges and opportunities

Introduction

Traditional marketing is a deliberate and planned process that proceeds carefully from an identification of markets and market needs (Roberts & Hall, 2003); however, the expansion of marketing from the corporate to the public domain has presented new challenges for marketers. This is clearly the case in community-based tourism—a sector largely dominated by small and medium enterprises, in a domain of experiences rather than traditional goods and services. In fact, some argue that destination (place) marketing might not be the best option for the communities, owing to a paradox inherent in tourism marketing: destinations often attempt to adapt their resources to satisfy the tourists' needs at the expense of the community (Haywood, 1990). In a world where places are becoming increasingly substitutable and difficult to differentiate (and where travelers are spoilt for choice of available destinations), can marketing help communities develop sustainable tourism product? Can a wisely and carefully crafted marketing strategy support tourism policy and strategic development plans in preserving the local culture, maintaining the quality of the environment of the destination, and improving the quality of life of the local residents, all while providing high quality experiences for the visitors (Buhalis, 2000; Pike, 2005; Ryan, 2002)? We believe the answer to this question is "yes." In fact, the Organization for Economic Co-operation and Development (OECD) has long encouraged small tourism operators to improve their marketing practices, as well as engage in collaborative marketing not only to sustain themselves as businesses, but also to sustain their communities and cultural landscapes (OECD, 1994). This chapter will review the opportunities and challenges for communities embarking on the path of sustainable marketing.

Planning For Tourism: SWOT Analysis

The first step in planning for destination tourism is to assess what is there to offer to tourists, and whether the destination can meet tourists' needs and wants in a sustainable manner. In other words, the first question that needs to be asked is whether tourism should be pursued at all. A *SWOT analysis* (defining community's strengths, weaknesses, opportunities, and threats) can provide an answer.

In order to be successful, any tourism development must rely on a thorough assessment to determine its economic, environmental, cultural, and social sustainability, as well as level of community support. An analysis of destination's strengths, weaknesses, opportunities, and threats determines the community's readiness for tourism and exposes concerns about tourism development (NOAA, 2007). To assess the community and its tourism potential, destination planners gather information on natural and cultural resources, policy environment, tourism industry interest, visitor patterns, and existing infrastructure. They can gather this information by using a variety of tools including existing materials, maps, interviewing residents, tour operators, and tourists, conducting surveys, and organizing community meetings and workshops in order to bring all stakeholders together.

The method of SWOT analysis is based on two tiers of analysis which are conducted separately (see Figure 5.1 for a sample template):–

Internal analysis (internal strengths and weaknesses)–Includes realities that affect the community and that community members have basic control over. For example, while having a status of a protected area would be considered an internal strength, poor communication between local tourism stakeholders would be a weakness.

External analysis (external opportunities and threats)–Includes realities that affect the community and that community members do not have immediate control over. For example, growth of a certain consumer market might be considered an opportunity, while competition from other destinations would be a threat.

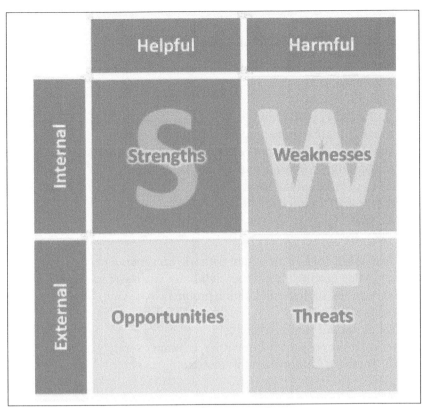

Figure 5.1. Sample SWOT Analysis Template

Once completed, SWOT analysis can provide policy makers with a clear picture of the tourism industry and can help them make appropriate policy decisions regarding the future growth and development of the industry. Obviously, it is nearly impossible to specify all the factors in each of the categories, but those of prime importance should be included. The essence of SWOT analysis is that strengths should be used, weaknesses eliminated, opportunities seized, and threats neutralized. Strengths in the model can be interpreted as resources, skills, and competences which improve the competitive position; weaknesses are internal negative factors that hinder development; opportunities are certain events and circumstances which can be used to achieve success, and threats are barriers or risks that hinder development and the achievement of objectives (Goranczewski & Puciato, 2010).

For communities, it is extremely important that a SWOT analysis is completed with input from local community members. The exercise can reveal key issues regarding strengths, weaknesses, opportunities, and threats, and how their impacts may balance or exceed each other; the overall attitude of the local participants toward tourism development; community cohesiveness and capacity to work together, as well as political and government structure of the area. The final decision will then reflect the community's readiness for tourism development, and the contents of the SWOT analysis will form the basis for all other elements of destination marketing (NOAA, 2007).

Examples of destination SWOT analyses are readily available, and some are of better quality than others. Table 5.1 provides an excerpt from the SWOT analysis of tourism in a town of Mammoth Lakes, California, a well-known skiing destination.

Table 5.1

SWOT Analysis of Tourism in Mammoth Lakes, California

Strengths
- Desirable natural product
- Breathtaking natural beauty
- Consistent, great weather year-round
- Exceptional terrain for both winter and summer activities
- Abundance and variety of winter and summer recreational activities
- Serves as training ground for/home to professional athletes
- Airport within close proximity of town
- Loyal visitor base out of Southern California
- World-class ski resort

Weaknesses
- Mammoth Lakes is known as a mountain with a town versus a town with a mountain
- Product offerings that extend beyond the "mountain" are lesser known
- Limited full-service and higher-end lodging product
- Air service/access is limited
- Perception that air service is unpredictable
- Guest experience lacks consistency (amenities, customer service)
- Perceived as a "Southern California-only" destination

Opportunities
- Marketing plan provides a longer term strategic road map and lessens reactive decisions
- Rise in adventure travel creates demand for what Mammoth Lakes has to offer
- An established brand identity when competitors don't have clear destination branding
- Diversification of winter product to reduce reliance on snow/ski/snowboard
- Increase capture ratio of overnight visitors passing through to national and state parks (Yosemite, Death Valley)
- Partnerships such as connection to Visit California

Threats
- The town is reliant on a strong winter season to carry rest of the year
- Summer and shoulder seasons have potential to be negatively affected by drought and wildfires
- Ski visitor is older
- Perception that accommodations and activities are too expensive in winter for the average family
- Fierce competition from other ski/snow destinations within key Southern California markets
- Many local businesses have limited digital and ecommerce capabilities when digital is number one medium for researching and booking travel
- Apathetic local community
- Limited to no investment in infrastructure limits business segmentation diversification (visitor profile heavily skewed to leisure/transient)

Source: Mammoth Lakes Tourism (2014)

The success of this method is mainly owed to its simplicity and flexibility. Its implementation does not require technical knowledge and skills (EU Science Hub, 2007). However, a good SWOT requires access to expert knowledge of the sector/region/area under analysis, thus making it costly and time consuming. In addition, SWOT analyses frequently do not prioritize factors that have to be taken into account, can be subjective and ambiguous, or even fail because of poor examination of opportunities and threats. The latter are especially critical for communities that need to stay abreast of industry trends, but have limited time and resources to invest in a thorough SWOT analysis.

Recently, *destination mapping* (building and protecting the destination brand) has emerged as an alternative to SWOT analysis. Two examples of the method include (1) *Foresight exercises* (also known as future studies, usually launched when a region/community finds itself facing a specific challenge), rather common in the European Union, and (2) the *DestinationNEXT tool* developed by Destination Marketing Association International (DMAI) with the vision of "providing Destination Marketing Organizations (DMOs) with practical, clear actions and strategies for sustainable success in a dramatically changing world" (DMAI/InterVISTAS Consulting, Inc., 2014, p.ii), launched in the United States. For those not familiar with the role of DMOs, these are organizations charged with representing a specific destination and helping the long-term development of communities through a travel and tourism strategy. In many communities, the role of DMOs is entrusted to local Convention and Visitors Bureaus (CVB) or Chambers of Commerce.

While exciting and innovative, destination mapping tools should not be seen as superior to the SWOT analysis, yet as alternatives that could be utilized by communities to develop successful marketing strategies.

Destination Marketing, Place Branding, and Positioning

Communities are destinations within a defined geographical region that are perceived by their visitors as a unique entity, with a political and legislative framework for tourism marketing and planning. They are amalgams of tourism products, offering an integrated experience to consumers (Buhalis, 2000). Destination marketing, as a subset of destination management, is typically designed to help the long-term development of a destination through a crafted travel and tourism strategy, and is carried out by destination marketing organizations (DMOs) that exist under a variety of names including Convention and Visitors Bureaus (CVBs), travel bureaus, visitors or tourism bureaus, welcome centers, information centers, etc. Their main charge is to represent a specific destination as a coherent brand.

Brand Management

Branding a place, whether it is a small village or a whole country, is probably the most complicated form of branding due to the fact that it is neither owned nor controlled by a single entity. And more often than not, many of the major stakeholders do not agree on what to do or how to do it. That is why the branding process is so important in place branding and destination marketing. It is not just about designing attractive logos and catchy tourism slogans but is a strategy of engagement with the outside world in a clear, coordinated, and communicative way (Lichrou, O'Malley, & Patterson, 2010).

Place branding. *Place branding*, as defined by editor emeritus of the *Place Branding and Public Diplomacy* journal, "Is not something you add on top: It is something that goes underneath" (Anholt, 2005, p. 121). The complexity of place branding can be illustrated with a simple example of a place name. In essence, the place name is the destination brand, and yet is most cases place names do not provide an explicit association with the position sought in the travel market(s) (Pike, 2005). Seeking clarity and precision, many communities design tourism slogans as a public articulation of their brand strategy; some go as far as to change their names so as to brand themselves (a town of Elston, Australia, changed its name to Surfers Paradise; Lee County in Florida is promoting itself as Lee Island Coast, and Hog Island in the Bahamas is now known as the Paradise Island) (examples from Pike, 2005). While the name-change examples are not so common, tourism slogans and brand associations have been used extensively to position destinations in a way as to reach the minds of busy consumers with a clear and succinct message. Creating an image, however, is not enough for effective and successful branding strategy; to work, the equation needs a critical component of brand identity (Cai, 2002).

Branding. *Branding* typically refers to a strategy used to differentiate products and companies (in case of tourism: destinations or communities). A brand can be treated as a legal instrument, logo, company, identity system, image, personality, relationship, and/or as adding value (Konecnik & Gartner, 2007). Chernatony and McDonald (2001) define successful brand as "an identifiable product, service, person, or place, augmented in such a way that the buyer or user perceives relevant, unique added values which match their needs most closely [and] its success results from being able to sustain these added values in the face of competition" (p. 20).

Brand identity. *Brand identity* refers to how a destination wants the visitors to perceive the brand and includes the visible elements of a brand such as colors, design, logo, and symbol(s). These elements together identify and distinguish the brand in the minds of consumers (Aaker, 1996). In addition, brand identity is concerned with the brand's vision, mission, culture, positioning, personality, relationships, and presentation; in other words, the destination's "DNA" (Kapferer, 2008).

Brand equity. *Brand equity* (often referred to as *brand value*) is a broader concept that deals with the brand from a visitor's perspective, and refers to destination's value from the return generated from a marketing strategy. In other words, brand equity is that incremental value that accrues to a destination when it is branded. Quoting Srinivasan, Park, and Chang (2006), if you can get your name to pop up in people's minds when they think of the (destination), you've won a big part of the battle. While difficult to quantify, brand equity of a destination can be understood as a function of (1) current and past arrivals (as measured by market share) and (2) future intentions as measured by travel preferences.

A model of customer-based brand equity for a tourism destination (CBBETD) was developed in 2005 by Konecnik and later empiricized by Konecnik and Gartner (2007). The model suggests that first and foremost, strategic marketing should carefully consider what the primary goal of destination branding is. With this goal in mind, proper marketing strategies should increase tourists' destination awareness (dimension 1), appeal to their image or quality perceptions (dimension 2), and influence visitor loyalty (dimension 3). Even though different markets may need different marketing strategies, all strategies should always align with the destination's brand identity.

Branding is perhaps the most powerful marketing weapon available to destinations confronted by tourists who are increasingly seeking lifestyle fulfillment and experiences. As more communities enter the tourism market, many argue that the future of tourism marketing will be a battle of brands, and that destinations are arguably the travel industry's biggest brands (Pike, 2005). Developing the right brand (or image) can determine the ability of the destination to satisfy visitors and allow the communities to develop realistic expectations (Buhalis, 2000).

Visitor expectations of any destination (community) are typically colored by their own previous experience, by what other people say, by the media, and also by how destinations choose to present themselves. The latter is the only one component communities have total control over, and is frequently accomplished using a strategy of market positioning.

Positioning

Positioning typically refers to the process of establishing and maintaining a distinctive place in the market (Lovelock, 1991). The goal of positioning is to create a distinctive place in the minds of potential customers; a position that evokes images of a destination in a way that differentiates the destination from the competition. Quoting Al Ries and Jack Trout (1969):

> Positioning is not what you do to the product; it's what you do to the mind of the prospect. It's how you differentiate your brand in the mind. Positioning compensates for our overcommunicated society by using an oversimplified message to cut through the clutter and get into the mind. Positioning focuses on the perceptions of the prospect not on the reality of the brand.

Positioning a destination can be quite difficult. As mentioned earlier in this chapter, destinations are amalgams of products, services and experiences provided locally. Decisions should be made which attributes are important enough to be included in the destination positioning in order to establish a distinct place of that destination in the minds of potential visitors (Gartner, 1989).

The typical destination positioning process involves the following stages:

- Identifying the target market
- Identifying competitive destinations serving the same target market
- Identifying motivations and benefits sought by visitors
- Identifying strengths and weaknesses of each competitive destination
- Identifying opportunities for differentiated positioning
- Implementing and monitoring the positioning strategy

Effective positioning is always clear and immediately resonates with a potential tourist. Not only does it help customers value the brand and identify with it, it helps people take ownership over the brand. And as Grimshaw-Jones (2012) argues, in today's digital world, this message is more relevant than ever. Most destinations have superb attractions; every country claims a unique culture, landscape, and heritage; each place describes itself as having the friendliest people; and high standards of customer service and facilities are now expected. So the need for destinations to create a unique identity is more critical than ever (ILO, 2012).

To be effective, however, the message has to be precise, clear, and to the point. Brands that try to appeal to everyone end up appealing to no one. A quick glance at some of the great brands—from Coca-Cola, Apple, and Starbucks, to Ikea, Under Armour, and McDonald's—upholds the unspoken truth that the most powerful brands in the world stand for singular ideas in the mind but are constantly updated to remain relevant.

One destination positioning strategy is to utilize destination tourism slogans, and it is not new. While the importance of creation of an ideal tourism slogan for destinations has long been acknowledged, there are very few destination tourism slogans that the wider market can easily identify and associate with. Successful slogans are the ones that encapsulate the image of a destination and strike an immediate chord with the tourist market. Below is a selection of some of the "20 most memorable destination slogans," as compiled by the CNN (Carrington & Veselinovic, 2015):

- **Las Vegas, Nevada:** "What happens in Vegas, stays in Vegas"
- **New Zealand:** "100% pure" (the campaign was so successful that the state of Michigan replicated it with the similar campaign "Pure Michigan")
- **California:** "Find yourself here"
- **Ethiopia:** "Thirteen months of sunshine"
- **New York City:** "I heart NY"

In addition to choosing the right theme for the advertisement, designing a catchy tagline, and highlighting the benefits—all in one message—for any positioning to be effective, the destination must live up to the expectations of its visitors. One of the latest strategic developments in marketing in this realm has been the one of experiential marketing. As services become increasingly commodified, customer perceptions of competitive advantage diminish, and so does satisfaction. To differentiate themselves from competitors and achieve sustainable competitive advantage, destinations are now starting to add experiential aspects to their products and services (Petkus, 2002). Enter the experience economy.

Marketing Tourism Experiences

Joseph Pine and James Gilmore introduced the concept of *experience economy* in 1998 issue of the *Harvard Business Review* with a birthday cake story:

How do economies change? The entire history of economic progress can be recapitulated in the four-stage evolution of the birthday cake. As a vestige of the agrarian economy, mothers made birthday cakes from scratch, mixing farm commodities (flour, sugar, butter, and eggs) that together cost mere dimes. As the goods-based industrial economy advanced, moms paid a dollar or two to Betty Crocker for premixed ingredients. Later, when the service economy took hold, busy parents ordered cakes from the bakery or grocery store, which, at $10 or $15, cost 10 times as much as the packaged ingredients. Now, in the time-starved 1990s, parents neither make the birthday cake nor even throw the party. Instead, they spend $100 or more to "outsource" the entire event to Chuck E. Cheese's, the Discovery Zone, the Mining Company, or some other business that stages a memorable event for the kids—and often throws in the cake for free. Welcome to the emerging experience economy. (p. 1)

The authors argue that an experience occurs when a company intentionally uses services as the stage, and goods as props, to engage individual customers in a way that creates a memorable event. Quoting the article, "commodities are fungible, goods tangible, services intangible, and experiences memorable" (Pine & Gilmore, 1998). In a later publication, Pine and Gilmore (1999) further explain:

> When a person buys a service, he purchases a set of intangible activities carried out on his behalf. But when he buys an experience, he pays to spend time enjoying a series of memorable events that a company stages to engage him in a personal way. (p. 2)

To design an experience customers will judge to be worth the price, destinations must first and foremost understand their distinct qualities and characteristics. Pine and Gilmore suggest we think about experiences across two bipolar constructs of customer participation (ranging from active to passive) and connection (ranging from absorption to immersion) (see Figure 5.2). Williams (2006) illustrates the participation construct with the examples of someone watching a film in a cinema (passive) versus someone dining in a restaurant (active), and the connection construct with the examples of someone watching a parade from a hotel balcony (absorption) versus someone on the street who is immersed in the sights, sounds and smells that surround them (immersion).

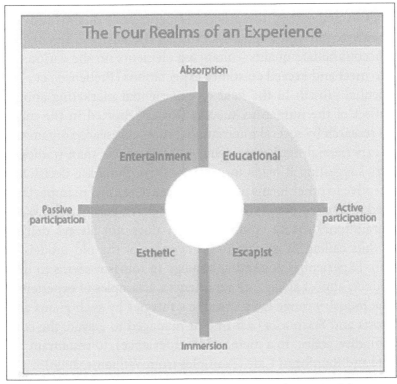

Figure 5.2. The four realms of an experience (Pine & Gilmore, 1998)

Most human experiences can be further understood when broken up in distinct phases—anticipation, participation, and reflection (Busser, 1993; Little, 1993). Tourism and leisure experiences, in particular, include two additional stages of traveling to and traveling from the destination, and therefore consist of five phases (Clawson & Knetsch, 1966):

- **Anticipation:** Travel planning occurs and key decisions are made—when to go, how to get there, how long to stay, what to take, what other things to do while there
- **Travel to:** Travelling to the venue, parking, costs and access
- **Participation:** Visitor experience onsite
- **Travel back:** The return journey
- **Reflection (recollection):** The many ways that outings and events are recalled, shared and commemorated

Prior to traveling (anticipation stage), tourists develop destination image as a set of expectations and perceptions based on past experiences, word of mouth, general information, and marketing campaigns (Buhalis, 2000). During the actual visit (participation stage) they "consume" destinations through various experiences, often without realizing that the elements of their experiences are produced by separate agencies. Destination marketing in this sense is none other than a great blend of strategic marketing elements of the hotel, tour operator, restaurant, museum, and other players participating in creation of visitor experiences. Product and service quality of the various providers are of paramount importance here since the degree of visitor satisfaction largely depends on the assessment of the perceived overall experience of the destination versus anticipated expectations and perceptions. It is therefore critical for communities to understand the process of experience quality and to identify the relative importance of the various phases of the experience for different groups in order to provide or accommodate quality-enhancing elements on the various phases of the journey so as to meet and exceed customer expectations (Prebensen et al., 2012).

The exponential growth in the field of experiential marketing appears to be the result of the effect of the numerous success stories reported in the media. Williams (2006) reviews research by several international market research organizations, only to conclude that experiential marketing delivers faster results than traditional methods, with consumers suggesting it leads to quick positive purchase decisions, and makes them more receptive to other forms of associated advertising (an important factor in an era of integrated marketing communication). Moreover, practice shows that increased spending on traditional media communication does not always deliver a growing market share, thus calling in question effectiveness of the old models of marketing communication. Experiential marketing strategy in tourism seems to be a natural fit, as tourism products almost always are experiences. Examples of experiential marketing successes in the industry range from creative strategies by such giants as Walt Disney Parks and Resorts and Starbucks (a firm that managed to elevate the consumption of a routine commodity, coffee, to a memorable experience), to restaurant chains such as Hard Rock Café and Rainforest Café (examples from Williams, 2006).

So what are the main strategies for experiential marketing in tourism? Pine and Gilmore suggest the following six design principles:

- **Theme the experience:** Sn effective theme is concise and compelling. It is not a corporate mission statement or a marketing tag line. It needn't be publicly articulated in writing. But the theme must drive all the design elements and staged events of the experience toward a unified story line that wholly captivates the customer.

- **Harmonize impressions with positive cues:** Impressions are the "takeaways" of the experience; they fulfill the theme. To create the desired impressions, companies must introduce cues that affirm the nature of the experience to the guest. Each cue must support the theme and none should be inconsistent with it.
- **Eliminate negative cues:** Ensuring the integrity of the customer experience requires more than the layering on of positive cues. Experience stagers also must eliminate anything that diminishes, contradicts, or distracts from the theme.
- **Mix in memorabilia (mementos):** From postcards and t-shirts, to key chains and bath towels
- **Engage all five senses:** The sensory stimulants that accompany an experience should support and enhance its theme. The more senses an experience engages, the more effective and memorable it can be.
- **Solicit customer feedback:** Experiential marketing requires a more diverse range of research methods in order to understand consumers, well beyond guest questionnaires.

Market Segmentation

Before any successful branding or positioning can take place, a destination needs to understand its markets through market segmentation and target marketing. It is critical that destinations clearly understand not only their active demand (current visitors) but also latent (potential) demand in order to develop a portfolio of tourism offerings to optimize the benefits and best serve their target markets (Buhalis, 2000; McKercher, 1995). To identify these target markets, destinations first need to segment the travel market, since breaking up the broad travel market makes it easier to manage separate segments.

Market segmentation is similar to tourist typology. It is another way of classifying tourists and understanding them. A broad range of criteria can be used for grouping tourists, including the purpose and features of the trip (business travelers vs leisure travelers), geographic segmentation (grouping of tourists based on their location), demographic segmentation (based on traveler characteristics such as gender, age, ethnicity, occupation, education, income, household size, and family situation), socio-cultural segmentation (religion, social class, lifestyle), product-related segmentation (grouping of tourists based on what they want and need in a particular good or service, as well as their loyalty), behavioral segmentation (activities undertaken, frequency of visit, expenditures), psychographic segmentation (visitor values, motives, expectations, and attitudes), and others.

According to Smith (1956), "market segmentation… consists of viewing a heterogeneous market (one characterized by divergent demand) as a number of smaller homogeneous markets" (p. 6). The obvious benefit of market segmentation is the ability of a destination to specialize on the needs of a particular group and become the best in meeting the needs and wants of this group, hence gaining an important competitive advantage. As a result, competition is narrowed to a certain segment, marketing becomes more focused, offerings can be tailored to best meet the needs of the established market, and as a result visitor satisfaction increases (Dolnicar, 2008).

Having segmented the market, the next step is to evaluate the segments. Useful segments typically meet the following criteria (Frank, Massy, & Wind, 1972; Wedel & Kamakura, 1998):

- A segment should be distinct (i.e., members of one segment should be as similar as possible to each other and as different as possible from members of other segments)
- A segment should align with the strengths of the destination
- A segment should be identifiable
- A segment should be reachable in order to enable destination management to communicate effectively
- A segment should be suitable in size (however, this does not mean that a bigger segment is necessarily better)

In practice, all market segmentation strategies are either *a priori* (commonsense) or *a posteriori* (post hoc, data-driven). Dolnicar (2008) explains:

In the first case, destination management is aware of the segmentation criterion that will produce a potentially useful grouping (commonsense) in advance, before the analysis is undertaken (*a priori*). In the second case, destination management relies on the analysis of the data (data-driven) to gain insight into the market structure and decides after the analysis (*a posteriori, post hoc*) which segmentation base or grouping is the most suitable one (p. 130).

Commonsense segmentation (also known as "profiling") remains the most common form of segmentation in tourism. This segmentation strategy involves selecting one criterion (variable)—such as age/gender/income/household size—to group the visitors. The advantage of this approach is that it is methodologically simple; on the other hand, it is possible to start off with the sub-optimal splitting criterion and produce merely descriptive results, insufficient for any distinct image building (Dolnicar & Kemp, 2009).

Data-driven segmentation strategy uses a set of consumer-based variables (mostly psychographic and behavioral variables), that are believed to be associated more closely to the destination (such as benefits sought) to determine market segments. The advantage of this approach is that clusters that are identified using this strategy may enable a more unique differentiation; on the other hand, these clusters are often constructed artificially for management and marketing purposes, as opposed to them occurring naturally in the tourism market.

Alternatively, destinations can take advantage of a combination of these two strategies to segment the market.

Following market segmentation, it is important to do the following:

- Create detailed profile of each selected segment
- Forecast market potential of each segment
- Estimate likely market share of each segment
- Decide which segment(s) to target
- Design an appropriate marketing mix for each target segment(s)/target market(s)

Rowett (2014a) goes even further and suggests the process of *ideal customer profiling*, or essentially identification of traits and predispositions of one single person you want visiting your community (see Figure 5.3). She suggests going into great details identifying characteristics of this very specific person such as:

- Exact age, gender, income, marital status, location, family status
- What books they like to read, what TV shows they watch, their favorite food, their hobbies
- What keeps them up at night, what gets them excited, what they value in life, and why they value it

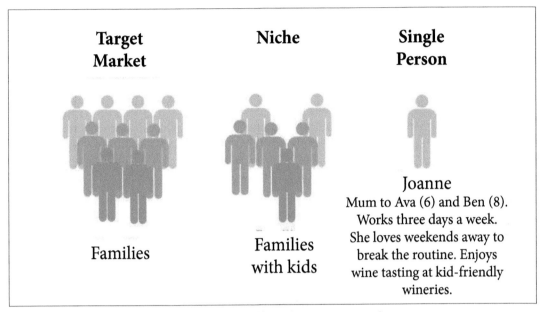

Figure 5.3. Ideal customer persona profiling (Rowett, 2014a)

Why go into such great detail? Rowett (2014a) argues that this is a foolproof strategy:

If you have identified this single person as being your most profitable prospect, then you only need to be communicating with them, where they are listening, and telling them what they want to hear or know. This means that the content you create in your marketing plan needs to only be directed at engaging with this one persona. Similarly, with the tactics that you deploy. So, if your ideal customer is not on Twitter, then you don't need to invest time in Twitter; and if they're not reading and being influenced by your regional visitor guide, then you shouldn't invest in advertising in your regional guide.

Approaching the right target market and providing the most appropriate combination of local tourism products and services is indeed the secret of successful destinations. Although small businesses may lack resources to carry out formal market segmentation, they are often close to their customers and in a strong position to know their needs (Anderson & McAuley, 1999). Not only do they know their customer base well enough to effectively respond to changing market demands, oftentimes they possess important knowledge (collect data) essential to effectively identify their target market(s) and subsequently develop an appropriate marketing mix for each of the identified target market(s).

Marketing Mix

Marketing mix is often associated with the four Ps: price, product, promotion, and place (distribution). The concept was introduced by Culliton (1948), who described a marketer as a mixer of ingredients, who sometimes follows a recipe as (s)he goes along, adapting a recipe to the ingredients immediately available, and experimenting with or inventing ingredients no one else has tried. McCarthy (1960) suggested the four Ps (representing price, promotion, product, and place distribution) as the primary ingredients of a marketing strategy, and Borden's (1964) article, *"The concept of the marketing mix"* widely popularized the concept. The model has been subsequently revised on numerous occasions, and several additional Ps have been introduced over time (such as packaging, positioning, people, politics, publics, partnerships, process, profit, etc.). In the 1990s, two modified models of four Cs were introduced as a more customer-driven replacement of four Ps (consumer, cost, communication, convenience and commodity, cost, communication, channel). The classic 4Ps, however, remains one the most fundamental concept of marketing, outlining the main parameters that marketing managers can control, subject to the internal and external constraints.

Product

Tourism product consists of the destination attractions, environment, services, facilities, accessibility, and imagery perceptions (Fyall & Garrod, 2005). It is therefore composed of both tangible and intangible aspects that provide features as well as benefits to the visitors. By buying the tourism product, visitors buy certain experiences. Product and service quality, therefore, are extremely important since they directly impact visitor experiences, and therefore determine visitor satisfaction.

In the business world, products are commonly viewed utilizing the framework of *product lifecycle,* consisting of the four stages of introduction, growth, maturity, and decline. This framework was adapted for destinations by Butler (1980) and is known as the *Tourism Area Life Cycle (TALC).* In his original article, Butler (1980) argued that resorts and other tourism products are normally developed and modified to meet the needs of specific markets in a similar way to the production of other goods and services. It therefore appeared to be reasonable to make the assumption that resorts would follow a generally similar pattern of development to that of most other products, or, in other words, would have a lifecycle (Catry & Chevalier, 1974). While rather simplistic, this model remains relevant in destination and tourism marketing as specifics of each stage of a destination's lifecycle call for different marketing strategies.

According to Butler (1980), stages of destination development include: exploration, involvement, development, maturity, and decline or rejuvenation (see Figure 5.4). The framework illustrates how tourism destinations (communities) move through a cycle beginning with almost non-existent tourism, to massive development and boom times and, oftentimes, to eventual stagnation and decline. The main stages of tourism development can be further described as follows (BBC, n.d.):

- **Exploration:** A small number of tourists visit the area. Destination remains relatively unspoiled, only a few tourist facilities exist.
- **Involvement:** Local people start to provide some facilities for tourists, beginning of a recognized tourist season.

- **Development:** The host country starts to develop and advertise the area, and it becomes recognized as a tourist destination.
- **Consolidation:** The area continues to attract tourists, however the growth is not as fast as before. Initial tensions develop between the host and the tourists.
- **Stagnation:** The facilities for the tourists may decline as they become old and run down; the numbers of tourists may decline too.
- **Rejuvenation:** Investment and modernization may occur which leads to improvements and visitor numbers may increase again.
- **Decline:** If destination is not rejuvenated (stage 6), then it will go into decline. People lose their jobs related to tourism; the image of the area suffers.

TOURISM LIFECYCLE

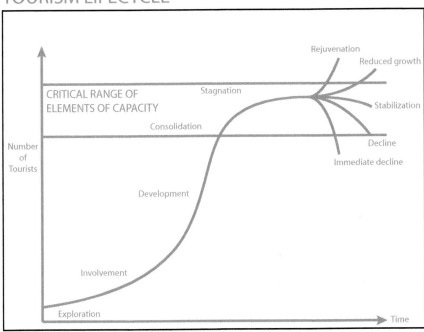

Figure 5.4. Tourism Area Life Cycle (TALC) (Butler, 1980)

Obviously, destinations are generally keen to avoid entering the stagnation, and even more so, decline stages (Pornphol & McGrath, 2010). Since its original publication, a number of destinations have benefitted from utilizing the model as an advisory expert system in order to design and implement various rejuvenation strategies (Beemer & Gregg, 2008).

Price

Price is the value that the consumer and provider establish to enable an exchange. For consumers, the price they are willing to pay equals the expected experience. On the provider side, the price is supposed to cover production costs and deliver the desired benefits (ILO, 2012). Price competitiveness is an essential component in the overall tourism competitiveness of a destination. There is a widely accepted evidence that price is one of the most important factors in decisions about whether, and where, to undertake a trip (Forsyth & Dwyer, 2009).

The key pricing factors that need to be considered include operating costs (fixed and variable costs), profit margin (how can you obtain a profit while retaining a competitive edge), and distribution network costs (also known as commissions or fees paid to distribute and sell your product). Additional pricing factors include competition (determines the maximum rate), demand (as generated by both existing and potential customers), target markets (including their needs, price sensitivity, length of stay, and disposable income), and seasonality (fluctuations in business between high and low seasons).

The two different rates that are common in the tourism industry include the *net rate* and the *retail rate* (also known as the gross, sell, or door rate). While the net rate is the absolute minimum the product could be sold for while still yielding a profit, retail rate also includes distributors' mark up or commission. Customers who book directly are quoted the retail rate; retail agents are quoted the retail rate (from which they deduct their 10% commission), and wholesalers are usually quoted 20% less than the retail rate. Consistency is extremely important in order to avoid the risk of customers comparing rates and discovering that one customer has paid much more than the other for the same service or experience (Destination NSW, 2012).

To maximize profit, destinations often utilize competitive pricing, including discounted pricing (often applied in the off season) and value-added pricing (adding features to your product that enhance the perceived value). Examples of the latter include purchase incentives, packages, and bundling the product with the other products in the area. Common package pricing methods include disguised pricing (when discounted package components such as accommodation, meals, entry fees, transport etc. are presented as one upfront cost), and visible pricing (offering a flexible package with each component priced separately and available for purchase individually).

Place

Place refers to the routes of exchange via which a tourist is able to access a tourism product, reserve, confirm, and pay for it (Middleton, 2001). It can refer to the physical location, as well as distribution of tourism products and services. The aspect of distribution encompasses distribution of information (trade shows, websites, direct mail, etc.), as well as the use of intermediaries (such as tour operators and travel agents) to distribute information about the destination (Godfrey & Clarke, 2000). The task of distribution is to connect the producer and the consumer.

Tour operators are companies that design and produce a large amount of tourist packages that are later sold through their own travel agencies or other wholesalers or retailers, under one or more brands. These businesses own and control various components of the tourism operation chain, such as airlines, hotels, bus companies, networks of retail travel agencies, insurance, etc. This gives them great autonomy, competitive prices, and considerable bargaining power (ILO, 2012).

Wholesalers provide retailers with travel packages comprising of two or more products supplied by different operators. These packages are put together in brochures, which are then distributed to networks of retail agents for display in their travel agencies.

Retailers provide customers with an accessible place to book or enquire about travel products. These agents usually provide a shopfront office for customers in shopping centers and downtown districts (Destination NSW, 2012).

Smaller operators typically sell directly to customers, and do not necessarily use distributors to sell their product. Entering a business with distributors does incur costs (also known as commission)—not upfront, but after the actual sale. As distribution operating costs are often high, many communities choose to employ direct provider-consumer sales in the distribution of their tourism products.

Of course, the right choice of distribution channels depends on the identified target markets and their purchase preferences, costs to work with a distributor, distributors' familiarity with the specific type of a tourism product, etc. If the decision is made to sell directly to consumers, travel planning and booking e-commerce platforms are a must. It is widely known that modern tourists turn to the Internet for access to extensive information to help make a selection from a variety of alternatives, and that customers consider online environment to provide convenient booking as well as a perceived price advantage (Destination NSW, 2012). Research indicates a steady growth of travelers investigating their travel options online, and the growth in online travel bookings has outpaced other online sales.

Promotion

Promotion is there to create a positive image and effectively position the destination in the tourism market. In other words, the goal of promotion is to stimulate preference for a destination by communicating a clear and consistent message (Cirikovic, 2014).

There exist a great variety of promotional instruments, and it is extremely important to select the best set of instruments within an established budget. Some of the most common promotional tools include advertising, public relations, sales promotions, personal selling, publicity, and direct marketing. However, it is worth stressing that word of mouth remains the main method of promotion, offering higher yields for small businesses at a lower cost.

A choice of the right promotional mix can be determined by answering the following questions (ILO, 2012):

- Who? (target audience)
- What? (clear, specific, and measurable objectives)
- How? (what is the key message)
- When? (the period in which the impact of the campaign will be most effective)
- Where? (which media and to what extent)
- How much? (the costs of the promotional activity)
- Evaluation (effectiveness should be measured in terms of meeting established goals and objectives)

Another strategy to determine which promotional mix to employ is to define where the customers are in their buying cycle, and to engage them through the appropriate mix of promotional instruments. Figure 5.5 illustrates online and offline marketing tactics for each of the stages of the so-called purchase funnel.

Purchase funnel describes the theoretical customer journey from the moment of the first contact with the brand, to the ultimate purchase decision. The model is typically depicted as a funnel to illustrate the natural loss of potential customers at each stage (many people may be aware of a particular brand, but this does not mean they'll purchase the product). The shape, number of stages, and duration of the process vary depending on both the consumer and the nature of the product, as well as other factors. Many different versions have been published, but the fundamental stages remain the same: awareness, consideration, preference, action, loyalty. The model above was modified to reflect stages typically observed in purchasing tourism products: awareness, consideration, sales conversion, loyalty, and advocacy.

Figure 5.5. Marketing tactics in tourism (Rowett, 2014b)

In tourism, purchase funnel is best represented by the Mathieson and Wall (1982) *travel buying behavior* model consisting of the following five stages:

- Need recognition (awareness)
- Information search (consideration)
- Evaluation of alternatives (preference)
- Purchase decision (action)
- Post- purchase evaluation (advocacy)

As Figure 5.4 depicts, there are numerous online and offline promotional opportunities for destinations to invest in. However, it is up to each community to identify their own unique mix of these tactics to achieve their marketing goals and objectives, that will be largely dependent on resources and customers segments (Rowett, 2014b). The authors provide the following tips on choosing the right promotional mix:

- Ensure your chosen tactics align with your target market(s)
- Select tactics your target markets trust (recommendations, branded websites, customer opinions online, editorial content like newspapers and articles. Online advertising is one of the least trusted tactics)

- Travelers are influenced most in the consideration phase of the buying cycle (that's when they read blogs, review sites, customer comments, social media sites, and third-party endorsements)
- Focus on tactics that encourage repeat visitation (typically, existing customers are ten times more likely to return; it costs anywhere from 4-10 times more to acquire a new customer than it is to retain a current customer. Example of a tactic that encourages repeat visitation is loyalty programs)
- Choose tactics that can be effectively measured

With that in mind, even though certain marketing tactics work best for certain stages of the buying cycle, there appear to be several cost-effective strategies most destinations can and should engage in; among them, setting up and managing a website, engaging in social media and other online content marketing strategies, strategic customer relationship management and marketing, strategic email marketing, building partnerships, and constantly measuring and reviewing marketing effectiveness (Rowett, 2014b).

Destination Marketing: Challenges and Opportunities

Recent developments in the fields of tourism and marketing provide communities with a number of challenges as well as opportunities for effective and successful destination marketing. Several of these are discussed below.

Marketing is Not Only About Promotion

Most small and medium tourism enterprises invest relatively little in marketing and related training (Lane, 1994; Ryan, 1991), and too often "marketing" efforts are slimmed down to the function of promotion with little attention being paid to the other marketing components. However, promotion is only one component of the marketing mix, and reducing marketing strategies to promotion only will render all marketing essentially ineffective. For destinations to be able to compete in the global market, it is critical to understand who their target market(s) are and provide highly satisfying experiences to meet the needs and wants of these markets. Moreover, it is important to develop a clear and concise branding and positioning strategies, as well as an appropriate marketing mix for each of the target market(s) identified. Ultimately, the role of destination marketing is to facilitate regional development goals and objectives in alignment with the tourism policies in place.

Sustainability Concerns

As many communities continue to adopt the narrow marketing perspective and equate marketing with promotion, frequently the focus of these efforts is to increase the number of visitors. Too often destination marketing is synonymous with creating images and "selling of places," and consists of creating tourism brochures and advertising campaigns (Jamrozy, 2007). But more tourist arrivals is not necessarily better; crowds of visitors can cause environmental pollution and degradation, loss of sociocultural authenticity, and may only benefit private businesses at the expense of the local residents. Such impacts not only harm the community but jeopardize the competitiveness of the region as a whole.

Although marketing has often been regarded as an enemy of sustainability, practice shows that it is possible to develop comprehensive marketing strategies to maximize economic benefits locally without damaging local resources. Indeed, resources in tourism are irreplaceable once destroyed, and therefore a planning strategy should ensure that their use is limited to the degree that does not threat their sustainability in the long term (Buhalis, 2000). Moreover, being sustainable does not necessarily require large investments; there are many small things destinations can do to be more sustainable while providing high-quality visitor experiences.

As destinations pursue more sustainable marketing approaches, several alternatives to the traditional forms of marketing have emerged, among them societal marketing, causal marketing, environmental (green) marketing, relationship marketing, and quality of life marketing (Jamrozy, 2007). The ultimate goal of these approaches is to develop marketing strategies that would contributing to the quality of life of tourists, tourism communities, and all other destination tourism stakeholders.

When Less is Better

Since destination marketing should not be used just as a sales tool but rather as a strategic mechanism in coordination with planning and management (Buhalis, 2000), destinations may decide to employ a tool of *demarketing* to manage demand. Typically, demarketing strategies aim at discouraging customers in general, or a certain type of customers in particular, from site visitation on either a temporary or permanent basis (Fullerton, McGettigan, & Stephens, 2010). The most common demarketing strategies include general demarketing (decreasing total demand), selective demarketing (discouraging certain market segments), and ostensible demarketing (creating a scarcity of product, and therefore increasing demand). The main demarketing tools include educating potential visitors, marketing to desirable markets, publicizing other sites as alternatives, limiting sites seasonally, and making access to fragile areas difficult (Sadiki, 2012). Most common techniques include some sort of prohibitive measures or changing premium prices.

Examples of destination demarketing strategies include the following:

- **Kingdom of Bhutan** (target market: low volume, high-value tourism)—limits number of entry visas, imposes a high daily fee
- **Galapagos Islands** (target markets: ecotourists, nature-based tourists)—allow tourists only at designated specific visitor sites
- **Island of Mauritius** (target market: high expenditure tourists)—does not allow charter flights
- **Antarctica** (target markets: educational tourists, adventure tourists)—restricts landings to one vessel at a time (per site), limits passengers on shore to 100 at a time
- **City of Venice**—strives to reduce mass tourism numbers by charging premium prices for all services offered
- **City of Cambridge** (target market: overnight visitors)—discourages day visitors by controlling their parking processes
- **Sites Machu Picchu and Mount Everest, city of Barcelona, Seychelles islands, Iceland**–are currently considering imposing a cap on the number of tourists

Beyond Conflicting Stakeholder Interests, Toward Collaboration/Cooperation/Coopetition

Destination marketing is an integral part of destination management, and as such is there to achieve a range of strategic goals and objectives to satisfy the needs and wants of various stakeholders—local residents, local businesses, visitors, and the region in general. Naturally, each stakeholder tries to maximize its own benefits and conflicts are often inevitable. However, it has been recognized that destination marketing, done individually and independently by different tourism stakeholders, cannot be conducive to developing a holistic image of the destination and will only impede chances for success in long term (Fyall & Garrod 2004). As Buhalis (2000) points out, managing often conflicting stakeholder interests makes destination marketing extremely challenging, however a compromise is critical to long-term success.

In an increasingly competitive marketplace, the ability to create greater levels of awareness of the destination through collaborative efforts provides an important competitive advantage for destinations (Palmer & Bejou, 1995). Pooling resources together and working collaboratively has also been shown to bring about many benefits to the broader tourism region. Clarke (1999) summarizes these benefits as follows:

- Greater leverage from limited marketing resources (in terms of finance, time, and marketing expertise)
- A more competitive position in the global marketplace
- Mechanisms for improving product quality and consistency without loss of the personal touch (especially important in community-based tourism)
- Strengthened product authenticity and local identity (counteracting the trend towards homogenization of destinations)
- The advantages of different forms of repeat business, rather than sole reliance on the classic repeat visitor and word of mouth recommendation

It is important to keep in mind that when various stakeholders participate in collaborative marketing, they can choose from several relationship forms ranging from loosely connected, to more formal and integrated relationships (Bailey & Koney, 2000). In addition to traditional relationships of *cooperation* or *competition*, today's business networks consist of a complex of different types of relationships—which at times require simultaneous coordination and cooperation among stakeholders (Wang & Krakover, 2008). From the outside, the destination might seem to be an amalgam of tourism businesses working together to offer a unified tourism product, however, within the destination there may be competition between these providers. A tourism business can be involved in several different relationships at the same time—competing with the others to get a bigger share of business, while simultaneously working along with the others to pool resources and achieve the common goals. When competition and cooperation merge, *coopetition* develops. Wang and Krakover (2008) emphasize the need for destination marketers to make sure that the local tourism industry understands that the wellbeing of the destination is more important than a single business's profit maximization from a long term perspective, and a win-win relationship is possible when each stakeholder contributes to the total value creation for the destination.

Enter the Mobile Revolution

The use of smartphone/tablet technology, social media, and apps is growing rapidly, to the point where online use from mobile devices outstripped traditional Internet use in 2014. To keep up with the pace of change, destinations need to consider the following trends:

- Not only do consumers have more choices than ever before, but increasingly they influence and are influenced through their online social networks. **Lesson: Power of word of mouth.**
- Social media are becoming increasingly ingrained in human behavior. **Lesson: Power of social media.**
- Growth of segments (beyond Millennials) practicing an "always on" lifestyle. **Lesson: You need to be "always on" yourself.**
- Expansion of 4G technology. **Lesson: Consumers have access to high-speed broadband Internet on their mobile devices.**

Add to these trends increasing customer confidence in booking online, and the fact that information can be accessed and disseminated 24/7, and no wonder that traditional marketing strategies no longer deliver expected outcomes. As Seth Godin eloquently summarized:

'Build it, and they will come' only works in the movies. Social media is a build it, nurture it, engage them, and they may come and stay.

Research by Tourism Northern Ireland (2013) suggests the following innovative strategies for destination marketers to reach modern-day consumers across the five phases of the travel cycle:

- **Stage 1—Dreaming:** Use social media as a source of inspiration and influence. Consider developing a social media strategy aimed at inspiring groups of potential visitors and creating a "snowball effect." Instead of using social media as a sales tool, encourage interaction by posting photos, links to articles, or competitions that will generate a reaction from your followers.
- **Stage 2—Planning:** Consumers are increasingly turning to the opinions of other tourists on travel review sites, and a large percentage of consumers take as much notice of online reviews as they do star ratings. Another piece of reality: no longer do tourists have all of their travel arrangements set in stone prior to departure; increasing number of travelers, for example, use their smartphones to book accommodation on the go.
- **Stage 3—Booking:** Make sure your website is mobile-optimized and can serve as an additional booking channel. Consumers want a hassle-free experience, and simplicity is the winning strategy here. Also, keep an eye on the rise of such collaborative networks as Couchsurfing, AirBnB, JustPark, and others.
- **Stage 4—Experiencing:** Mobile technology now has the capability to enhance and enrich visitor experiences (i.e., through geolocation and vision-based augmented reality apps).
- **Stage 5—Sharing:** As consumers become more socially connected and technology makes it easier to review their experiences, it will continue to

be important for destinations to monitor, respond to and act upon feedback received through online review sites.

Finally, destinations can greatly improve their marketing efforts by engaging in *social customer relationship marketing* (whereby you can retrieve background information about your target market(s) and monitor social media conversations about your destination), supporting *mobile payments* (which can be used for marketing promotion and customer profiling), and developing *mobile apps* to engage the customers in co-creating their unique destination experiences.

Summary

This chapter sought to examine principles and practices of community-based (destination) tourism marketing. As Anthony Climpson (currently serving as a chair of the Framework for English Tourism "Wise Growth" Action Plan) pointed out:

> Visitors who are well informed before they visit, welcomed when they arrive, and well cared for during and after their stay, tend to be happier visitors. Happier visitors will also tend to understand more, spend more, behave well and enjoy a better overall experience during their stay (VisitEngland, 2014, p. 2).

The role of destination marketing, therefore, is to support tourism policy and strategic development plans in preserving the local culture, maintaining the quality of the environment of the destination, and improving the quality of life of the local residents, all while providing high-quality experiences for the visitors. This chapter outlines several processes and strategies of sustainable destination marketing—including SWOT analysis, destination branding and positioning, market segmentation, target marketing, and marketing mix; it also discusses new and emerging trends that are greatly impacting marketing practices, and suggests strategies and tactics to utilize these trends in the most effective manner.

Key Concepts

- SWOT analysis
- Branding, brand identity, and brand equity
- Market positioning
- Experience economy
- Experiential marketing
- Service quality
- Market segmentation
- Target marketing
- Customer profiling
- Marketing mix
- Product lifecycle
- Purchase funnel and travel buying behavior
- Customer relationship marketing
- Sustainable marketing
- Destination mapping

Useful Sites, Exercises, and Resources

1. Visit Brand USA website at http://www.thebrandusa.com. Brand USA is the destination marketing organization for the United States. Go to "Research and analytics" tab, review destination branding reports and marketing research conducted to support and enhance marketing the United States as a premier travel destination.
2. Explore DestinationNEXT website at http://www.destinationmarketing.org/destinationnext.
3. Conduct a SWOT analysis for your community using the guidelines provided in the chapter.

Questions for Review and Case Problems

1. Discuss the main marketing concepts including SWOT analysis, destination mapping, destination branding and positioning, market segmentation, target marketing, and marketing mix.
2. What is experiential marketing, and how does it differ from product or services marketing?
3. Discuss the main strategies for destination/ community marketing.

References

BBC. (n.d.). Tourism in the UK: Models of tourist development. Retrieved from http://www.bbc.co.uk

Beemer, B. A., & Gregg, D. A. (2008). Advisory systems to support decision making. *Handbook on decision support systems*. Berlin: Springer.

Borden, N. H. (1964). The concept of the marketing mix. *Journal of Advertising Research, 4*(June), 2–7.

Buhalis, D. (2000). Marketing the competitive destination of the future. *Tourism Management, 21*(1), 97–116.

Busser, J. A. (1993). Leisure programming: The state of the art. *Journal of Physical Education, Recreation and Dance, 64*(8), 25–33.

Butler, R. W. (1980). The concept of the tourist area life-cycle of evolution: Implications for management of resources. *Canadian Geographer, 24*(1), 5–12.

Cai, L. (2002). Cooperative branding for rural destination. *Annals of Tourism Research, 29*, 720–742.

Carrington, D., & Veselinovic, M. (2015, June 1). 20 most memorable destination slogans. CNN. Retrieved from http://www.cnn.com/2015/06/01/travel/gallery/20-most-memorable-destination-slogans/index.html

Catry, B., & Chevalier, M. (1974). Market share strategy and the product life cycle. *Journal of Marketing, 38*(4), 29–34.

Cirikovic, E. (2014). Marketing mix in tourism. Retrieved from http://www.dukagjinicollege.eu/research

Clawson, M., & Knetsch, J. L. (1966). *Economics of outdoor recreation*. Washington, D.C.: Resources for the Future.

Culliton, J. (1948). *The management of marketing costs.* Boston, MA: Division of Research. Graduate School of Harvard School of Business Administration.

Destination NSW. (2012a). *Tourism business toolkit. Volume 2: A guide to developing your tourism product.* Department of Trade and Investment NSW. Retrieved from http://www.destinationnsw.com.au

DMAI/InterVISTAS Consulting, Inc. (2014). Destination NEXT: A strategic road map for the next generation of global destination marketing. *Destination Marketing Association International.* Retrieved from https://www.destinationmarketing.org/destinationnext

Dolnicar, S. (2008). Market segmentation in tourism. In A. G. Woodside and D. Martin (Eds.), *Tourism management: Analysis, behavior, and strategy* (pp. 129–150). Cambridge, MA: CAB International.

Dolnicar, S., & Kemp, B. (2009). Tourism segmentation by consumer-based variables. In Kozak, M. & Decrop, A. (Eds.), *Handbook of tourist behavior: Theory and practice* (pp. 177–194). New York, NY: Routledge.

EU Science Hub. (2007). *The FOR-LEARN online Foresight guide.* Retrieved from http://forlearn.jrc.ec.europa.eu/guide

Forsyth, P., & Dwyer, L. (2009). Tourism price competitiveness. *The travel and tourism competitiveness report 2009.* World Economic Forum. Retrieved from http://www.weforum.org

Frank, R. E., Massy, W. F., & Wind, Y. (1972). *Market segmentation.* Englewood Cliffs, NJ: Prentice-Hall.

Fullerton, L., McGettigan, K., & Stephen, S. (2010). Integrating management and marketing strategies at heritage sites. *International Journal of Culture, Tourism and Hospitality Research, 4*(2), 108–117.

Godfrey, K., & Clarke, J. (2000). *The tourism development handbook: A practical approach to planning and marketing.* London, UK: Continuum International Publishing Group Limited.

Goranczewski, B., & Puciato, D. (2010). SWOT analysis in the formulation of tourism development strategies for destinations. *Tourism, 20*(2), 45–53.

Grimshaw-Jones, N. (2012). What is brand positioning? Retrieved from http://www.touchmarketing.co.nz

Haywood, M. K. (1990). Revising and implementing the marketing concept as it applies to tourism. *Tourism Management, 11*(3), 195–205.

Jamrozy, U. (2007). Marketing of tourism: A paradigm shift toward sustainability. *International Journal of Culture, Tourism and Hospitality Research, 1*(2), 117–130.

Kapferer, J.-N. (2008). *The new strategic brand management: Creating and sustaining brand equity long term* (4th ed.). London, UK: Kogan Page Ltd.

Konecnik, M., & Gartner, W. G. (2007). Customer-based brand equity for a destination. *Annals of Tourism Research, 34*(2), 400–421.

Little, S. L. (1993). Leisure program design and evaluation. *Journal of Physical Education, Recreation, and Dance, 64*(8), 26–29, 33.

Mammoth Lakes Tourism. (2014). Destination marketing plan 2014. Retrieved from http://mltindustryinsider.com

Mathieson, A., & Wall, G. (1982). *Tourism: Economic, physical, and social impacts.* London, UK: Longman.

McCarthy, E. (1960). *Basic marketing: A managerial approach.* Homewood, IL: Irwin.

McKercher, B. (1995). The destination-market matrix: A tourism market portfolio analysis model. *Journal of Travel and Tourism Marketing, 4*(2), 23–40.

Middleton, V. (2001). *Marketing in travel and tourism.* Oxford, UK: Butterworth-Heinemann.

NOAA. (2007). Assessment for sustainable tourism. Retrieved from http://sanctuaries.noaa.gov

Pike, S. (2005). Tourism destination branding complexity. *Journal of Product and Brand Management, 14*(4), 258–259.

Pine, B. J., & Gilmore, J. H. (1998). Welcome to the experience economy. *Harvard Business Review* (July/August), 97–105.

Pine, B. J., & Gilmore, J. H. (1999). *The experience economy.* Boston, MA: Harvard Business School Press.

Pornphol, P., & McGrath, G. M. (2010). Implementation of the tourism area life cycle model as an advisory decision support system. In *Proceedings of the 14th Pacific Asia Conference on Information Systems*, Association for Information Systems Electronic Library, Taipei, Taiwan, pp. 1743–1750.

Prebensen, N. K., Woo, E., Chen, J. S., & Uysal, M. (2012). Experience quality in the different phases of a tourist vacation: a case of northern Norway. *Tourism Analysis, 17*(5), 1–11.

Rowett, P. (2014a). Ideal customer persona profiling: The strategic approach to tourism marketing. Retrieved from http://tourismeschool.com

Rowett, P. (2014b). Our top 7 marketing tactics for all tourism businesses. Retrieved from http://tourismeschool.com

Ryan, C. (1991). Tourism and marketing: A symbiotic relationship. *Tourism Management, 12*(2), 101–111.

Sadiki, F. A. (2012). *Sustainable tourism marketing strategies at UNESCO World Heritage Sites.* UNLV Theses/Dissertations/Professional Papers/Capstones. Paper 1477.

Srinivasan, V. S., Park, C. S., & Chang, D. R. (2006). Calculating the dollar value of brand equity. *Standford GSG News.* Stanford Graduate School of Business.

Tourism Northern Ireland. (2013). Tourism in the midst of a mobile revolution. Retrieved from http://www.nitb.com

VisitEngland. (2014). Keep it real for destinations: A guide to incorporating Wise Growth in your communications with visitors, residents, and businesses. London, UK: VisitEngland.

Wang, Y., & Krakover, S. (2008). Destination marketing: competition, cooperation or coopetition? *International Journal of Contemporary Hospitality Management, 20*(2), 126–141.

Wang, Y., & Xiang, Z. (2007). Toward a theoretical framework of collaborative destination marketing. *Journal of Travel Research, 46*(1), 75–85.

Wedel, M., & Kamakura, W. (1998). *Market segmentation: Conceptual and methodological foundations.* Boston, MA: Kluwer Academic Publishers.

Williams, A. (2006). Tourism and hospitality marketing: fantasy, feeling and fun. *International Journal of Contemporary Hospitality Management, 18*(6), 482–495.

CHAPTER 6

BUSINESS CONCEPTS/ ENTREPRENEURSHIP

"Small business isn't for the faint of heart. It's for the brave, the patient and the persistent. It's for the overcomer."

–Unknown

CHAPTER OBJECTIVES

- Define and discuss the concept of small and medium-sized enterprises (SMEs) in tourism including their characteristics, typology, and role in community and economic development.
- Define and discuss the concept of entrepreneurship in tourism including characteristics, typology, motivations and characteristics of entrepreneurs.
- Discuss the concepts of lifestyle and family entrepreneurship.
- Introduce and briefly discuss the role of innovation in tourism entrepreneurship.
- Discuss the role of entrepreneurship policy framework, education and training, and sustainability practices.
- Discuss the concepts of clusters, networks, and alliances in tourism.
- Outline and discuss small business development lifecycle.

Introduction

Tourism is a complex industry that involves a broad range of businesses, organizations, and government agencies working together at different levels to deliver a complete tourism package (Government of Western Australia, n.d.). Small and medium-sized enterprises (SMEs) are the backbone of local economies and form the majority of businesses in the tourism industry. Small, locally owned enterprises tend to enhance community stability, do less harm to the physical environment, and greatly improve the business climate (Loucks, 1988). They are also key drivers of the local economies, with small business entrepreneurship frequently touted as a low-cost strategy of economic and social development (Echtner, 1995).

Operating a small business is not easy. Owners/managers are accountable for planning, decision-making, and management of all aspects of the tourism business. They must continuously review and update business plans, check budget figures, monitor accounting and cash control procedures, and ensure the overall operation is in line with the expectations (go2 Tourism HR Society, 2015). They also operate alongside such key players as governments (that control infrastructure, marketing, licensing, and regulations), other businesses (partners and/or competitors), and local communities. To succeed in an increasingly competitive and fast paced environment, small businesses need to continuously adapt, innovate, and stay abreast of current trends and opportunities.

This chapter will review the main business concepts in community based tourism, with a special emphasis on entrepreneurship. It will discuss the nature of small businesses in tourism, tourism entrepreneurship, innovation, entrepreneurship policies, and strategies to gain and maintain competitive advantages, among them formal and informal education and training, sustainability practices, participating in clusters, networks, and alliances, and understanding the small business development lifecycle.

Small Businesses in Tourism

There is no single and commonly acceptable definition of a small firm; in fact, definitions of small businesses vary from firms employing fewer than 10 people, fewer than 100 people, fewer than 200 people, 1-500 people, etc. (Storey, 1994). The most common criteria are the number of employees, annual turnover, total balance sheet, and sometimes, independence.

According to the Organization for Economic Co-operation and Development (2005):

> Small and medium-sized enterprises (SMEs) are non-subsidiary, independent firms which employ fewer than a given number of employees. This number varies across countries. The most frequent upper limit designating an SME is 250 employees, as in the European Union. However, some countries set the limit at 200 employees, while the United States considers SMEs to include firms with fewer than 500 employees. Small firms are generally those with fewer than 50 employees, while microenterprises have at most 10, or in some cases 5, workers. (p. 17)

Types of Small Businesses

SMEs account for over 95% of firms and 60% to 70% of employment in OECD economies; 99% of all companies employ fewer than 250 workers (OECD, 2000). In the United States, the estimated 28 million small businesses represent more than 99% of all firms, employ half of the private sector workforce, and create two of three net new American jobs (U.S. Small Business Administration, 2011). Family firms specifically create an estimated 70% to 90% of global GDP annually; in the U.S., they account for half of the GDP (Family Firm Institute, 2015).

Karen Mills (a former administrator in the U.S. Small Business Administration) suggests that most small businesses fall within one of the four segments (see Table 6.1).

Table 6.1

The Four Main Types of Small Businesses

Types of Firms	Number of Firms	Description
Nonemployee businesses	23 million	*Sole proprietorships* They employ a large number of people but do not necessarily create jobs; these businesses operate in a wide range of sectors, from consultants and IT specialists to painters and roofers.
Main Street	4 million	*Main Street businesses: local businesses serving consumers and other local businesses.* They employ a significant portion of the workforce, yet exist largely to support a family and are not principally focused on expansion. These are local retailers, restaurants, "mom and pop" shops, car repair operations, etc. Main Street operations are known to shape and reflect a community's identity and values.
Suppliers	1 million	*Suppliers: commercial and government supply chains.* These businesses are often focused on growth, domestically or through exports. Suppliers generate high paying jobs and are critical to the success of large companies and growth startups.
High-growth	200,000	*High-growth startups: fast-growing, innovation-driven businesses.* They exist in all industries, but seem to be overrepresented in the services sector. These companies are outstanding job creators, and are also known as "gazelles." The term "gazelles" was coined in 1979 by David Birch, who estimated that this type of firms account for only 4% of all U.S. companies, yet generate 70% of all new jobs. The growth pace of "gazelle" companies far outpaces that of the Fortune 500 "elephants" and Main Street "mice" (Investopedia, 2015).

Source: Mills (2015)

This heterogeneity of small businesses is further complicated by the sectoral differences: for example, small manufacturing businesses markedly differ from small service businesses, and is would be unwise to ignore the differences between, say, a small IT company and a bed and breakfast operation. And obviously, small firms differ from large businesses. Unlike large companies, small businesses have greater financial constraints, lack specialized management, have an increased likelihood of management or structural changes, are less likely to invest in research, and face greater uncertainty in terms of the market as a result of a limited customer base. At the same time, they are closer to their customers, and therefore are more likely to respond to niche markets (Burns, 1996; Dewhurst & Burns, 1993; Storey, 1994).

Small Businesses in Tourism

It has been well documented that most tourism destinations around the world are characterized by the predominance of small, local businesses. These businesses include accommodation providers, travel intermediaries, transportation services (including car rentals), convention, meetings and events management, attractions and services (cultural, natural, adventure, etc.), restaurants and food services, and tourism research companies (Al-Azri & Cai, 2009). While statistics vary, it is believed that close to 80% of all hotels worldwide are SMEs; in Europe, this figure is 90% (World Economic Forum, 2009).

Reliability of the available statistics on the number of SMEs in tourism is questionable since businesses operating below the tax threshold or in the informal economy (e.g., too few rooms) are often not accounted for, therefore the official statistics leave out a large number of small and especially micro businesses (Morrison, 1998; Williams & Thomas, 1996). The predominance of SMEs in tourism, however, does not result in a large turnover/share of business. In fact, over half of the total turnover is generated by the large companies (those that employ in excess of 500 people) that are also disproportionately significant in terms of employment. In the hotel and restaurant sector, for example, this category accounts for only 0.1% of all businesses, yet is responsible for creating almost 40% of employment and 41.5% of total sectoral turnover (Thomas, 2000).

The fact that most of the companies that depend on tourism have the structure of a small business reflects the preferences of the consumer and the need for personalized services in tourism (Keller, 2004). Among other reasons justifying the high number of small businesses in tourism are low capital and lack of specific qualifications and professional requirements needed to start a business, localized demand, ability to quickly respond to changing customer needs and expectations, and many businesses being owned and managed by families (Jaafar et al., 2011).

Strengths and Weaknesses of Small Businesses in Tourism

Small business in tourism are extremely vulnerable to failure, particularly in their early years of operation. Buhalis (1996) reports that up to 40% of small firms in tourism tend to fail within the first three years, and 60% close within 10 years. Family businesses have odds stacked against them as well: according to the Family Firm Institute (2015), by the second generation, about 70% are no longer in family ownership, only 12% pass into the third generation, and less than 3% endure into the fourth generation or beyond.

Some of the main causes of the inability of small firms to overcome strategic problems are a shortage of financial resources, a lack of management and marketing skills, a lack of industry expertise and strategic vision, a lack of quality management, and resistance to change or advice (Seppala-Esser et al., 2009; Jaafar et al., 2011). The majority of the problems are believed to be caused by the small size and deficient resources, and they undoubtedly contribute to the fact that almost a third of small businesses are struggling, and another third should not have been started (Wanhill, 2000).

It is important that SMEs view their weaknesses as competitive disadvantages and design strategies to overcome them. Review of best practices suggests the following three management priorities: marketing knowledge and activities, networking and relationship management, and quality and customer focus (Breen et al., 2005). Finally, cooperation appears to play a critical role in determining survival and possible growth of the small businesses (Seppala-Esser et al., 2009).

Among the main strengths of small businesses in tourism is their ideal position to provide high-quality personalized services, yet remain flexible enough to detect and promptly respond to the changes in travelers' wants and needs. Their focus on repeat business, however, makes it difficult for these companies to change, adapt, and innovate (Keller, 2004).

Entrepreneurship in Tourism

We will return to the discussion of innovation later in this chapter. First the concept of entrepreneurship will be discussed.

Understanding Entrepreneurship

The term *entrepreneurship* comes from the French verb *entreprendre*, which means *to undertake* (Couger, Higgins, & McIntyre, 1990). It was introduced by Richard Cantillon in the early 18th century and discussed by many well-known economists, including Adam Smith, David Ricardo, John Stuart Mill, Alfred Marshall, and Joseph Schumpeter, among others (Burnett, 2000). Entrepreneurship should be distinguished from *intrapreneurship* (intrapreneurs are typically employees in large companies who behave innovatively). Over time, entrepreneurs have been characterized as risk bearers, visionaries, managers, coordinators and organizers, gap fillers, leaders, and innovators, or creative imitators. Sociologists further contributed to the discussion by introducing concepts of a classical entrepreneur (business innovator), an *artisan entrepreneur* (focused on employment satisfaction and independence), and a *managerial entrepreneur* (emphasizing management skills). Table 6.2 outlines several most frequently used typologies of entrepreneurship.

Tourism entrepreneurs are different from other entrepreneurs in a number of ways: (1) they work with intangible offerings and have a higher service content, (2) they are highly impacted by seasonality, (3) their offers are immobile (meaning the customers must come to them, not the other way around), and (4) they do not own many of their attractions (for example, national parks or historic sites) (Koh & Hatten, 2002). They typically have two routes into the industry: starting from scratch, or acquiring a franchise; both have their strengths and weaknesses, and directly impact business growth and innovation.

Table 6.3 outlines typology of tourism entrepreneurs (Koh & Hatten, 2002). The authors suggest two approaches to categorizing tourism entrepreneurs: the extent of product differentiation, and entrepreneurs' behaviors. Using the extent of product differentiation as the categorization criterion, three basic types of tourism entrepreneurs may be identified; a behavioral approach produces six types of tourism entrepreneurs.

Table 6.2

Types of Entrepreneurship

Smith, 1967
- *Craftsmen:* risk-averse entrepreneurs, driven by making a comfortable living
- *Opportunistic entrepreneurs*

Katz, 1995
- *Growth entrepreneurs:* those who measure their success by business size and growth
- *Autonomy-seeking entrepreneurs:* those wishing to be their own boss

Shaw and Williams, 1998
- *Real entrepreneurs:* are driven by profit and growth
- *Nonentrepreneurs:* as lifestyle entrepreneurs, they typically lack business experience and enter the small business world not to make profits, but rather to enjoy a chosen destination while generating income to sustain their lifestyle; many are retired or semi-retired and self-employed
- *Constrained entrepreneurs:* young people with interest in business growth and innovation, and often with professional experience in tourism; they rely on personal/family capital and are also driven by lifestyle motives

Getz and Carlsen, 2000
- *Family-first entrepreneurs:* are driven by quality of life and use the business for the betterment of the family, potentially across more than one generation; they account for over two-thirds of the total in developed economies
- *Business-first entrepreneurs:* are driven by profit and growth

Shaw, 2004
- *Business-oriented entrepreneurs:* are driven mainly by economic motives
- *Lifestyle entrepreneurs:* are motivated less by profit and more by noneconomic factors; within this group are *nonentrepreneurs* (semi-retired in a tourism destination of their choice, mainly motivated by a certain type of lifestyle) (Shaw & Williams, 1998), and *lifestyle entrepreneurs* interested in developing certain types of niche tourism products (Ateljevic & Doorne, 2000)

Among the types of tourism entrepreneurs outlined above, the largest and most significant category is that of a lifestyle entrepreneurship. In fact, the vast majority of tourism entrepreneurs are "lifestylers" that do not aspire to grow and are often motivated by non-financial factors (Thomas, 2000). This category includes *social* and *family entrepreneurs* (including so called *copreneurs*, or married couples operating a business) who make conscious decisions to forego growth and pursue motives other than economic.

Table 6.3
Typology of Tourism Entrepreneurs

Criterion 1: The extent of product differentiation

- *Inventive tourism entrepreneurs:* Those whose offerings are truly new to the tourism industry (e.g. first Thomas Cook travel agency, American Airlines' frequent flyer program)
- *Innovative tourism entrepreneurs:* Those whose offerings are somewhat new (e.g., Disneyland as a twist on traditional amusement parks, casino-hotels merging several offerings in one)
- *Imitative tourism entrepreneurs:* Those whose offerings have no significant differences from established offerings (e.g., hotels, restaurants, franchises)

Criterion 2: Tourism entrepreneurs' behaviors

- *Social tourism entrepreneurs:* Those who establish nonprofit tourism enterprises (e.g., nonprofit gardens, museums, art galleries, etc.)
- *Lifestyle tourism entrepreneurs:* Those who launch tourism enterprises to support their desired lifestyle and have little to no interest in business growth
- *Marginal tourism entrepreneurs:* Those who operate their enterprises in the informal sector (e.g., street vendors, unlicensed tour guides, etc.)
- *Closet tourism entrepreneurs:* Those who operate tourism enterprises alongside a full-time job
- *Nascent tourism entrepreneurs:* Those who are in the process of creating a tourism enterprise
- *Serial tourism entrepreneurs:* Those who have established more than one tourism enterprise

Source: Koh & Hatten (2002)

Understanding Lifestyle Entrepreneurship

There is a broad support of the assumption that profit seeking is not the only motive for entrepreneurship. For example, Morrison (2006, p. 197) suggests a number of other "entrepreneurial behavioral" cues, among them to "buy" oneself or a family member a job, to avoid unemployment, and to pursue independence or a flexible lifestyle. Tourism industry is especially attractive for those entrepreneurs driven by motives other profit and growth. As Peters et al. (2009) explain:

> The leisure and tourism industries have always attracted a large number of small businesses and nongrowth-oriented owners-entrepreneurs. The perceived nice life, often close to the beach or the alpine regions or at attractive parts of city, has frequently motivated entrepreneurs to leave their job and adventure in tourism and hospitality. Quite often this implied primarily following a dream, often with no experience, training or expertise in these areas. Sometimes this is financed with savings from property or previous careers and is propelled by plenty of optimism that things will work out. The prospect of living in the attractive region, where entrepreneurs may have visited as tourists made all other business aspects that come with that look irrelevant or secondary. The prime motivation was to enjoy the perceived quality of life and do something on the side, to sustain a certain lifestyle and economic status. (p. 397)

Lifestyle entrepreneurship firms form the backbone of development in rural areas and small towns, even if only few jobs are created. They earn money that tends to stay in the local economy, contribute to the vitality of destinations, and help sustain natural environments, crafts, and traditions that might otherwise disappear (Getz & Carlsen, 2000; Getz & Petersen, 2005; Morrison, 2006). In other words, they "comprise a seedbed of entrepreneurial and enterprise 'culture' on which much of the profit and employment prospects of big businesses ultimately depends" (Middleton, 2001, p. 198).

Lifestyle entrepreneurs are markedly different from entrepreneurs as defined by economic theory (Table 6.4). They lack career ambition, merge family and business, are mostly driven by quality of life aspirations, and have generally low motivations for innovation and growth. Table 6.4 outlines main characteristics of lifestyle entrepreneurs suggested by Peters et al. (2009).

Table 6.4
Characteristics of Lifestyle Entrepreneurs

- Motivated by quality of life and lifestyle rather than growth
- Making most decisions without return on investment in mind
- Underutilizing capital investments
- Possessing limited marketing and product development expertise
- Lacking management training
- Low awareness of quality management techniques
- Lacking innovation
- Dependent on tourism intermediaries
- Reluctant to accept professional advice or external involvement
- Resistant to change
- Not very innovative
- Unwilling to cooperate
- Low involvement within industry structures
- Underutilizing modern technologies
- Unwilling to let go or to sell their ventures

Source: Peters et al. (2009)

Instead of pursuing traditional entrepreneurial goals of profit maximization, competiveness, market, and/or business expansion, lifestyle entrepreneurs in tourism emphasize personal life aspirations. These entrepreneurs can be found across a number of tourism sectors including farm and rural tourism, small accommodation providers (bed and breakfasts, one and two star inns and guest houses), adventure tourism, and cultural tourism, among others (Bohn, 2013).

Entrepreneurship and Innovation

An important caveat needs to be made here. While the previous discussion centered on small businesses and enterprises in tourism, the two concepts are not synonymous. In fact, many businesses (including small businesses) are not entrepreneurial at all, especially if we endorse the view that a central tenet of entrepreneurship is innovation.

Using the formal definition of innovation as "the specific tool of entrepreneurship, the means by which they exploit change as an opportunity for different business or a different service" (Drucker, 1985, p. 19), one can argue that the tourism industry is possibly less innovative than other industries (Hjalager, 2002, 2009). Small tourism businesses are especially criticized for being less innovative than larger tourism enterprises, as well as preventing innovation and growth (Thomas et al., 2011). In fact, several authors suggest that truly entrepreneurial firms are the minority in tourism.

Blichfeldt (2009) describes entrepreneurial firms in tourism as follows:

> Critical issues separate the entrepreneurial venture from other small businesses. These issues are that the entrepreneurial enterprise goes beyond other small businesses in terms of growth potential, strategic objectives, and innovation. In practice, this means that a small business (for example the 37th bed and breakfast operation established in a specific area within the last 7 years) may not be entrepreneurial at all if it is operated and organized in the same way as the other 36 B&Bs; if it does not offer customers anything "new" compared to the offerings of the other B&Bs; and if it is only initiated in order to make an additional income by means of renting out existing, spare rooms. (pp. 416–417)

Arguably, a relatively small number of entrepreneurial firms in tourism could be explained by the nature of the industry. As we have seen, most small firms in tourism are so-called "passive entrepreneurs" (quoting Morrison et al., 1999), or lifestyle and autonomy oriented, and only small fraction of small tourism businesses are innovative and entrepreneurial (Getz & Petersen, 2005).

However, innovation in tourism is not the same as in other industries. Unlike traditional product/process/market innovation outlined by Schumpeter (1934), innovation in tourism includes process, management, logistical, institutional, and experiential innovation (Hjalager, 2002; Shaw & Williams, 2009; Voss & Zomerdijk, 2007). Innovative ideas usually come from within the firm (owners or staff), or from external sources (suppliers, customers, competitors, other industries, educational institutions, alliances, partnerships, and networks) (Baker & Hart, 2007; Hjalager, 2002; Weiermair, 2003). Other possible sources of entrepreneurial innovation include changes within the firm or industry (the unexpected success or failure, the incongruity between reality and desired state, process needs, or changes in the market), and changes outside the firm or industry (demographic, changes in perceptions, or a new knowledge) (Drucker, 1985).

Entrepreneurship and innovation can be a double-edged sword for small firms in tourism. While small businesses (especially family-run firms) can often create space for risk-taking, staying with what has worked sometimes proves to be the chosen pathway. However, the long held notion that one great idea can last three generations is no longer valid; in fact, each new generation and change of leadership is now expected to create at least three great new ideas to stay viable in today's global economy (Entrepreneurship and Innovation Institute, 2015).

Finally, innovation does not just happen, it needs to be nurtured. There are many ways in which policymakers can boost innovation and spur growth by building on local strengths and ensuring the development of an environment supportive of innovation.

A closer look at the world leaders in innovation validates the argument that investing in education and research is essential for staying ahead in the global race for successful innovation. For example, the Global Innovation Index 2015 ranks Switzerland, the United Kingdom, Sweden, the Netherlands, and the United States of America as the world's five most innovative nations, and China, Malaysia, Viet Nam, India, Jordan, Kenya, and Uganda among a group of countries outperforming their economic peers (Cornell University et al., 2015). Similarly, 2014 Legatum's Prosperity Index lists Denmark, Sweden, the United States of America, Finland, the United Kingdom, Norway, Ireland, Singapore, Iceland, and Canada as the most innovative nations in the world (Legatum Institute, 2014). A strong entrepreneurial climate in these countries comprises of a number of factors, among them low costs of starting a business, public perception of a good entrepreneurial environment, a country's ability to commercialize innovation, and existing Information and Communication Technology (ICT) infrastructure. Interestingly, when a country increases the likelihood that entrepreneurial activity will pay off, and when individuals experience the satisfaction that comes from earning their success, a society's prosperity increases overall (RealClearWorld, 2015).

"Innovation holds far-reaching promise for spurring economic growth in countries at all stages of development. However, realizing this promise is not automatic," argues Francis Gurry, Director General of the World Intellectual Property Organization, and he further adds that "each nation must find the right mix of policies to mobilize the innate innovative and creative potential in their economies" (The Global Innovation Index, 2015). The following section will further explore the role of entrepreneurial policies in cultivating environment favorable for innovation and entrepreneurship in tourism.

Entrepreneurship Policy Framework

As we have seen, small businesses and enterprises in tourism are very heterogeneous, a fact that needs to be recognized by policymakers, since different types of firms require different support systems and policies to succeed. It can be disastrous to single out and focus on only one segment—such as businesses creating most jobs—and ignore, for example, lifestyle entrepreneurs. As Mills (2015) explains:

Sure, the local dry cleaner isn't going to employ radically more people next year than it did this year. But these businesses employ a lot of Americans—as many as 57 million—and the policies they need are not the same as the ones required by startups. If policymakers really want to help small businesses—and they should—they need to understand that not all of them are alike. Each type has a way it contributes to employment and the vibrancy of the American economy.

Treating all small businesses the same can lead to potentially misleading declarations, and bad policy. For example, a "mom and pop" Main Street shop has different financing needs than a high-tech startup. One might need a bank loan while the other might need a patient equity investor like an angel or venture capitalist. Setting up an innovation ecosystem around a university or an emerging technology helps potential high-growth entrepreneurs, while downtown revitalization can help local businesses [on the Main Street].

However, as Getz and Petersen (2005) point out, economic development policies in many countries noticeably favor growth-oriented entrepreneurs who create jobs. It is often assumed that growth-oriented entrepreneurs are more likely to innovate and therefore maximize tourism competitiveness of the destinations. This creates a dilemma for policymakers as to how to design an entrepreneurial climate that would work best for a specific community. Unfortunately, there is no simple answer to this question, just as there is no consensus as to what would be the best solution. On one hand, Getz and Petersen (2005) argue that "cultivating the purely autonomy and lifestyle-oriented owner will not produce many jobs, nor necessarily lead to industry competitiveness and community stability" (p. 240), while Peters et al. (2009) counter that "in most cases, the financial support is allocated on the condition that enterprises commit to growth objectives, which in reality do not positively influence lifestyle entrepreneurs. Recognizing the entrepreneurial realities and motivations as well as designing policy measures that address the quality of life balance is thus paramount for those incentives to be effective (p. 400).

Ultimately, any policy needs to be rooted in the context of the destination and aligned with the vision and goals of the tourism development. If job creation is the goal, then perhaps assistance should be channeled to growth-oriented entrepreneurs, whereas a remote destination might benefit from growth in the number and improvement in the quality of micro and small businesses (Getz & Petersen, 2005). Moreover, policies related to lifestyle tourism entrepreneurship must include lifestyle objectives as a significant element in policy decision-making (Hollick &Braun, 2005; Mottiar, 2007).

Finally, effective policies are those informed by research, and designed with the small business in mind. Quoting Thomas et al. (2011), "too often, those involved in delivering business support do not assume to enter the world of the small business (to establish what matters to them or what their needs might be) but instead focus too much on the supply of interventions such as consultancy, training programs or other forms of business support" (p. 7). Unfortunately, such policies do little to support and nurture entrepreneurship climate.

While policies are indeed important, a favorable entrepreneurial climate alone will not automatically produce entrepreneurs. Cultivating entrepreneurship should also involve nurturing people to behave entrepreneurially (Koh & Hatten, 2002). Among the strategies to create such an environment are public recognition of successful entrepreneurs, promoting entrepreneurial behaviors (such as critical thinking, communication skills, etc.), as well as creating opportunities to learn and experience entrepreneurship in action.

Gaining and Maintaining Competitive Advantages in Tourism

Strategy I: Education and Training

If destinations are to deliver high-quality tourism services and products, they need to have access to well-educated and well-trained professionals, as well as provide formal and informal training for their current employees. Both of these are great challenges for small tourism enterprises. First of all, even though small tourism and hospitality firms do not have major difficulties recruiting new staff, that is mainly because of the lower perceived need for skilled staff (Kitching & Blackburn, 2002; Peacock, 1993; Thomas et al., 2000). Dewhurst et al. (2007) partially support this argument by citing a number of studies by the UK-based Hospitality Training Foundation which found communication skills, initiative, customer service, and willingness to learn (generic skills) to be most valued in the hospitality sector.

Second, the issue of training. A report by the European Commission (2014) provides the following observations (pp. 47–49):

- Small businesses are less likely than larger companies to provide training for their employees, and the level of engagement in training is strongly related to their limited financial resources and time constraints.
- The tourism industry is known for its poor training record; for example, a study by Dewhurst et al. (2007) concluded that less than half of tourism enterprises engage in training, and close to 75% of employees report having received no job-related training.
- Smaller employers provide less formal training than larger companies; SMEs have less incentives to provide training opportunities as they often face difficulties retaining trained staff. When tourism SMEs do take advantage of training, it is mostly driven by legislation.
- Training among small tourism enterprises is not restricted to the traditional education offer, instead much training in the tourism sector is informal and takes place "on the job."
- Successful organizations often adopt an informal approach to training, which is also less costly and can be contextualized and tailored to meet specific training needs.
- The likelihood of tourism enterprises engaging in external training provision increases with the firm size.

The report further suggests that it is important to keep in mind that training can take different forms and that it does not always involve formal education and learning methods. Instead, it can include formal structured training in a traditional classroom setting or online, as well as informal training and learning through seminars, workshops, conferences, or printed materials (European Commission, 2014). Dewhurst et al. (2007) add that effective and successful training programs are those that are short, inexpensive, easily applied, and with visible personal and business benefits. Moreover, small businesses in particular need easily accessible training provision that is tailored to their specific needs.

Finally, as we have repeatedly demonstrated, the vast majority of tourism entrepreneurs are lifestyle oriented and do not exhibit typical entrepreneurial attitudes; this makes it nearly impossible to predict the extent to which such businesses would engage in business development measures such as training (Dewhurst et al., 2007). What is needed is a better understanding of the owner-managers' goals for success and associated business strategies, in order to tailor training provision to match such priorities (Brownlie, 1994; Dewhurst & Horobin, 1998).

Strategy 2: Sustainability Practices

Education, innovation, and entrepreneurial success go hand in hand. Today, another critical variable in this equation is the one of sustainability. Ensuring that the small business is successful and sustainable for future generations requires patience, honesty, and planning. Beginning early, involving stakeholders, and remaining innovative can steer many businesses in a positive direction (Entrepreneurship and Innovation Institute, 2015).

Even though the concept of sustainability has generated a lot of research activity, few tourism academics have paid attention to the role of small firms. Moreover, the literature on sustainable tourism and small businesses provides limited guidance for policymakers. This is quite disappointing for those advocating change, particularly in the absence of leadership from elsewhere (Clarke, 2004).

A recent study of around 900 tourism enterprises in 57 European protected areas outlined the following main motives for engaging in sustainability (Font et al., 2015):

- **Cost-reduction competitiveness: Enterprises will undertake sustainability actions that can provide a competitive advantage.** Many small tourism enterprises have low sustainability literacy and perceive sustainability practices to be expensive and complex (Dodds & Holmes, 2011; Revell & Blackburn, 2007; Vernon et al., 2003); these beliefs often result in shallow sustainable behaviors that rarely disturb the status quo (Font et al., 2015). Introduction of responsible practices is frequently viewed in terms of their relationship with financial performance, and consequently businesses favor those practices that lead to easily gained financial bottom line improvements. However, research has not yet found conclusive associations between sustainability and financial performance (or corporate social responsibility and financial performance), and only few small enterprises consider non-economic outcomes. At the moment, tourism businesses are mainly motivated by "green" taxes, incentives or subsidies to change behaviors.

- **Societal legitimization: Enterprises will undertake sustainability actions for visibility or to meet expectations by others.** This can be linked to the development of social capital and creating competitive advantage through protecting reputation. Especially in case of small firms, it appears that industry associations or destination-wide efforts to introduce sustainability values may encourage small tourism enterprises to consider sustainability practices; sharing best practices can further reaffirm that they are "doing the right thing."

- **Lifestyle-value drivers: Enterprises will undertake sustainability actions because of personal choices and habits, sometimes without consideration of a possible economic gain.** Many small tourism firms fall into the category of lifestyle entrepreneurs, consciously foregoing profits to maintain a certain lifestyle. Sustainability practices by these firms often reflect owners'/managers' personal values, beliefs, and choices, and thus become the part of the firm's DNA. Interestingly, such decisions are very much appreciated by the customers, and frequently lead to higher satisfaction and loyalty levels.

It can be argued that many owners/managers of small tourism firms have a good grasp of sustainability concepts without knowing the theory (Fassin et al., 2011). In the tourism industry, sustainability perfectly fits with lifestyle, habits, and routines for most small enterprises, and is positively correlated with improving performance. However, small firms make limited use of their sustainability potential and are often shy to communicate their sustainability messages. Clearly, there is no "one-size-fits-all" strategy to remedy this; however, sharing best sustainability practices and tailoring them to the specifics and realities of the region can encourage many small tourism enterprises to reconsider and expand their sustainability behaviors.

As researchers continue to try to explain why some firms are, or might become, sustainably engaged while others are not, some have advocated the need to institutionalize the principles of sustainability in tourism policy (Getz, 2009). Others, such as Dredge and Whitford (2010), have cautioned against interpretation of sustainable development as a "higher truth" or correct way of doing things, and instead suggested rebalancing of the social, environmental and economic values that characterize sustainable development, and refocusing what is important.

A brief review of policy instruments and project incentives to encourage or coerce sustainable behaviors (such as corporate social responsibility, accreditation schemes, and eco-labels to ensure the sustainable protection of the destinations) suggests that for the most part, they have failed to generate any action. And since it is neither feasible nor desirable to coerce small enterprises to be sustainable, at the end it is up to the owners/managers to decide how to grow and develop their firms; therefore decisions regarding sustainable practices are typically driven by owners'/managers' personal values and lifestyles, or anticipated cost savings (Garay & Font, 2012).

Among many reasons to support locally grown entrepreneurs is that they do appear to be more sustainable and conservation-inclined (Carlsen, Getz, & Ali-Knight, 2001). Interestingly, "companies with local roots are [also] more likely to become involved in partnerships" (Davies, 2001, p.168). Working with others via networks, clusters and alliances can indeed greatly benefit all parties involved and ultimately benefit the tourism destination as well (Crotts & Turner, 1999).

Strategy 3: Clusters, Networks, and Alliances in Tourism

One of the key challenges for small tourism enterprises is to move from increasing individual "size of the slice" to increasing the "size of the pie" in order to benefit everyone involved in the local tourism industry (Buhalis, 1996). While the definition of success varies from one business to another, research suggests that cooperation appears to be critical to survival and possible growth of small enterprises (Seppala-Esser et al., 2009). Buhalis and Cooper (1998) emphasize that cooperation at the destination is essential for reinforcing the competitiveness of both small tourism enterprises as well as their respective destinations. Friel (1998) further adds that cooperation allows small firms to enjoy many of the advantages of larger businesses, while sustaining the advantages of being small, and Keller (2004) points out the vital role of cooperation in positioning and marketing tourism services, as well as increasing productivity and bringing down costs.

In order to cope with the threats of global competition and develop strategic positioning, tourism destinations should encourage formation of tourism clusters, networks and alliances/partnerships among private businesses, but especially between the public and the private sector (Breda, Costa, & Costa, 2006). Specifically, the purpose of clusters and networks is to promote the destination and to get the small businesses that would normally work in isolation to cooperate and build a successful tourism product in the region (Novelli et al., 2006).

The main characteristics of networks, clusters, and alliances is briefly discussed below:

- **Networks.** Networks are usually viewed as organizational structures with two or more organizations involved in long-term relationships. In fact, the entire economy may be viewed as a network of organizations with a vast hierarchy of subordinate, crisscrossing networks (Thorelli, 1986). Knoke and Kuklinski (1983) see networks as a specific type of relation linking a set of persons, objects, or events, and Jarillo (1993) further argues that networks are sets of companies that work together toward a common goal, and that network coordination is not achieved by mergers and acquisitions, but rather through the creation of a "strategic network" of companies, working together toward the same goals.
- **Clusters.** Clusters are defined as "geographic concentrations of interconnected companies and institutions in a particular field, linked by commonalities and complementarities" (Porter, 1998, p. 78). Tourism clusters are the result of the co-location of complementary businesses which may not necessarily be involved in the same sector (Novelli et al., 2006). Indeed, some argue that clusters are one of the best tools available in fostering economic growth and tourism development, since they combine a broad range of services and products to deliver the specific experience that tourists seek (Michael, 2003).
- **Strategic alliances.** Pansiri (2008) outlines the following eight types of strategic alliances found in tourism: joint ventures, equity participating alliances, brand sharing, franchises and licensing, marketing and distribution agreements, joint selling or distribution, sharing information technologies, and joint purchasing and equipment/office sharing.

Nordin (2003) further explains the main differences between networks and clusters:

Networks have restricted membership, clusters have open 'membership.' Networks are based on contractual agreements, clusters are based on social values that foster trust and encourage reciprocity... Networks are based on cooperation, clusters require both cooperation and competition. Networks have common business goals, clusters have collective visions. (pp. 13–14)

Networks and clusters are rather common in the tourism industry. Their popularity is reinforced by a deep belief that contacts and cooperation with other firms makes one better equipped to succeed, as compared to individual companies and industries acting separately without the benefit of resources that complement each other (Arzeni & Pellegrin, 1997; Ingley, 1999). Soteriades et al. (2009) lists the following benefits of networks and clusters: economies of scale, a focus on cooperation and innovation, increased synergies and productivity, knowledge transfer, joint marketing, increased competitiveness, and sustainable competitive advantage. At the same time, as Peters et al. (2009) observe, the vast majority of small tourism entrepreneurs are independent minded, and have difficulty in participating in networks/clusters or accepting external advice. This applies particularly to lifestyle entrepreneurs who are not profit motivated. In reality, in myriad disconnected networks that typically exist in a destination, the cultural norm is the one of divergence and competition rather than cooperation (Braun, 2003). Consequently, when clusters do arise, it is mostly for the purposes of marketing, which is not surprising given a dominant culture of competition and autonomy in the tourism industry.

Speaking of strategic alliances, Pansiri (2008) observes that failure of many alliances can be traced to partner selection at the planning stage, and suggests forming alliances with compatibility, capability, commitment, control (the four Cs), as well as trust in mind. *Compatibility* refers to sharing values, principles, and future goals; *capability* is often viewed in terms of resources and core competencies; *commitment* can be described as a pledge to commit resources and undertake actions to achieve common goals, and *control* determines the level of authority to develop alliance capabilities in a way so as to prevent one member from becoming dominant. Finally, *trust* is a source of confidence in partner cooperation. In practice, the most effective and least expensive types of alliances appear to be marketing and distribution agreements, sharing information technologies, joint selling or distribution, and franchises and licensing.

It is incredibly important that alliances are mutual and collegial, as opposed to relying on legal contracts. Success of many alliances also greatly depends on personal relationships and friendly ties between owners/managers that enhance partner commitment, capability, compatibility and trust (Pansiri, 2008).

Strategy 4: Understanding the Small Business Development Lifecycle

As we have illustrated so far, small tourism enterprises operate in a complex environment. To make matters even more interesting, small businesses are not static on their own either; they change and develop over time. And even though no two small businesses are alike, most firms experience common problems arising at similar stages in their development. These points of similarity can be organized into a framework that increases our understanding of the nature, characteristics, and problems of businesses (Churchill & Lewis, 1983). Obvious benefits of such framework include better assessment of current challenges, ability to anticipate the key requirements at various points, ability to diagnose problems and find solutions, and improved evaluation of the impacts of regulations and policies. Moreover, the emphasis on the pathways of firm development as opposed to the classic approach to "births" and "deaths" of firms provides more useful framework for small businesses.

The small business development lifecycle model was developed by Churchill and Lewis (1983), and later adapted for the tourism industry by Morrison et al. (1999) who kept the original five stages (see Figure 6.2).

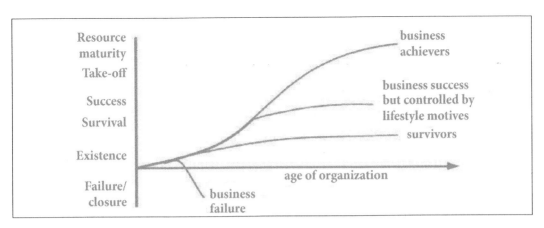

Figure 6.2. Stages of small business development over time. *Source:* Morrison et al. (1999)

Table 6.5 outlines each of the five stages of small business development.

Table 6.5
Stages of Small Business Development

Stage	Main Characteristics
Existence	Businesses focus on obtaining customers and delivering the product or service; the organization is simple, formal planning minimal or nonexistent. The company's strategy is simply to remain alive
Survival	Businesses have enough customers and satisfy them sufficiently; the organization is still simple, and planning mainly focuses on forecasting cash flow. A large number of tourism businesses never progress beyond this stage, whether for the lifestyle reasons or because they are constrained in some other way (Shaw, 2004)
Success	Businesses are faced with two options – stability (essentially, maintain the status quo; adapting only to survive) or growth (requires developing new management structures and the ability to expand resources)
Take-off	Businesses that have made it to this stage have to determine how to grow rapidly and how to finance that growth
Resource maturity	Businesses entering this stage have to balance the tasks of consolidating and controlling the profits generated by growth, while retaining the advantages of small size. The organization is now more sophisticated, with adequate staff and financial resources to engage in detailed planning

Source: Churchill and Lewis (1983)

Knowing the current stage and what lies ahead enables managers, consultants, and investors to make more informed choices, and to prepare themselves and their businesses for later challenges. For example, the first phases of business development are especially critical for the food and accommodation sectors, since the research shows that these firms display statistically significantly lower survival rates as compared to the other sectors. Family businesses are similarly vulnerable: as Getz and Carlsen (2000) note, only a few family businesses endure through a complete lifecycle, and those businesses who manage to survive their incubation period, usually face serious strategic problems including high levels of debt (Peters et al., 2009).

In addition to outlining the stages of small business development, the framework also suggests a number of factors that are prominent in determining ultimate success or failure of small enterprises. Among these are financial resources (cash and borrowing power), personnel resources (numbers and quality of people), systems resources (sophistication of information and planning systems), business resources (customer relations and marketing), and owner's goals and abilities (operational, managerial, and strategic). As firms move from one stage to another, the importance of each of these factors changes, therefore the ability to anticipate and manage the factors as they become important to the company is critical to the success of the business. Moreover, understanding the underlying dynamics of the small business development over time can provide useful insights regarding the timing of change or growth, and a careful balanced management of the factors is what most likely differentiates "survival" firms from "growth" firms (Shaw, 2004).

Summary

This chapter sought to examine the main business concepts in community based tourism, with a special emphasis on entrepreneurship. Without a doubt, SMEs play an important role in small communities, and are critical to the development of villages and small towns (Getz and Carlsen, 2005). They suffer less economic leakages, provide higher multiplier effects as compared to larger businesses, and contribute to the vitality of destinations (Morrison, 2006; Wanhill, 2000). However, the rapid pace of changes in the tourism industry leaves many small businesses vulnerable to the threats emerging from the external environment.

Entrepreneurship and innovation in tourism are all around us, and entrepreneurs in reality are ordinary human beings, seeking to do good for themselves in terms of material gain and social status (Pearce, 1980). Their risky endeavors, however, have greatly changed the world and have significantly contributed to material progress in society: just think of the iconic tourism entrepreneurs such as Walt Disney (co-founder of the Walt Disney Company), Conrad Hilton (founder of the Hilton Hotels chain), Thomas Cook (founder of the Thomas Cook & Son travel agency), and Richard Branson (founder of the Virgin Group), among others (examples from Morrison, 2006).

How can destinations and communities nurture and support tourism entrepreneurship? This chapter reviewed a number of tools that are available including formal and informal education and training, sustainability practices, and clusters, networks, and alliances, among others. Many of these form the core of a sound favorable policy environment to nurture innovative and entrepreneurial climate.

And what about small firms that are not entrepreneurial? It is essential for them to first and foremost improve their understanding of marketing knowledge and activities, networking and relationship management, and quality and customer focus, and turn these into competitive advantages.

In order to succeed in an increasingly competitive and fast-paced environment, small businesses need to continuously adapt, innovate, and stay abreast of current trends and opportunities. This chapter outlined complexities of small business entrepreneurship, discussed unique characteristics of small businesses in tourism, and suggested several key essentials of successful tourism entrepreneurship.

Key Concepts

- Small and medium-sized enterprises (SMEs)
- Entrepreneurship
- Lifestyle entrepreneurship
- Innovation
- Education and training
- Sustainability
- Clusters, networks, and alliances
- Small business development lifecycle

Useful Sites, Exercises, and Resources

1. Visit Government of British Columbia website at http://www2.gov.bc.ca. Go to "Menu" tab, then select "Employment, Business & Economic Development," "Business," "Small business." Review examples of governmental support for small businesses in British Columbia, Canada.
2. Review "Keeping British Columbia in Business" at http://www.businessinfocusmagazine.com/2014/06/ministry-for-tourism-and-small-business. What is the role of the Ministry for Tourism and Small Business in British Columbia in supporting small tourism businesses?

Questions for Review and Case Problems

1. What are the main strength and weaknesses of small businesses in tourism?
2. Discuss entrepreneurship in tourism. How are tourism entrepreneurs different from other entrepreneurs?
3. Discuss the concepts of lifestyle and family entrepreneurship.
4. What are the main strategies of gaining and maintaining competitive advantages in tourism?
5. Discuss the role and importance of clusters, networks, and alliances in tourism.

References

Al-Azri, H. I., & Cai, L. (2009). Uniqueness of tourism SMEs: Strategic marketing framework propositions. *Tourism Issues, (8)*, 142–151.

Arzeni, S., & Pellegrin, J.-P. (1997). Entrepreneurship and local development. OECD Observer, 204 (Feb./March), 27–29.

Ateljevic, I., & Doorne, S. (2000). "Staying within the fence": Lifestyle entrepreneurship in tourism. *Journal of Sustainable Tourism, 8*(5), 378–392.

Baker, M., & Hart, S. (2007). *Product strategy and management* (2nd ed.). New York, NY: Financial Times/Prentice Hall.

Birch, D. L. (1979). *The job generation process.* Cambridge, MA: MIT.

Blichfeldt, B. S. (2009). Innovation and entrepreneurship in tourism: the case of a Danish caravan site. *PASOS: Revista de Turismo y Patrimonio Cultural, 7*(3), 415–431.

Bohn, D. (2013). *No ordinary business: Lifestyle entrepreneurs and their tourism products: Insights from Finnish Lapland.* Thesis, Rovaniemi University of Applied Sciences, School Of Tourism and Hospitality Management.

Braun, P. (2003). SME networks: Clustering for regional innovation purposes. *Proceedings of the 16th Annual Small Enterprize Association of Australia and New Zealand,* 28 Sept-1Oct, Ballarat, Victoria.

Breda, Z., Costa, R., & Costa, C. (2006). Do clusters and networks make small places beautiful? The case of Caramulo (Portugal). In L. Lazzeretti & C. Petrillo (Eds.), *Tourism local systems and networking* (pp. 67–82). Advances in Tourism Management Series. Oxford, UK: Elsevier.

Breen, J., Bergin-Seers, S., Jago, L., & Carlsen, J. (2005). *Small and medium tourism enterprises: The identification of good practice.* Queensland: Cooperative Research Centre for Sustainable Tourism.

Brownlie, D. (1994). Market opportunity analysis: A DIY approach for small tourism enterprises. *Tourism Management, 15*(1), 37–45.

Buhalis, D. (1996). Enhancing the competitiveness of small and medium sized tourism enterprises at the destination level by using information technology. *Electronic Markets, 6*(1), 1–6.

Buhalis, D., & Cooper, C. (1998). Competition or co-operation: The needs of small and medium-sized tourism enterprises at a destination level. In E. Laws, B. Faulkner, & G. Moscardo (Eds.), *Embracing and managing change in tourism* (pp. 324–346). London, UK: Routledge.

Burnett, D. (2000). Hunting for heffalumps: The supply of entrepreneurship and economic development. Retrieved from http://technopreneurial.com/

Burns, P. (1996). Introduction: The significance of small firms. In P. Burns & J. Dewhurst (Eds.), *Small business and entrepreneurship* (2nd ed.). Basingstoke, UK: MacMillan.

Carlsen, J., Getz, D., & Ali-Knight, J. (2001). Environmental attitudes and practices of family businesses in the rural tourism and hospitality sectors. *Journal of Sustainable Tourism, 9*(4), 281–297.

Čavlek, N. (2002). Business in tourism: SMEs versus MNCs. *Zagreb International Review of Economics and Business, 5*(2), 39–48.

Cornell University, INSEAD, & World Intellectual Property Organization. (2015). *The Global Innovation Index 2015: effective innovation policies for development.* Ithaca and Geneva: Fontainebleau.

Couger, J. D., Higgins, L. F., & McIntyre, S. C. (1990). *Differentiating creativity, innovation, entrepreneurship, intrapreneurship, copyright and patenting for I.S. products/processes.* University of Colorado, Colorado Springs: Center for Research on Creativity and Innovation, College of Business.

Churchill, N. C., & Lewis, V. L. (1983). The five stages of small business growth. *Harvard Business Review, 6*(3), 30–50.

Crotts, J. C., & Turner, G. B. (1999). Determinants of intra-firm trust in buyer-seller relationships in the international travel trade. *International Journal of Contemporary Hospitality Management, 11*(2/3), 116–123.

Davies, J. S. (2001). *Partnerships and regimes.* Aldershot, UK: Ashgate.

Dewhurst J., & Burns, P. (1993). *Small business management* (3rd ed.). Basingstoke, UK: Macmillan.

Dewhurst, H., Dewhurst, P., & Livesey, R. (2007). Tourism and hospitality SME training needs and provision: a sub-regional analysis. *Tourism and Hospitality Research, 7*(2), 131–143.

Dewhurst, P., & Horobin, H. (1998). Small business owners. In R. Thomas (Ed.), *The management of small tourism and hospitality firms* (pp. 19–38). London, UK: Cassell.

Echtner, C. M. (1995). Entrepreneurial training in developing countries. *Annals of Tourism Research, 22*(1), 119–134.

Entrepreneurship and Innovation Institute. (2015). Five tips for family businesses: beating the odds of succession. Retrieved from https://www.johnson.cornell.edu/Entrepreneurship-and-Innovation-Institute

European Commission. (2014). Mapping skills and training needs to improve accessibility in tourism services. Retrieved from http://ec.europa.eu/

Family Firm Institute, Inc. (2015). Retrieved from http://www.ffi.org

Getz, D., & Carlsen, J. (2000). Characteristics and goals of family and owner-operated businesses in the tourism and hospitality sectors. *Tourism Management, 21*(6), 547–560.

Getz, D., & Petersen, T. (2005). Growth and profit-oriented entrepreneurship among family business owners in the tourism and hospitality industry. *International Journal of Hospitality Management, 24*(2), 219–242.

go2 Tourism HR Society. (2015). Small business owner/operator. Retrieved from https://www.go2hr.ca/careers/small-business-owneroperator

Government of Western Australia. (n.d.). The broader tourism industry. Small Business Development Corporation. Retrieved from http://www.smallbusiness.wa.gov.au/TourismBoost/

Hjalager, A.-M. (2002). Repairing innovation defectiveness in tourism. *Tourism Management, 23*(5), 465–474.

Hjalager, A.-M. (2009). A review of innovation research in tourism. *Tourism Management, 31*(1), 1–12.

Hollick, M., & Braun, P. (2005). Lifestyle entrepreneurship: the unusual nature of the tourism entrepreneur. *Proceedings of the Second Annual AGSE International Entrepreneurship Research Exchange 2005*, Melbourne, Australia.

Ingley, B. (1999). The cluster concept: cooperative networks and replicability. *Proceedings of the 44th World Conference of the International Council of Small Business*, June 20-23, Naples, Italy.

Investopedia. (2015). Gazelle company. Retrieved from http://www.investopedia.com/

Jaafar, M., Abdul-Aziz, A. R., Maideen, S. A., & Mohd, S. Z. (2011). Entrepreneurship in the tourism industry: issues in developing countries. *International Journal of Hospitality Management, 30*(4), 827–835.

Jarillo, J. C. (1993). *Strategic networks: Creating the borderless organization.* Oxford, MA: Butterworth-Heinemann.

Keller, P. (2004). Introduction: The future of SMEs in tourism. In P. Keller & T. Bieger (Eds.), *The future of small and medium-sized enterprises in tourism* (pp. 7–34), 54th AIEST Congress, Petra, Jordan, vol. 46.

Kitching, J., & Blackburn, R. (2002). *The nature of training and motivation to train in small firms.* Kingston, UK: Kingston University.

Knoke, D., & Kuklinski, J. (1983). *Network analysis.* Los Angeles, CA: Sage.

Koh, K.Y., & Hatten, T. S. (2002). The tourism entrepreneur: the overlooked player in tourism development studies. *International Journal of Hospitality and Tourism Administration, 3*(1), 21–48.

Loucks, K. E. (1988). *Training entrepreneurs for small business creation: Lessons from experience.* Management Development Series No. 26. Geneva, Switzerland: International Labour Office.

Legatum Institute. (2014). *The 2014 Legatum Prosperity Index.* London, UK: Author.

Michael, E. J. (2003). Tourism micro-clusters. *Tourism Economics, 9*(2), 133–145.

Middleton, V. (2001). The importance of micro-businesses in European tourism. In L. Roberts & D. Hall (Eds.), *Rural tourism and recreation: Principles to practice* (pp. 197–201). Wallingford, Oxon: CABI.

Mills, K. (2015). The 4 types of small businesses, and why each one matters. *Harvard Business Review* (April 30). Retrieved from https://hbr.org/2015/

Morrison, A. (2006). A contextualisation of entrepreneurship. *International Journal of Entrepreneurial Behaviour and Research, 12*(4), 192–209.

Morrison, A., Rimmington, M., & Williams, C. (1999). *Entrepreneurship in hospitality, tourism, and leisure industries.* London, UK: Butterworth-Heinemann.

Mottiar, Z. (2007). Lifestyle entrepreneurs and spheres of inter-firm relations: The case of Westport Co. Mayo, Ireland. *The International Journal of Entrepreneurship and Innovation, 8*(1), 67–74.

Nordin, S. (2003). *Tourism clustering and innovation: Paths to economic growth and development.* Östersund, Sweden: European Tourism Research Institute.

Novelli, M., Schmitz, B., & Spencer, T. (2006). Networks, clusters and innovation in tourism: a UK experience. *Tourism Management, 27*(6), 1141–1152.

OECD. (2000). *Small and medium-sized enterprises: Local strength, global reach.* Policy brief (June).

OECD. (2005). *OECD SME and entrepreneurship outlook: 2005.* Paris, France: OECD.

Pansiri, J. (2008). The effects of characteristics of partners on strategic alliance performance in the SME dominated travel sector. *Tourism Management, 29*(1), 101–115.

Peacock, M. (1993). A question of size. *International Journal of Contemporary Hospitality Management, 5*(4), 29–32.

Pearce, I. (1980). Reforms for entrepreneurs to serve public policy. In A. Seldon (Ed.), *Prime mover of progress: The entrepreneur in capitalism and socialism.* London, UK: The Institute of Economic Affairs.

Peters, M., Frehse, J., & Buhalis, D. (2009). The importance of lifestyle entrepreneurship: a conceptual study of the tourism industry. *Journal of Revista de Turismo y Patrimonio Cultural, 7*(2), 393–405.

Porter, M. E. (1998). Clusters and the new economics of competition. *Harvard Business Review, 76*(6), 77–90.

RealClearWorld. (2015). Global prosperity analysis: Ten most innovative countries in the world. Retrieved from http://www.realclearworld.com/topic/global_prosperity_analysis

Seppala-Esser, R., Airey, D., & Szivas, E. (2009). The dependence of tourism SMEs on NTOs: the case of Finland. *Journal of Travel Research, 48*(2), 177–190.

Shaw, G. (2004). Entrepreneurial cultures and small business enterprises in tourism. In A. A. Lew, C. M. Hall, & A.M. Williams (Eds.), *A companion to tourism* (pp. 122–134). Oxford, MA: Blackwell Publishing.

Shaw, G., & Williams, A. M. (1998). Entrepreneurship, small business culture and tourism development. In D. Ioannides & K. G. Debbage (Eds.), *The economic geography of the tourist industry* (pp. 235–255). London, UK: Routledge.

Shaw, G., & Williams, A.M., (2009). Knowledge transfer and management in tourism organizations: an emerging research agenda. *Tourism Management, 30*(3), 325–335.

Soteriades, M. D., Tyrogala, E. D., & Varvaressos, S. I. (2009). Contribution of networking and clustering in rural tourism business. *Tourismos: An International Multidisciplinary Journal of Tourism, 4*(4), 35–56.

Storey, D. J. (1994). *Understanding the small business sector.* London, UK: Routledge.

The Global Innovation Index. (2015). Press release "Global Innovation Index 2015: Switzerland, UK, Sweden, Netherlands, USA are leaders." Retrieved from https://www.globalinnovationindex.org/content/page/press-release

Thomas, R. (2000). Small firms in the tourism industry: Some conceptual issues. *International Journal of Tourism Research, 2*(5), 345–353.

Thomas, R., Lashley, C., Rowson, B., Xie, G., Jameson, S., Eaglen, A., Lincoln, G., & Parsons, D. (2000). *The national survey of small tourism and hospitality firms: 2000 skills demand and training practices.* Centre for the Study of Small Tourism and Hospitality Firms, Leeds Metropolitan University, Leeds.

Thomas, R., Shaw, G., & Page, S. J. (2011). Understanding small firms in tourism: A perspective on research trends and challenges. *Tourism Management, 32*(5), 963–976.

Thorelli, H. B. (1986). Networks: Between markets and hierarchies. *Strategic Management Journal, 7*(1), 37–51.

U.S. Small Business Administration. (2011). Frequently asked questions. Retrieved from http://www.sba.gov/

Voss, C., & Zomerdijk, L. (2007). Innovation in experiential services: An empirical view. In Department of Trade and Industry (Eds.), *Innovation in service* (pp. 97–134). Occasional Paper no. 9. London: Department of Trade and Industry.

Wanhill, S. (2000). Mines, a tourist attraction: Coal mining in industrial South Wales. *Journal of Travel Research, 39* (August), 60–69.

Weiermair, K. (2003). Product improvement or innovation: What is the key to success in tourism? *Proceedings of the OECD Conference on Innovation & Growth in Tourism,* September 18-19, Lugano, Switzerland.

CHAPTER 7

Community Issues, Concerns, and Planning

"The trouble is that success in tourism is measured in terms of volume."
—William Bryan, Tour Operator

CHAPTER OBJECTIVES

- To build an awareness of the impacts of tourism
- To understand how to measure community concerns for tourism
- To understand the factors that lead to sprawl and uncontrolled development
- To understand the community tourism planning process
- To gain insight into community participation mechanisms

Introduction

Tourism will likely have both positive and negative effects on a host community and its residents. However, tourism planning, development, and management can be practiced responsibly to at least sustain the relationship it must rely on—the relationship between the local community, the visitor, and the environment that they share (Knowles-Lankford & Lankford, 2000). Many examples abound with regard to tourism impacts and planning. For example, Grybovych and Hafermann (2010) analyzed how the community of Ucluelet, B.C. Canada facing a threat of uncontrolled tourism development embraced practices of participatory planning using a proactive approach to guide development and inform developers. Tourism is incremental in that it happens over time and changes the structure, density, and character of a place (Knowles-Lankford & Lankford, 2000). Communities oftentimes find they are spending considerable resources on police, fire, transportation and traffic management, and waste management. Essentially, the community was totally unprepared for the build out of the area which began with possibly a single development or event.

Importantly, research by Long et al. (1990) on 28 rural Colorado communities indicated that residents' favor of tourism development increased initially, but became less favorable after a threshold level of development was reached. Essentially, the sustainability of the community and what makes it special becomes an issue. Sustainable tourism development occurs when the planning and management processes embrace a number of philosophic and procedural dimensions (Figure 7.1, adapted from Knowles-Lankford & Lankford, 2000). First, local community members must participate in the development process. Second, education of the host population, the developers and visitors must occur. Third, wildlife habitat, use of energy, and microclimate must be understood and respected. The fourth area is the importance of transportation and the means to reduce at least use of fossil fuels within the visitor complex. Lastly is an economy of means, implying getting the most benefit from the least energy. For example using local labor and business skills to develop the tourism industry. A community process of development will promote a healthy relationship between the community, visitor and environment and add economic vitality in a sustainable fashion.

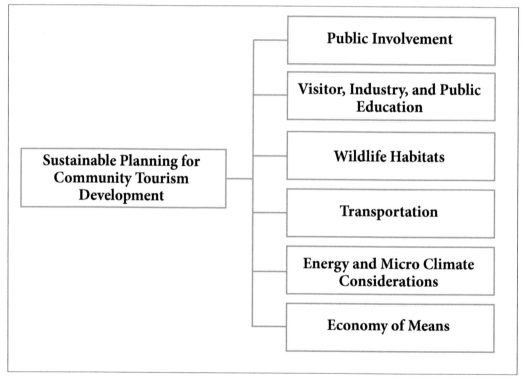

Figure 7.1. Sustainability and Community Tourism

Impacts of Tourism

Numerous conceptual models have dealt with the typical courses of community development. For example, Doxey (1975), in a well-cited and elaborated model, provided what is called the index of tourist irritation. The model (Figure 7.2) implies that residents' perception of the impacts of tourism increase as the industry matures and passes through four stages: from euphoria through apathy, to irritation to antagonism. Intuitively this model makes some sense. As one can imagine, at the first stages, the community is supportive of new jobs, then later takes the industry for granted and is somewhat apathetic. Later, as the industry gains a stronger presence in the community, people become more concerned about impacts and crowding, and finally are outwardly antagonistic toward tourists and industry supporters. It is important to note that on-going monitoring of concerns for tourism, appropriate planning, and civic engagement strategies and efforts, will help to alleviate the more negative actions of some stakeholders. Many cases of youth throwing rocks at tour buses, vandalizing cars of out-of-state visitors, and even assaults on tourists have occurred. One could only guess why, but managing the industry as described will help minimize these negative experiences.

STAGE	HOST COMMUNITY ATTITUDE	CHARACTERISTICS
Stage 1	**Euphoria**	• Small number of visitors • Visitors seek to merge with the local community • Host community welcomes tourism • Limited commercial activity in tourism
Stage 2	**Apathy**	• Visitor numbers increase • Visitors are taken for granted • The relationship between tourists and the host community is more formalized
Stage 3	**Irritation**	• The number of tourists grows significantly • Increased involvement of external commercial concerns • Increased competition for resources • Locals concerned about tourism
Stage 4	**Antagonism**	• Open hostility from locals • Attempts to limit damage and tourism flows

Figure 7.2. Irridex Model of Tourism Attitudes

The impacts of tourism can be considered from a range of viewpoints (pro and con) and disciplines. Specifically, these are economic (jobs, higher property taxes, higher wages, higher cost of living), environmental, social, cultural, crowding and congestion, public services and infrastructure, and community support and attitudes. It is important to note that some communities may or may not experience all of the impacts, but a recognition of the potential and monitoring of the impacts is crucial to the success of the industry. Table 7.1, adapted from Kreag (2001) and Lankford and Howard (1993), provides examples of these impacts.

Stakeholders and Perceptions of Tourism Impacts

Usually there are various groups of community members who take divergent positions on the industry. Those who have a stake in the tourism industry, such as business owners, convention bureaus, hotels, chambers of commerce, builders, and those employed or who could be employed in tourism, would be more supportive and also less likely to concede the problems the industry causes. There may be environmental groups, historical groups, recreation and sports clubs, civic organizations, etc. that also may be more cautious or more supportive for a variety of reasons.

Table 7.1

Examples of Positive and Negative Impacts of Tourism

Impact	Positive	Negative
Economic	Increased standard of living	Increased prices of goods, services, cost of living
	Employment/jobs	Imported labor
	Increased tax revenue	Increased taxes for roads/ infrastructure
	Improved infrastructure	Profits exported by nonlocal owners
Environmental	Protection of important habitats and preserves	Destruction of flora and fauna, artifacts, etc.
	Improvement of areas appearance and landscape	Degradation of landscape and historic sites, advertising is obtrusive
	Clean industry	Water shortage, sewer issues, litter
Social/Cultural	Improved understanding of others	Unwanted lifestyle changes
	Enhances historical and cultural amenities	Displacement of residents for tourism
	Preserves local cultural identify	Language, culture, and changes in values
Crowding/ Congestion	Concentrates tourist facilities	Congestion and traffic
	Old buildings reused	Overbuilt, out-of-scale development
	Management schemes to reduce use	Conflicts and overcrowded recreation areas
Public Services	Increased recreation services	Neglect of local recreation services
	Higher quality police and fire	Increased pressure to serve tourists

It is important to discover the specific interests of each stakeholder group and where their interests diverge and overlap. Figure 7.3 demonstrates the divergent interests. In this model, Kreag (2001) demonstrates that group A is comprised of businesses and residents interested in jobs, while group B is comprised of people who are displaced by visitors, while group C is comprised of environmental groups who are concerned about plant and wildlife habitats. Even though the groups are divergent, that does not mean they cannot be educated about the industry and its impacts. It means there is an opportunity to put these concerns into action within the planning process and plan. The important component is to have civic engagement to identify issues and develop solutions with the support of the groups. Figure 7.4 demonstrates the overlapping interest areas where we find common ground to work with the stakeholders. Recognizing, measuring, documenting, and developing ongoing dialogue about these issues builds trust and support. Some authors support involving groups such as government employees, local and regional administrators, professional planners, and local business owners to reveal discrepancies between the levels of support of every group (Ayers & Potter, 1989; Lankford, 1994; Ritchie, 1988; Uysal et al., 1994). The more the residents are involved in the process of change, the more favorably they perceive that process.

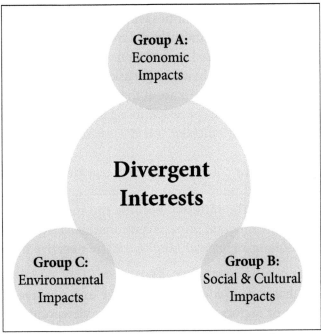

Figure 7.3. Divergent Interests in Tourism Impacts

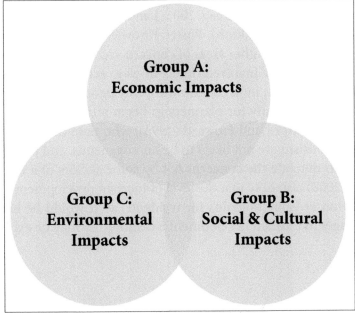

Figure 7.4. Overlapping Interests in Tourism Impacts

Table 7.2 (adapted from Lankford, 1994) provides an example of the differences stakeholders have regarding tourism impacts within the Columbia River Gorge using the standardized Tourism Impact Attitude Scale (TIAS, Lankford & Howard, 1993, which is described in more detail later in this chapter). The Gorge has been popular with residents of the Portland, Oregon metropolitan area, is a designated National Scenic Area administered by the U.S. Forest Service and the interstate (Oregon and Washington) regional commission known as the Columbia River Gorge Commission. The Gorge has year-round tourism, is a significant wind-surfing attraction, near Mt. Hood ski area, with fishing, hiking, and camping. The study, part of a monitoring project, surveyed 1,436 randomly selected stakeholders in the Gorge, for a 74.1% response rate, which represented the 13 cities and 6 counties within the National Scenic Area. As one can see, the resident population significantly differed from business owners, government employees and elected/appointed government leaders on all of the items in the scale. The notations by the column labeled H (Kruskal-Wallis H statistic) can be interpreted as follows: a = all significance levels are at the <.01 level; b = residents significantly differ from the other three groups; c = residents significantly differ from government employees and elected/appointed officials; and d = residents significantly differ from government employees.

Generally, residents were less convinced about the economic benefits, yet all agreed that tourism will have a continued economic impact and provide jobs. However, residents did not want to see the industry become the main industry. Residents felt noise, crime, litter and environmental impacts have increased. Residents were skeptical about the effectiveness of long-range planning to control negative impacts.

Factors Influencing Support for Tourism

There are reasons that stakeholders have negative and positive views of tourism. Generally, the predictors or factors that influence these viewpoints can be personal or based on other factors that are related to the issues as noted above in Figures 7.3 and 7.4. Figure 7.5 identifies some of the factors from the literature which are known to influence support for tourism (adapted from Kreag, 2001; Lankford & Howard, 1993; Lankford & Knowles-Lankford, 1995; and Lankford, Pfister, Knowles-Lankford, & Williams, 2003). The three main areas (there are other areas of concern according to some research) area individual characteristics, how involved one is in civic activities and the community, and perceptions of recreational impacts. Knowing why people react to tourism the way they do provides an opportunity for planners to begin a dialog on the issues. Rollins (1997) concurs with Lankford and Howard (1993), who note that even in rural areas resident attitudes to tourism are not likely to be homogeneous, and public consultation will be imperative to mitigate the concerns felt by some sectors of a host community. Wang and Pfister (2008) also note that the level of tourism development plays a notable role in the formation of value domains for residents, so it would be helpful to know more about the stages of tourism development a community may be experiencing.

Table 7.2

Mean Scores and Kruskal-Wallis H Values Between Stakeholder Groups: TIAS–Concern For Local Tourism Development

Scale Item	Residents	Government Employees	Elected Officials	Business Owners	H[a]
I am against new tourism facilities, which will attract more tourists to my community.	2.78	2.02	2.21	1.98	59.33[c]
I believe tourism should be actively encouraged in my community.	3.18	3.75	3.68	4.00	44.69[b]
Columbia Gorge communities should not try to attract more visitors.	2.73	2.17	2.38	2.01	34.51[b]
I believe tourism should be actively encouraged in the Columbia River Gorge.	3.25	3.86	3.70	4.11	44.78[b]
The community should encourage more intensive development of tourist facilities.	3.00	3.67	3.58	3.76	55.19[b]
I support tourism as having a vital role in our community.	3.18	3.73	3.74	4.01	47.09[b]
The city/county government was right in promoting tourism facilities in this community.	3.18	3.77	3.64	3.76	50.64[b]
My community should become more of a tourist destination.	2.87	3.58	3.42	3.72	52.33[b]
Tourism has negatively impacted the environment.	2.94	2.46	2.74	2.44	19.97[b]
The noise level from the existing tourism facilities is not appropriate for this town/ community.	2.71	2.38	2.56	2.31	16.43[c]
There is more litter in my community from tourism.	3.35	2.91	3.25	3.00	17.61[d]
Tourists are valuable.	3.39	4.00	3.72	3.88	41.83[b]

Table 7.2 (cont.)

More outdoor recreation development is not desirable.	2.66	2.07	2.24	2.00	42.54[b]
Tourism has increased crime in my community.	3.05	2.64	2.76	2.78	21.70[c]
The benefits of tourism outweigh the negative consequences of tourism development.	2.95	3.42	3.40	3.62	33.75[b]
I support tourism and would like to see it become the main industry in my community	2.40	2.89	2.88	3.07	41.73[b]
Long-term planning by my city/county can control the negative impacts of tourism on the environment.	3.49	4.01	3.95	3.80	36.51[d]
Tourism development in my community will provide more jobs for local people.	3.32	3.87	3.85	3.76	39.98[c]

Note: 1= Strongly Disagree; 5 = Strongly Agree

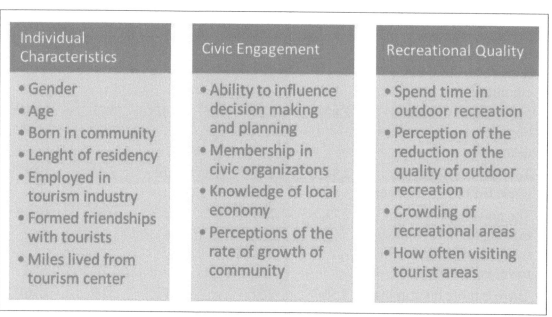

Figure 7.5. Factors Influencing Support for Tourism

Use of the TIAS has also provided some statistical evidence of the importance of various reasons why people hold the positive or negative views of tourism that they have. Table 7.3 provides a comparison of some of the places (it has also been used in Connecticut, Illinois, South Carolina, U.K., The Netherlands, Turkey, and Africa to our knowledge) that the TIAS has been employed, and the resulting predictors that explain peoples' attitudes toward tourism in their community. What is most surprising, is the comparison of the reasons for these attitudes across very different communities, specifically cultural, social, and environmentally different places at varying levels of tourism development. Obvious examples include being employed in the industry provides a favorable view of tourism. By comparing the common predictors in Figure 7.5 in this chapter, we can see that individual, civic and recreational concerns provide a framework for reviewing Table 7.3 with regard to the explanation of the attitudes toward tourism within the comparison of these communities.

A Framework for Measuring Impacts

As has been noted, it is important to gauge support for tourism and monitor perceived and real impacts upon the community. In response to this need, Lankford and Howard (1993) developed and tested a scale, the Tourism Impact Attitude Scale (TIAS) for this purpose. Drawing on earlier work, they pretested the scale in two tourism communities, Bend (mountain community) and Cannon Beach (coastal community) Oregon. Both communities have been successful in delivering visitor services and are impacted by tourism. Figure 7.6, (Lankford, 1994) describes the process used to develop the TIAS. One can see the level of testing of the scale and attention to detail in developing the 27 items for measuring community attitudes. Importantly the response rates (rather high, minimizing nonresponse bias error), sampling process (systematic random) and sample frame (actual community members in tourism based economies) provide some level of assurance about the development of the scale and its application.

Table 7.4 provides a review of the TIAS used in four international communities and six North American/U.S. sites. The term "factors" refer to a grouping of questions that have some statistical relevance or relationship to one another. Interestingly, the factor structure and topics vary by place, due to local conditions. However, what is more important is that the interpretation of these factors suggest the same concerns no matter where the scale is used. Equally important is that the internal reliability of the 27 item TIAS seems to be a reliable measure for tourism attitudes (alpha reliability over .6 is acceptable, ranging from 0-1). Wang and Pfister (2008) noted that the TIAS reliability and validity have been tested by using it in various tourism settings over the past decades (i.e., Lankford & Howard, 1993, in Oregon and Washington States; Lankford, Chen, & Chen, 1994 in Taiwan; Rollins, 1997, in British Columbia; Vesey & Dimanche, 2001, in New Orleans, Louisiana; and Harrill & Potts, 2003, in Charleston, South Carolina.

Plans and the Planning Process

After acknowledging and measuring tourism impacts in a community, it is important that the planning process for tourism incorporate these considerations. A clear statement of the community's values and vision of tourism should be central to the plan and process. Kreag (2001) notes that active planning can direct tourism toward the goals of the community, and clarifies tourism's role and unites multiple interests.

Table 7.3

Multiple Regression Analysis: Influence of Independent Variables on the 27 Items Tourism Impact Attitude Scale (TIAS) Dependent Variable: Attitude Toward Tourism as Measured by TIAS

Independent Variables	Pacific Northwest[a] (n=1436)	China[a] (n=917)	Hawaii[a] (n=217)	Canada[a] (n=346)	Bend[a] (n=199)	Cannon[a] (n=186)	Washington, North Carolina[b] (n=122)	Austria[c] (n=1758)	Charleston, South Carolina[d] (n=404)	New Orleans French Quarter[e] (n=227)	Monteville, Connecticut[f] (n=218)
							Beta weights				
Reduce the quality of outdoor recreation	-.41***	-.15***	-.14*	-.16***	-.18**	-.12*					-.178
Ability to influence tourism decision making	-.34***	.10**		.24***	.11*	.17**					
Are you employed in a job related to tourism[1]?	.12**				.20***	.13**		-.27	.235	.115	-.037
Have formed relationships with tourists[2]	-.12**		.13*					-.27			
How long have you lived in this are?	-.10**						.047	-.14	.377		
Rate of growth in community	-.09*	.37***		.09*			.159			.117	
Knowledge of main industries in area.	.08*										
Local recreation programs have expanded due to tourism	.15**	.16***	.42***		.15**	.11*					.336
Decision makers listen to residents	.12	.05**	.18**		.22***					.078	.211
Most people do not like tourists	-.06	-.18***				-.22***					
Tourists are crowding local areas				-.31***							
Tourists interfere with employment of place	-.40	-.12**	-.25***		-.40***	-.36***					-.332
Frequency of talking with tourists[3]		.06**		.20***				-.27		.096	
Frequency of visiting tourists areas[4]	.04	.04*									
Age	-.04	.07**									.027
Income[5]		.05*				.13**	.271				.029
Sex[6]		.04*					.217		-.149		.024
Number of civic organizations		.04*									
Pleasant conversations with tourists[7]				.27***							
Size of tourism industry in Nanaimo				.11**							
Should provide recreation facilities for local people rather than tourists	-.09		-.13*		-.12*	-.13*					

Note 2, 3 & 4: Never=1, Occasionally=2, Often=3
Note 5: Under 8,000=1, 8,000-18,000=2, 18,000-28,000=3, 28,000-38,000=4, 38,000-48,000=5, 48,000-58,000=6, Above 58,000=7
Note 6: Male=1, Female=0
Authors: Lankford[a], Wang & Pfister[b], Bachleitner & Zins[c], Harrill & Potts[d], Vesey & Dimanche[e], Jones[f]

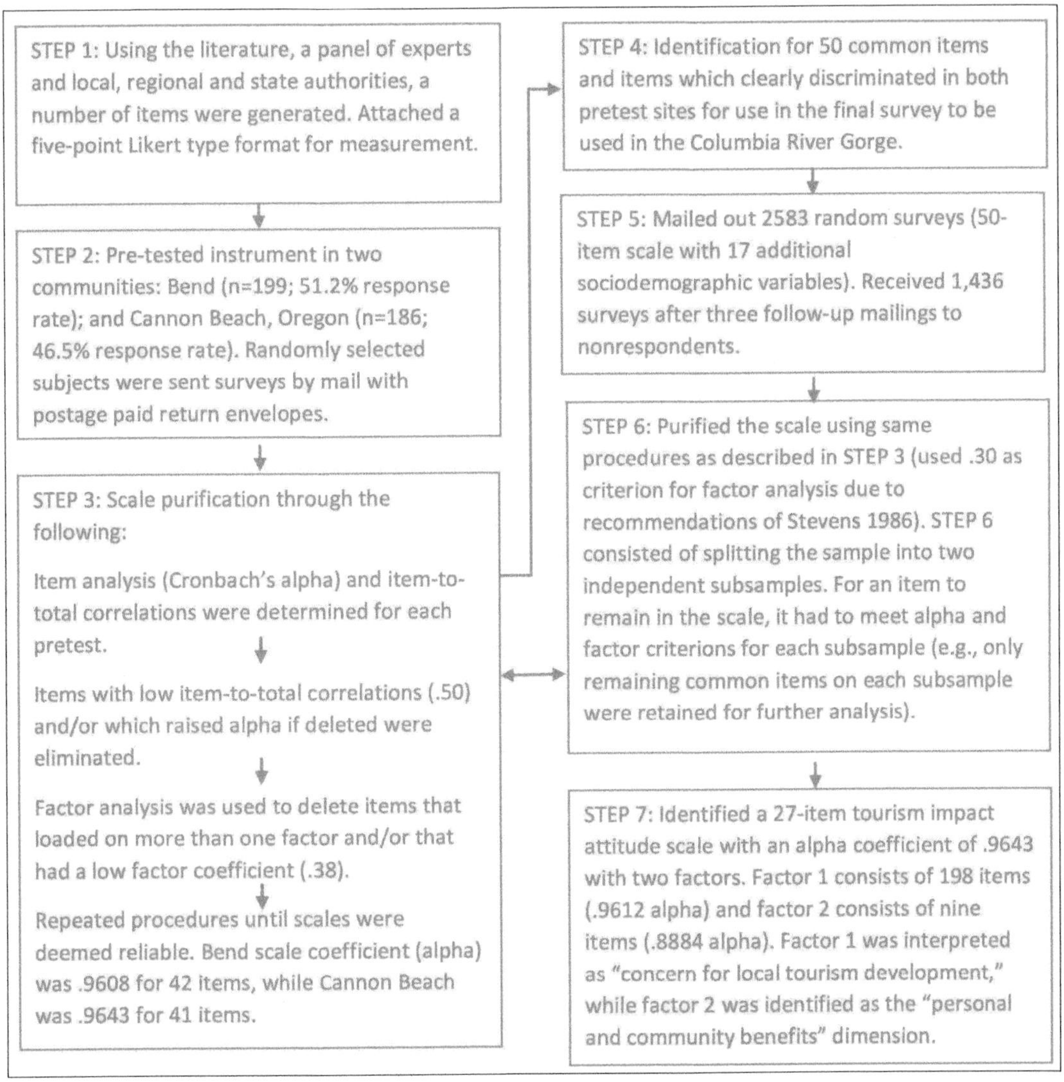

STEP 1: Using the literature, a panel of experts and local, regional and state authorities, a number of items were generated. Attached a five-point Likert type format for measurement.

STEP 2: Pre-tested instrument in two communities: Bend (n=199; 51.2% response rate); and Cannon Beach, Oregon (n=186; 46.5% response rate). Randomly selected subjects were sent surveys by mail with postage paid return envelopes.

STEP 3: Scale purification through the following:

Item analysis (Cronbach's alpha) and item-to-total correlations were determined for each pretest.

Items with low item-to-total correlations (.50) and/or which raised alpha if deleted were eliminated.

Factor analysis was used to delete items that loaded on more than one factor and/or that had a low factor coefficient (.38).

Repeated procedures until scales were deemed reliable. Bend scale coefficient (alpha) was .9608 for 42 items, while Cannon Beach was .9643 for 41 items.

STEP 4: Identification for 50 common items and items which clearly discriminated in both pretest sites for use in the final survey to be used in the Columbia River Gorge.

STEP 5: Mailed out 2583 random surveys (50-item scale with 17 additional sociodemographic variables). Received 1,436 surveys after three follow-up mailings to nonrespondents.

STEP 6: Purified the scale using same procedures as described in STEP 3 (used .30 as criterion for factor analysis due to recommendations of Stevens 1986). STEP 6 consisted of splitting the sample into two independent subsamples. For an item to remain in the scale, it had to meet alpha and factor criterions for each subsample (e.g., only remaining common items on each subsample were retained for further analysis).

STEP 7: Identified a 27-item tourism impact attitude scale with an alpha coefficient of .9643 with two factors. Factor 1 consists of 198 items (.9612 alpha) and factor 2 consists of nine items (.8884 alpha). Factor 1 was interpreted as "concern for local tourism development," while factor 2 was identified as the "personal and community benefits" dimension.

Figure 7.6. Tourism Impact Attitude Scale Development Process

Table 7.4
Demonstration of the Use of the TIAS

Area	Number of Factors	Sub-Factor Names	Percent Variance Explained	Factor Reliability Range	Overall Scale Alpha
Columbia River Gorge, USA[a]	2	Concern for promotion and development, personal and community benefits	57	0.89-0.96	0.96
Cannon Beach, OR, USA[b]	2	Concern for development, personal and community benefits	56	0.88-0.96	0.96

Table 7.4 (cont.)

Bend, OR USA[b]	2	Concern for Development, personal community benefits	55.7	0.87-0.92	0.93
Nanaimo, BC Canada[c]	4	General benefits, community benefits, negative impacts, personal benefits	56.8	0.72-0.93	0.92
Charleston, SC, USA[d]	3	Negative impacts, economic impacts, cultural impacts	57.6	0.78-0.82	0.84
Washington, NC, USA[e]	2	Support for tourism development, contributions to community	51	0.81-0.91	0.90
Penghu, Taiwan[f]	5	Promote/positive, anti-promotion, impacts, public services, benefits of tourism	54.6	0.53-0.89	0.90
Bali, Indonesia[g]	3	Promotion, benefits, negative impacts	47.4	0.70-0.80	0.73
Amman, Jordan[g]	5	Economic benefit, public services, negative impacts, personal benefit, promotion	49.9	0.55-0.73	0.71
Suwa, Japan[g]	3	Economic benefit, promotion, impacts	53.8	0.61-0.89	0.89

[a]=Lankford & Howard (1993), n=1,436, mail survey
[b]=Lankford (1992), n=186 for Cannon Beach, 199 for Bend, mail surveys
[c]=Rollins (1997), n=405, telephone survey
[d]=Harrill & Potts (2003), n=404, telephone survey
[e]=Wang & Pfister (2008), n=136, mail survey
[f]=Lankford, Chen, & Chen (1994), n=971, random drop-off pick-up surveys
[g]=Schneider, Lankford, & Oguchi (1997), n= 257 for Bali, n=177 Amman, n=112 Suwa, on-site interviews random for Bali and Suwa, onsite interview convenience sample for Amman

The importance of regional plans cannot be overemphasized. Communities are not isolated, so ignoring surrounding local communities is a mistake. Travelers often stop at numerous places for their travel. Communities in a region do not operate in isolation, but are part of a system for the traveler to explore. Importantly, if a regional planning approach is used, mitigation of impacts is often easier to address on a larger scale. For example, if a community has a significant nature based tourism program, the Texas Parks and Wildlife (2015) recommends creating a regional community-based nature tourism development plan. Recommendations for the plan suggest a need to:

- Inventory existing infrastructure and decide what may be needed to accommodate present and future visitation.
- Decide, from a balanced perspective, which kinds and intensities of nature tourism activity are appropriate for the resource.
- Evaluate community tourism plans (if any exist), and then strive to determine needs of nature tourism operators for potential businesses in the resource region. Look for common ground.
- Consider creating a regional nature-based tourism development plan based on these activities.
- Consider regional cooperative marketing opportunities.
- Institute regular natural resource impact assessments and revise management strategy to achieve goals for careful resource use and protection.
- Consider creating a process for evaluating and reinventing the nature tourism plan, including bringing fresh and future ideas and suggestions for careful resource use and conservation.

Often, tourism planning for a community is undertaken as an economic development strategy. A recommended approach is to first identify methods to improve the economic conditions. Second is to have a team of planners and stakeholders assess the feasibility of developing specific destination resort facilities within the community. Third, investigate ways and means of making the community more attractive and economically viable. Attention must be given to resident, visitor, and business interests and needs. Major planning phases need to be completed for tourism. These are as follows:

1. **Development potential and feasibility analysis.** The community planners would examine the existing and potential demand, with particular attention paid to the existing market area, measurement of current and future demand for private and public tourism services. A review of existing land use requirements and restrictions is also required. Results of any public meetings, committee meetings, surveys of visitors and resident populations needs to be available for review. Analysis of the sociodemographic characteristics of the resident and visitor population is needed. An inventory of land use potential and limitations are also presented in this phase.

2. **Access and visibility identification.** The goal here is to identify appropriate design formats for signage and way finding, and the best and most pleasing locations. Recommended guidelines for signage should be adopted by the community so as to not detract from the aesthetics of the community. Particular attention should be given to materials, size, shape, color etc. Signage should be considered for use in directing traffic off highways, and for directing traffic (foot, bicycle and car) to businesses and places of interest. This phase also incorporates the analysis and recommendations for circulation, access, parking, pedestrian traffic, visibility, and signage for the highways.

3. **Design guidelines.** This phase of the plan should address unique and existing architectural and landscape elements. The design process has four critical steps:
   a. Design suggestions and guidelines for the community entrances
   b. Design suggestions and guidelines for revitalizing the business district

c.   Specific building site guidelines for future development

d.   Guidelines for the improvement of lighting in the community

4. **Development proposals, design, and cost estimates.** This pertains to the estimated costs of recommended improvements for the community and priorities for funding. This phase also involves identifying sources of funding and strategies for acquiring funding. Recommendations are made for the development potential, feasibility of recommendations and proposals for future development, to include design concepts and finance.

It is important for communities to review state mandates for planning and community involvement. We do know that some states are highly structured in their planning requirements and some are nonexistent. Not all have state guidelines that can be problematic and at times disastrous for tourism based communities. Once the development starts in a community without proper plans and land use controls, the pace and type of development can be detrimental to tourism. Sprawl, inappropriate signage, inadequate and poorly designed buildings all detract from what made the community special in the first place. An example of how Oregon guides development of resorts is included at the end of the chapter. Goal 8 of the Oregon land use requirements addresses recreation needs and siting of resorts. No matter what the planning process that is adopted, it must reflect resident opinion and address local concerns regarding tourism. We do know that places with high levels of community involvement, are more successful in the long term.

Community Participation and Planning

The community of Government Camp, Oregon on Mt. Hood completed a tourism development plan in the 1990s that required three years of planning work (Lankford, Knowles-Lankford, & Povey, 1996). That plan has been in the implementation phase for over 20 years. A review of the plan and the actual development that was implemented reveals that the plan is being followed to some degree. In fact, the plan utilized a variation of the four phases mentioned above. The plan received recognition from the Oregon Chapter of the American Planning Association due to the level of community participation. It is believed that the community and plan is successful in part due to the input that the stakeholders had with regard to the tourism plans that were adopted in Government Camp. The following community engagement efforts were made for this plan (Table 7.5).

There are numerous issues in mobilizing the residents of a community for planning. Putnam (2001), in Bowling Alone identified problems of society as primarily having individuals insulated from one another, and therefore preventing meaningful interactions, which has resulted in a loss of social capital. This has created less interest and involvement in civic related and community service activities. Putnam notes that there is a need for greater opportunities for bonding and social bridging. Unfortunately, many communities today lack the opportunities to engage in meaningful and purposeful activities, and much communication and engagement is being replaced primarily now through technology. Engström, Mattsson, Järleborg, and Hallqvist (2008) (Figure 7.7) developed a model to represent two dimensions and two aspects of social capital. Importantly, a community must provide the structural system to engage the public (structural), but also find means to ensure the public trusts the political system (cognitive). Efforts must be made equalize power relationships. We know that when the public feels they have access to the decision-making process and that they can help influence local decisions, they are more supportive of tourism (Lankford & Howard, 1993).

Table 7.5

Community Engagement Methods for the Government Camp Tourism Plan

Techniques	Occurrences
Facilitated Meetings–Nominal Group Methods	
Recreation Association and Government Officials	2 Sessions
Visitors and Business Owners	1 Session
Residents	1 Session
Public Meeting Presentations by Planning Teams	3 Sessions for Residents 2 Sessions for Visitors, Residents, and Public Officials
Telephone Interviews	All Government Service Departments City Officials, County Officials Federal Agencies Businesses
Mail Surveys	Resident, Visitors, Other Destination Resorts, Convention Centers
Intercept Surveys	Visitors
Structured Interviews	Businesses and Public Services Departments
Design Workshop*	Resident, visitor, business, investors, government officials (local, county, state, and federal)
Radio, TV, Newspaper, and Public Displays of Reports, Plans and Designs	During 3 Years**

*Three professional design teams presented and stakeholders voted on aspects of each design scenario and what they supported

**All meeting notices, results and plan information was constantly provided to the media

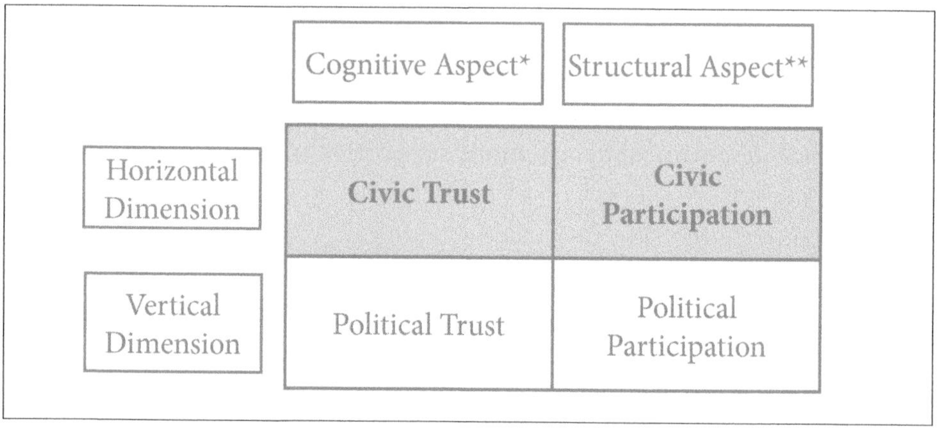

	Cognitive Aspect*	Structural Aspect**
Horizontal Dimension	**Civic Trust**	**Civic Participation**
Vertical Dimension	Political Trust	Political Participation

* People's perception of the level of interpersonal trust, sharing, and reciprocity
** Density of social networks, or patterns of civic engagement

Figure 7.7. Dimensions and Aspects of Social Capital

Perhaps an answer to the dilemma of a lack of civic engagement lies in the philosophy of the community leaders and public policy. The notion of deliberative democracy, which is not new but is noteworthy for this discussion. Deliberative democracy as noted by Grybovych and Hafermann (2010) offers a way of engaging citizens in deciding upon the matters that directly affect their lives and by doing so fosters the creation of livable communities characterized by community cohesion, existing norms of trust and reciprocity, civic engagement, and participatory governance. Weeks (2000 & 2003) noted the characteristics and philosophy of deliberative democracy include the following:

- Broad and representative public participation
- Informed public judgement
- Deliberate public participation
- Highly credible and methodologically sound outcomes and results

The goals of deliberative democracy are to revitalize civic culture, improve public discourse, and generate the political will to take action. Grybovych and Hafermann (2010) suggest that embracing deliberative democracy sets high standards for community planning processes, provides important guidance for designing and implementing processes that would ensure meaningful citizen involvement in tourism planning and development. The importance here is that planning which encourages civic engagement will strengthen social capital, which will enhance social sustainability. In communities where public controversy over plans is highly charged, little progress is made in implementing and realizing those plans. Where civic engagement is high, issues discussed and some effort made to recognized concerns and mitigate impacts, significant progress is realized. In practice, the application of the principles of deliberative democracy remains an ideal to for which to strive. This ideal is often constrained by the issues of power, inequality of resources, and legal and policy regulations among others (Grybovych, 2008).

Summary

This chapter introduced sustainable tourism planning and its dimensions in tourism. Tourism issues and impacts were presented that have been documented in various studies. The Irridex Model by Doxey (1975) was used to demonstrate the gradual levels of irritations that may occur in a community if no planning interventions occur. Differences by stakeholder groups were noted and presented. The monitoring system Tourism Impact Attitude Scale (TIAS) was introduced as one means of measuring support for tourism. The development of the TIAS was presented, along with information on where the scale was implemented. Planning and citizen engagement guidelines were reviewed and discussed.

Key Concepts

- Tourism Impacts
- Sustainable Tourism Planning
- Irridex Model
- Stakeholders
- TIAS
- Measurement of Impacts
- Planning
- Community Involvement and Participation

Useful Internet Sites, Exercises, and Resources

American Planning Association
https://www.planning.org/cityparks/briefingpapers/tourism.htm

UNWTO
http://sdt.unwto.org/en/content/guidelines-policy-making-and-planning

Washington State
http://sdt.unwto.org/en/content/guidelines-policy-making-and-planning

Nova Scotia
https://novascotiatourismagency.ca/community-tourism-development-guide

Questions for Review and Case Problems

1. A quote in the article by Tourtellot (2000) in the *National Geographic* notes that travel has suddenly become such a huge industry that it's threatening to wreck the places we love. In a small group, identify a place you have visited, perhaps in your own town and comment on a) how the place is being wrecked; b) why it is being wrecked; and c) what is being done to save it or what can be done?
2. Find a tourism development plan. Trace how it documents resident concerns and how they were incorporated. If they were not, what was the citizen involvement process? How would you develop a process for tourism development?

Example of Planning Requirements for Resorts

Regulating Resort Siting Within Land Use Laws: The Case of Oregon's Statewide Planning Goals & Guidelines GOAL 8: RECREATIONAL NEEDS. Oregon's land use planning process specifically addresses resort siting requirements under the Goal 8: Recreational Needs. Specifically, "to satisfy the recreational needs of the citizens of the state and visitors and, where appropriate, to provide for the siting of necessary recreational facilities including destination resorts." Land use planning laws cover other tourism development like any other land use within a community. Some of the pertinent language is as follows:

Destination Resort Sitting

Comprehensive plans may provide for the siting of destination resorts on rural lands subject to the provisions of state law, including ORS 197.435 to 197.467, this and other Statewide Planning Goals, and without an exception to Goals 3, 4, 11, or 14.

(1) "Small destination resorts" may be allowed consistent with the siting requirements of section (1), above, in the following areas: (a) On land that is not defined as agricultural or forest land under Goal 3 or 4; or (b) On land where there has been an exception to Statewide Planning Goals 3, 4, 11, or 14. Siting Standards

(1) Counties shall ensure that destination resorts are compatible with the site and adjacent land uses through the following measures:

(a) Important natural features, including habitat of threatened or endangered species, streams, rivers, and significant wetlands shall be maintained. Riparian vegetation within 100 feet of streams, rivers, and significant wetlands shall be maintained. Alterations to important natural features, including placement of structures that maintain the overall values of the feature, may be allowed.

(b) Sites designated for protection in an acknowledged comprehensive plan designated pursuant to Goal 5 that are located on the tract used for the destination resort shall be reserved through conservation easements as set forth in ORS 271.715 to 271.795. Conservation easements adopted to implement this requirement shall be sufficient to protect the resource values of the site and shall be recorded with the property records of the tract on which the destination resort is sited.

(c) Improvements and activities shall be located and designed to avoid or minimize adverse effects of the resort on uses on surrounding lands, particularly effects on intensive farming operations in the area. At a minimum, measures to accomplish this shall include:

(d) Establishment and maintenance of buffers between the resort and adjacent land uses, including natural vegetation and where appropriate, fences, berms, landscaped areas, and other similar types of buffers. (ii) Setbacks of structures and other improvements from adjacent land uses. (iii) Measures that prohibit the use or operation in conjunction with the resort of a portion of a tract that is excluded from the site of a destination resort pursuant to ORS 197.435(7). Subject to this limitation, the use of the excluded property shall be governed by otherwise applicable law.

The land use regulations define, for the purposes of planning compliance, what a destination resort is and is not. This allows for the community to designate lands for various uses, protects local recreational areas and addresses the recreation needs of the resident, and also informs developers of the requirements to "do business" in the community. A destination resort in Oregon is defined as:

A self-contained development providing visitor-oriented accommodations and developed recreational facilities in a setting with high natural amenities, and that qualifies under the definition of either a "large destination resort" or a "small destination resort" in this goal. A large destination resort is:

(1) The resort must be located on a site of 160 acres or more except within two miles of the ocean shoreline where the site shall be 40 acres or more.

(2) At least 50 percent of the site must be dedicated as permanent open space excluding yards, streets and parking areas.

(3) At least $7 million must be spent on improvements for onsite developed recreational facilities and visitor-oriented accommodations exclusive of costs for land, sewer, and water facilities and roads. Not less than one-third of this amount shall be spent on developed recreational facilities.

(4) Commercial uses allowed are limited to types and levels necessary to meet the needs of visitors to the development. Industrial uses of any kind are not permitted.

(5) Visitor-oriented accommodations including meeting rooms, restaurants with seating for 100 persons, and 150 separate rentable units for overnight lodging must be provided.

To qualify as a "small destination resort" under Goal 8, a proposed development must meet standards (2) and (4) under the definition of "large destination resort" and the following standards:

(1) The resort must be located on a site of 20 acres or more.

(2) At least $2 million must be spent on improvements for onsite developed recreational facilities and visitor-oriented accommodations exclusive of costs for land, sewer, and water facilities and roads. Not less than one-third of this amount must be spent on developed recreation facilities.

(3) At least 25 but not more than 75 units of overnight lodging shall be provided.

(4) Restaurant and meeting rooms with at least one seat for each unit of overnight lodging must be provided.

(5) Residential uses must be limited to those necessary for the staff and management of the resort.

(6) The county governing body or its designee must review the proposed resort and determine that the primary purpose of the resort is to provide lodging and other services oriented to a recreational resource that can only reasonably be enjoyed in a rural area. Such recreational resources include, but are not limited to, a hot spring, a ski slope, or a fishing stream.

(7) The resort shall be constructed and located so that it is not designed to attract highway traffic. Resorts shall not use any manner of outdoor advertising signing except:

(a) Tourist oriented directional signs as provided in ORS 377.715 to 377.830; and

(b) Onsite identification and directional signs.

Developed Recreation Facilities

Are improvements constructed for the purpose of recreation and may include but are not limited to golf courses, tennis courts, swimming pools, marinas, ski runs and bicycle paths.

Open Space

Means any land that is retained in a substantially natural condition or is improved for recreational uses such as golf courses, hiking or 6 nature trails or equestrian or bicycle paths or is specifically required to be protected by a conservation easement. Open spaces may include ponds, lands protected as important natural features, land preserved for farm or forest use and lands used as buffers. Open space does not include residential lots or yards, streets or parking areas.

Overnight Lodgings

Are permanent, separately rentable accommodations that are not available for residential use. Overnight lodgings include hotel or motel rooms, cabins, and time-share units. Tent sites, recreational vehicle parks, manufactured dwellings, dormitory rooms, and similar accommodations do not qualify as overnight lodgings for the purpose of this definition.

Recreation Areas, Facilities and Opportunities

Provide for human development and enrichment, and include but are not limited to open space and scenic landscapes; recreational lands; history, archaeology and natural science resources; scenic roads and travelers; sports and cultural events; camping, picnicking, and recreational lodging; tourist facilities and accommodations; trails; waterway use facilities; hunting; angling; winter sports; mineral resources; active and passive games and activities.

Recreation Needs

Refers to existing and future demand by citizens and visitors for recreations areas, facilities and opportunities.

Self-Contained Development

Means a development for which community sewer and water facilities are provided onsite and are limited to meet the needs of the development or are provided by existing public sewer or water service as long as all costs related to service extension and any capacity increases are borne by the development. A "self-contained development" must have developed recreational facilities provided on-site.

Tract

Means a lot or parcel or more than one contiguous lot or parcel in a single ownership. A tract may include property that is not included in the proposed site for a destination resort if the property to be excluded is on the boundary of the tract and constitutes less than 30% of the total tract.

Visitor-Oriented Accommodations

Are overnight lodging, restaurants, meeting facilities that are designed to and provide for the needs of visitors rather than year-round residents.

References

Doxey, G. V. (1975). *A causation theory of visitor-resident irritants: Methodology and research inferences.* The Impact of Tourism, Sixth Annual Conference Proceedings, Travel Research Association, pp. 195–198.

Engström, K., Mattsson, F., Järleborg, A., & Hallqvist, J. (2008). Contextual social capital as a risk factor for poor self-rated health: A multilevel analysis. *Social Science and Medicine, 66*(11), 2268–2280.

Grybovych, O. (2008). *Deliberative Democratic practices in tourism planning: Towards a model of participatory community tourism planning.* (Doctoral Dissertation, University of Northern Iowa, 2008). ProQuest Dissertations and Theses. (UMI No. AAT 3321006).

Grybovych, O., & Haftermann, D. (2010). Sustainable practices of community tourism planning: Lessons from a remote community. *Community Development, 41*(3), 354–369.

Harrill, R., & Potts, T. (2003). Tourism planning in historic districts. *Journal of American Planning Association, 69*(3), 233–244.

Kreag, G. (2001). *The impacts of tourism.* Minnesota Sea Grant, Publication Number T13.

Knowles-Lankford, J., & Lankford, S. (1995). Sustainable practices: Implications for tourism and recreation development. In S. F. McCool A. E. & Watson (Eds.), *Linking tourism, the environment, and sustainability.* Proceedings of a special session of the annual meeting of the National Recreation and Parks Association; 1994 Oct. 12-14; Minneapolis, MN. Gen. Tech. Rep. INT-GTR-323. Ogden, UT: U.S. Department of Agriculture, Forest Service, Intermountain Research Station.

Lankford, S. (Sept.-Oct. 1988). Encouraging economic development in an Unincorporated Alpine Community: Government Camp, Oregon. *Small Town, 19* (2), 12–21.

Lankford, S. (1992). *Tourism Impact Assessment, Bend, Oregon and Cannon Beach, Oregon.* Community Planning Workshop, University of Oregon.

Lankford, S. (1994). Attitudes and perceptions toward tourism and rural regional development. *Journal of Travel Research, 32*(3), 35–43.

Lankford, S. V., Chen, J. S. Y. & Chen, W. (1994). Tourism's Impacts in the Penghu National Scenic Area, Taiwan. *Tourism Management, 15*(3), 222–227.

Lankford, S., & Howard, D. (1993). Developing a tourism impact attitude scale. *Annals of Tourism Research, 21*(1), 121–139.

Lankford, S., & Knowles-Lankford, J. (1995). Impacts of tourism in the Republic of China's Penghu National Scenic Area. In S. F. McCool & A. E. Watson (Eds.), *Linking tourism, the environment, and sustainability.* Proceedings of a special session of the annual meeting of the National Recreation and Parks Association; 1994 Oct. 12-14; Minneapolis, MN. Gen. Tech. Rep. INT-GTR-323. Ogden, UT: U.S. Department of Agriculture, Forest Service, Intermountain Research Station.

Lankford, S. V., Knowles-Lankford, J., & Povey, D. (1996). Instilling community confidence and commitment in tourism: Community participation and public participation in Government Camp, Oregon. In L. Harrison & W. Husbands (Eds.), *Practicing responsible tourism: International case studies in tourism planning, policy, and development* (pp. 330–349). New York, NY: John Wiley & Sons.

Long, P. T., Perdue, R. R., & Allen, L. (1990). Rural resident tourism perceptions and attitudes by community level of tourism. *Journal of Travel Research, 28*(3), 3–9.

Lankford, S., Pfister, R., Knowles, J., & Williams, A. (2003). An exploratory study of the Impacts of tourism on resident outdoor recreation experiences. *Journal of Park and Recreation Administration – Special Issue on Sustainable Places, 21*(4), 30–49.

Putnam, R. D. (2001). *Bowling alone: The collapse and revival of the American community.* New York, NY: Simon and Schuster.

Rollins, R. (1997). Validation of the TIAS as a tourism tool. *Annals of Tourism Research, 24*(3), 740–756.

Schnieder, I., Lankford, S. V., & Oguchi, T. (1997). Cross-cultural equivalency of the TIAS: Summary results. *Annals of Tourism Research, 24*(4), 1994–1998.

Texas Parks and Wildlife. (2015). Community planning for nature tourism. Retrieved from http://tpwd.texas.gov/landwater/land/programs/tourism/your_business/guidance/

Tourtellot, J. B. (2000). The tourism wars, special report. *National Geographic,* October 2000, pp.110–119.

Wang, Y., & Pfister, R. (2008). Residents' attitudes toward tourism and perceived personal benefits in a rural community. *Journal of Travel Research,47*(1). Retrieved from http://journals.sagepub.com/doi/abs/10.1177/0047287507312402

Weeks, E. C. (2000). The practice of deliberative democracy: Results from four large-scale trials. *Public Administration Review, 60*(4), 360–372.

Weeks, E. C. (2003 Spring). Deliberative democracy. *PPPM Circle, 7*(4).

CHAPTER 8

Main Street

"All of us, if we are reasonably comfortable, healthy, and safe, owe immense debts to the past. There is no way of course, to repay the past. We can only repay those debts by making gifts to the future."

—Jane Jacobs

CHAPTER OBJECTIVES

- To build an understanding of Main Street development and its relationship to community tourism
- To understand the relationship between Main Street revitalization, smart growth and new urbanism
- To understand the function of the National Main Street Center
- To understand the role Main Street plays in supporting community tourism.

Introduction

Main streets developed around the need or desire to trade goods and services. However much more than goods and services were traded and Main Streets often became not only the economic center, but the social center for the community. They provided the context for building community. Typically main streets are located on either a current or historic "path" facilitating the exchange of goods and services. Accordingly, main streets reflect the heart of the community, at least at some point in their development. For this reason, communities often focus attention on Main Street as a measure of their vitality.

In many situations, main streets have suffered economically with a change in use often due to a change in the dominant transportation route or the development of alternative commercial districts catering to auto transport (i.e., mall development). Efforts to reinvigorate main street areas have often included tourism development. Expanded range of services, and organizational, promotion, and marketing strategies are developed to serve a visitor population. These efforts cater to a range of local and visitor needs depending on particular local conditions in the community. Some communities target visitor populations almost entirely while others provide a mix of community and visitor services. Either way, Main Street areas and organizations play both an indirect role through attractions, services and entertainment and a direct role through festivals and events in community tourism. The focus on Main Street revitalization is often supported by a range of local, regional, and national organizations and programs.

Main Street Programs

Several countries have organized Main Street programs to support and reinvigorate Main Street development including Australia, Canada, Great Britain and the United States. Canada has organized since 1980 to support historic preservation and main street revitalization through the Heritage Canada Foundation, a national nonprofit organization and charity in Canada. This program is modeled after the U.S. National Main Street Center of the National Trust for Historic Preservation. The U.S. program has served as a model for main street revitalization for over 34 years, assisting over 2,000 communities in their revitalization efforts. Many more communities nationwide have revitalized their Main Street independent of the National Main Street Center.

In the U.S., the National Main Street Center provides support to state and local agencies and organizations for Main Street redevelopment through developing and disseminating information, technical assistance and research; and providing conferences, publications, training, and certification. The effort is guided by a four-point approach, including organization, promotion, design, and economic restructuring. Staff provide technical assistance and training to new and existing Main Street programs for small towns, business and cultural districts, and neighborhoods. Services include site seminars and workshops, field services, and an annual conference.

The on-site seminars and workshops address the four point approach, including organizational development, commercial district design, promotion and marketing, and economic revitalization. There are a number of seminars and workshops offered under each area of the four-point approach. In addition, training sessions can be developed to assist specific locations and their particular conditions. Table 8.1 lists the types of seminars and workshops available through the National Main Street Center.

Additional topics addressed in seminars and workshops include revitalization experienced by selected Main Street organizations, trends and smart growth strategies related to main street development. The field services provided address similar topics and can be tailored to the experience of specific state and local Main Street organizations.

Data is collected annually on the preservation, revitalization, and economic activities in communities that participate in the Main Street Program. Data include net gain in income, net gain in jobs, number of building rehabilitations, and number of dollars reinvested in rehabilitation. Table 8.2 displays the total cumulative statistics gathered from 1980 through 2014 for all designated Main Street communities nationwide (National Main Street Center, http://www.preservationnation.org/main-street/about-main-street/reinvestment-statistics-1.html)

Table 8.1
List of National Main Street Center Seminars and Workshops

Organizational Development	Commercial District Design	Promotion & Marketing	Economic Revitalization
Introduction to Main Street Organization	Introduction to Main Street Design	Introduction to Main Street Promotions	Introduction to Main Street Economic Revitalization
How to Organize a Board Retreat	Designing Design Guidelines	Marketing Your Commercial District	Economic Trends in Main Street Commercial Districts
How to Facilitate Effective Meetings	Streetscape Survival Training		Market Analysis
Managing Main Street Staff	Urban Planning for Main Street Programs		Business Retention Activities
Recruiting and Managing Volunteers	Developing a Commercial District Master Plan		Business Recruitment
Promoting Your Organization	Auditing Your Comprehensive Planning and Zoning Ordinance		Finding and Fostering Entrepreneurs
Membership Campaigns			Facilitating Business Transitions
Turning Special events into Fund-Raisers			
Developing a Fund-Raising Plan			

Table 8.2
Cumulative Reinvestment Statistics

Dollars Reinvested:	$61.7 billion
Total reinvestment from public and private sources	
Number of building rehabilitations:	251,838
Net gain in jobs:	528,557
Net gain in businesses:	120,510
Reinvestment Ratio (i):	$26.52:$1

Note: The Reinvestment Ratio measures the amount of new investment that occurs, on average, for every dollar a participating community spends to support the operation of its Main Street program, based on medial annual program costs reported to the National Main Street Center by its coordinating programs. This number is not cumulative and represents investment and organization budgets from January 1, 2013 to December 31, 2014.

Main Street Design

Design is important to Main Street revitalization. Often Main Streets are enveloped in subsequent development and have lost not only their function as a commercial center but also their character based on the influence of the automobile on society and an emphasis of mobility over accessibility. The focus of Main Street design is to "preserve" the architectural character of existing buildings and to recapture a pedestrian scale in the articulation of buildings and sidewalks.

The focus on pedestrian scale in Main Street development complements the development trends of smart growth and new urbanism. Smart growth is an urban planning and transportation theory that promotes concentrated development where services are accessible to residents by walking, biking, or using alternative modes of transportation. Smart growth is aligned with sustainable development in its promotion of reducing resource consumption through the provision of services close to residents. Smart growth and new urbanism share the philosophy of developing walkable communities or neighborhoods that provide a range of services in close proximity to residents. Smart growth and new urbanism encompass new development where Main Street revitalization focuses on a historical framework of development. New urbanism, in particular, has adopted many design elements of Main Street development.

Building Renovation

Main Street development occurred largely during the 19th and early 20th centuries. During this time frame, architectural styles and materials changed influencing building appearance. Consistent use of materials created a typical pattern of Main Street development using a 19th century structural framework with 20th century modifications and additions. In fact several modifications could have occurred over the history of the structures. Jackson (n.d.) notes that "Main Streets typically do not represent a single era of commercial architecture since most Main Streets are a 150-year collage of evolving storefront designs." Jackson provides an illustrated description of this evolution in *Storefronts on Main Street: An Architectural History through the Illinois Historic Preservation Agency.* Figure 8.1 illustrates the change in building appearance that often takes place with building renovation. The image on the left is more typical of the 19th century framework with relatively minor changes since construction. The figure on the right illustrates the how façade modifications on the "Thrift Shop" can change the appearance of a structure. Note how in both illustrations the structural framework is similar with structures built on the property line. The image on the right is a good example of how buildings were "modernized during the time frame from 1940-1960, where facades were encased with new materials.

The most common Main Street pattern is a "wall" of two story structures built on the property line at a 25-foot spacing. Properties were generally platted at a 25-foot width due to the construction materials used at the time. A wood joist during this era of construction could span 22 feet. This dimension together with the thickness of a one foot masonry wall created the pattern or rhythm of structures prevalent in Main Street architecture and can be found throughout the world (Jackson, n.d.). This architectural rhythm was accentuated by the manufacture of six- to eight-foot iron lintels or beams which set the distance between columns. This space typically accommodated storefront windows. The resulting architectural pattern was scaled to the pedestrian. This 25 foot spacing of buildings accommodates a range of services within a relatively compact area and provides the framework for Main Streets.

Figure 8.1.Comparison of Main Street Architectural Framework

Since many of the buildings on Main Street are over 100 years old, renovations are common. The trends in architectural style and materials used at the time when the renovation occurred are reflected in the building appearance. Buildings "modernized" from 1940 through the 1960s were often encased with new materials covering the entire structure (See Figure 8.1 right side). This façade update covered decaying façade elements and gave a modern "sleek" appearance, often covering unused upper stories of the structure. This new façade provided a background for large signage elements. Since 1970, it is often these more recent applications that are removed and original building elements or elements from older renovations are revealed or recreated.

Streetscapes

Since Main Streets were typically located on the main transportation route of a generation past, many have lost their definition with subsequent development. In other situations, the main transportation route has bypassed the Main Street to accommodate more auto traffic traveling at higher speeds. Whichever the case, Main Street typically must address the interface between automobile and pedestrian traffic.

The dimension of many Main Streets started out with a 60- to 100-foot-wide right-of-way. This space accommodated the ability of a horse and wagon to turn around. The public right-of-way was shared by all users. As use of the automobile became accessible to more people, the shift toward an "auto-centered" right of way developed. This design shift often created an environment less conducive to people walking.

The current focus in Main Street revitalization, smart growth, and new urbanism is to accommodate all modes of transportation in the public right of way. The public right of way, which encompasses the street, parking, and sidewalks, can be designed to provide for accessibility and safety for all users. Oregon published a guide to Main Street development called *Main Street . . . When a Highway Runs Through It: A Handbook for Oregon Communities* (1999) funded by the Transportation Growth Management Program. This guide addresses roadway design considerations and strategies including bikeways, travel lane width, travel lane removal, refuge islands, textured cross walks and pavement and parking, among other topics. In addition, the guide provides sidewalk area design considerations including curb extensions, driveways, maintenance, sidewalk dimensions and materials, street furniture, trees and plantings, and utilities. The focus is on creating an interesting environment catering to the pedestrian. These strategies and design considerations are consistent with "Complete Streets," a smart growth strategy to enable safe access for all users, regardless of age, ability, or mode of transportation. Ideally, public sidewalk improvements are coordinated with associated businesses. Figure 8.2 illustrates public sidewalk amenities including paving, street trees and planters, bollards, lighting, and trash receptacles complement business. Additional space to accommodate outdoor seating supports the fronting restaurant business. These elements are all part of the public right of way.

Figure 8.2. *Sidewalk amenities in Winters, California*

Signage

Main Street revitalization typically addresses signage. Signage can either contribute or detract from business. Too many signs without design parameters can create visual chaos. An effective signage program establishes unifying design elements. There are two categories of signage in a community. The city or town provides directional signs, such as the location of historic districts, special attractions, parking areas and street names (see Figure 8.3). Individual businesses provide their business signs.

Signs provided by the city or town can provide important information particularly to visitors unfamiliar with the community. It is important for this signage to display some unifying elements that help visitors to find their destination or discover new destinations within the community.

Figure 8.3. Example of city directional signage

Communities often use "gateways" to mark Main Street. Figure 8.4 provides an example of how a community has marked Main Street.

Figure 8.4. Example of a community gateway

Figure 8.5. Examples of a Banner Marking a Neighborhood District

Districts often use banners to identify a particular district. Figure 8.5 provides an example of how banners are used to identify the Alberta Arts District in Portland, Oregon.

Each business relies on signage for advertising their goods and services. Although diversity in signage creates interest, too much diversity can be distracting and detract from the overall appearance of the district. Signs that share some common element among businesses such as the type of sign holder, form of illumination, or the location on the building tend to contribute to the entire district.

Many communities adopt sign design guidelines. Sign guidelines typically address the types of permitted signs, permitted sign area, placement, sign message and lighting. Sign guidelines are implemented to prescribe specific design parameters without compromising flexibility and creativity. Signs that work well often reflect the essence of the business and are in scale with their façade. Figure 8.6 illustrates how signs can illustrate this goal. Soft Horizons is a business specializing in fibers. The sidewalk sign "Thicket" is a sign for a neighborhood nursery selling plants.

Design Guidelines

Communities often adopt design guidelines to address the appearance and "feel" of Main Street revitalization. Guidelines can be integrated with municipal ordinances, be advisory in nature, or a combination of both. The City of Portland uses a two-track process. A development proposal can be reviewed through the design review board following design guidelines established for a particular district. The alternative track is through objective standards delineated in the zoning ordinance through a plan check process. The City of Portland design guidelines are divided into three sections including Portland personality, pedestrian emphasis and project design. Figure 8.7 illustrates a page from the Portland personality guidelines.

Figure 8.6. Examples of signage that reflect business services

The following photographs and illustrations provide examples of how a particular desired site and building design features may be accomplished in the 122nd Avenue Station Area (see Figure 8.7).

On-site Open Areas

Landscaping and open/green space is an important feature in residential development.

The photo and diagram below show an approach to on-site open space.

The buildings form a courtyard protecting the open space from traffic, which creates a safe open space for residents that is buffered from street noise.

Residential Development on Busy Streets

Livability is a key factor in multi-dwelling and mixed-use developments. The photo and diagram below show an example of how ground floor residential units may achieve a greater sense of privacy by elevating units above sidewalk grade, using landscaping, and by increasing the front yard building setback.

Figure 8.7. Example of City of Portland design guidelines

Figure 8.7. (cont.). Source: City of Portland Bureau of Planning (1998, Updated September 2008). Community Design Guidelines

Working Together

Since Main Street districts generally have evolved over several generations and the societal changes which reflect each generation, many issues or concerns must be addressed. Table 8.3 identifies some typical concerns associated with Main Street revitalization.

Table 8.3

Typical Main Street Concerns

Safety	Can't walk to stores Can't turn left safely Bikes use the sidewalks
Security	Downtown doesn't feel safe There is too much graffiti
Comfort	Noisy Unsightly Nowhere for kids or the elderly
Speed	Traffic exceeds posted speed Drivers don't slow down
Crossing	Stop sign or signal wanted Crosswalks aren't marked Kids can't cross safely
Access	Not enough parking Delivery trucks block street Median not acceptable to businesses Downtown not accessible to the disabled
Congestion	Too much traffic and delay Highway doesn't meet performance standards Too many trucks Cut-through traffic in neighborhoods

Source: Oregon.gov (1999)

Addressing these concerns in revitalizing Main Street districts requires a coordinated effort among stakeholders in the community. The more that people and groups work together to imagine and develop a revitalized Main Street, the more likely the effort will be successful. Reviewing Table 8.3 clearly indicates a need for coordination between residents, businesses and city planning and transportation officials.

A coordinated effort can not only address existing concerns but create a range of new opportunities. For example, Cleveland was experiencing what many Main Street districts experience: an abundance of empty buildings. In an effort to facilitate small business, Cleveland developed the "Small Box Program," which turned old shipping containers into retail spaces for start-up small businesses in the downtown warehouse district without the big price tag of downtown rent. (http://www.preservationnation.org/main-street/main-street-news/story-of-the-week/2015/small-box-a-creative-retail.html).

Although a successful revitalization effort requires a coordinated effort, the list of stakeholders is unique to each community. Table 8.4 lists a variety of potential stakeholders.

Table 8.4
Benefits and Impacts of Downtown Revitalization Program

Stakeholders	Benefits
Merchants	Greater opportunity for growth and expansion Expand customer base Less financial risk
Property Owners	Stable or higher rents Increased occupancy rates/improved marketability of property Higher property values
Financial Institutions	Expanded business customer base Expanded residential customer base Improved public image and goodwill Fulfillment of community reinvestment mandate
Professionals and Service Businesses	Ready-made customer base of district employees Location near government, banks, post office and other institutions Nearby amenities for clients and staff
Chambers of Commerce	Potential new business members Healthier overall business climate Potential partnerships or joint projects
Residents	Local accessibility to goods and services Opportunities for volunteerism and leadership development Preservation of community for future generations More employee opportunities Stronger tax base to support other community initiatives (schools, parks, trails) Investment in existing downtown infrastructure is more cost-effective than extending new services to outlying areas

Table 8.4 (cont.)

Local Government	Increased property tax base Protection of property values and infrastructure investment Reduced cost of services such as police and fire protection Reduced pressure for sprawl development
Community Partners (Business Improvement Associations, civic clubs, historic preservation organizations, arts organizations, etc.)	Improved quality of life Expanded capacity to undertake additional projects New membership potential among residents Achievement of common goals Preservation of community history
Schools	Youth involvement in civic projects Potential employment and business opportunities More places to go and more activities in which to take part Use of downtown as "classroom" for school projects
Businesses outside of down town	Increased visitor traffic to community Improved municipal services throughout community Increased business through overall healthier economy Additional amenities for employees and clients
Industry	Improved quality of life makes recruiting and retaining employees easier

Source: Heritage Canada Foundation (2009)

Ashland, Oregon provides an interesting illustration of how Main Street programs develop and operate. Ashland is home to a Shakespearean Festival that attracted over 100,000 individuals in 2014, 15% of whom are from the local area. The economic impact of the festival in 2014 was over $260 million (Oregon Shakespeare Festival, 2015). This is the largest regional repertory theater in the U.S., offering 11 classical and contemporary plays in three theaters from February through October. The establishment of the Festival, which contributes to the local culture and economy, is built on the history of Ashland, originally home to the Shasta tribes. Settlers from the westward movement had established Ashland by 1852 as a milling center; first lumber, then wheat, then woolens. The Ashland Academy was founded in 1872, and later became Southern Oregon University. Like many communities, Ashland is located on a main transportation route between the major port cities of San Francisco, California, and Portland, Oregon, and the railroad traveled through the town until 1927. This location provided an opportune site for the Chautauqua, a traveling program delivering arts, education, and entertainment nationwide. Although the original structures built for Chautauqua performances no longer stand, the foundation of the original Chautauqua walls inspired a young English teacher, at what was then the Southern Oregon Normal School, to propose a "festival" of two plays to be performed at the site of the original Chautauqua. This site reminded him of sketches he had seen of Elizabethan theatres. This became the evolving foundation upon which the Ashland Shakespearean Festival was born. Had it not been for the location of the community between two major ports, the establishment of a normal school, and the inspiration of an English teacher, Ashland would be a very different community today. Southern Oregon University, part of the state's regional comprehensive higher education system, provides library, computing, and community outreach resources to serve the region and complements the many artistic, musical, and theatrical opportunities available here.

Summary

Communities are "recapitalizing" on their "Main Streets" or historic commercial districts. These areas are characterized by small businesses offering a range of services often specialized or distinct to a particular locale. The historic development pattern locates residential uses in close proximity to services and supports people walking with sidewalk amenities, business orientation, and more detailed signage directed to the pedestrian. These historic commercial districts often rely on community historic preservation efforts to restore traditional facades baring the original building materials and street-facing presentation. This type of community preservation effort is intended to revitalize and attract residents and visitors.

Historic preservation is often viewed as an expensive "fix" that stands in the way of economic development. However, recent research has found that historic preservation is an important economic development tool. In addition, Laurie (2008) notes that historic preservation,, clustered with the tourism, the film industry, housing and environmental management, supports each industry more effectively as a cluster rather than individually.

The focus of main street redevelopment is often based on nostalgia, the perception of a past era where "life was good." The memory of what was positive is much easier to rekindle than the difficulties that main streets faced in the past. Regardless, small businesses provided for the needs of the community, both in durable goods and services and social exchange—the weather, the kids, the goats, or the garden. Society depended on a local market, and the presence of corporate services was not as pervasive as it is in today's economy. In order to reinvigorate main streets across the nation, communities have had to diversify services and expand their market base. This is why tourism is often used or seen as an important component of main street development. The visitor expands the market base. There is no prescribed ratio for the degree to which tourism is developed or to which visitors are catered. Some redeveloped main streets focus solely on visitor services while others develop a mix of services for both local community members and visitors.

The community of Galena, Illinois, was one of the pilot communities for the Main Street effort. The pilot project was extremely successful in terms of historic preservation and reinvestment in historic buildings. Paradis (2000) notes that property values doubled or tripled within a three-year period in Galena. This process of gentrification occurs with economic disparity. In the case of Galena, the influx of people from Chicago to a rural community like Galena exemplifies this disparity. While people from Chicago thought property values, commercial and residential, were so affordable, they drove prices well above what local Galena residents could afford.

Every community has their own set of circumstances and qualities to celebrate, enhance or use as inspiration. Ashland, Oregon embraces theater. Idaho Falls celebrate the falls in the river on which the community is located. Mineral Point values the labor of miners who settled the region and built beautiful stone structures. These qualities or assets are the inspiration for the community. Although it takes many hands to highlight or celebrate a specific quality, it is often from the inspiration of one leading to the next inspiration which leads to the building a great community.

Ashland developed its theater district based on the inspiration of an English teacher who was inspired by the ruins of a former national movement established in the community because it was a convenient stop on a popular route. It is serendipitous. This serendipity can lead to great community.

Key Concepts

- Main street revitalization
- Economic impacts of main street revitalization
- Gentrification
- Pedestrian scale
- Smart growth
- New urbanism

Useful Internet Sites, Exercises, and Resources

Exercise 1

Define the four-point system as developed by the US Main Street Center. http://www.preservationnation.org/main-street/

Exercise 2

Locate a Main Street Community in a state of your choice and describe how the four point system of the National Main Street Center has been applied to your selected community.

Exercise 3

Identify techniques to address pedestrian scale in a Main Street development.

Internet Sites

http://www.oregon.gov/lcd/tgm/docs/mainstreet.pdf

https://www.illinois.gov/ihpa/Preserve/Documents/Storefronts-Shopfronts-Facades.pdf

http://www.oregon.gov/lcd/tgm/docs/mainstreet.pdf

http://www.nps.gov/tps/standards/rehabilitation/rehab/index.htm

Questions for Review and Case Problems

1. Select a community and illustrate how main street development supports or fails to support community tourism.

2. Discuss how smart growth and new urbanism support community tourism development. Select a city and identify how the main street development reflects smart growth and new urbanism.

3. Identify the Main Street coordinating agencies in selected states and their organizational structure. Describe the types of services the Main Street coordinating agency provides to local governments and organizations.

References

City of Portland Bureau of Planning. (1998, updated September 2008). *Community Design Guidelines.* Portland, OR: Author.

Heritage Canada Foundation. (2009). *The Main Street program: Past and present.* Retrieved from http://www.pcs.gov.sk.ca/MSProgramHCF

Jacskon, M. (n.d.). *Storefronts on main street: An architectural history.* Illinois Preservation Series, 9. Illinois Historic Preservation Agency.

National Trust for Historic Preservation. (2017). National Main Street Center Four Point Strategy. Retrieved from http://www.preservationnation.org/main-street/about-main-street/the-approach/#.VgyAUH1Bfvo

Oregon.gov. (1999). Main street…when a highway runs through it: A handbook for Oregon communities. Retrieved from http://www.oregon.gov/lcd/tgm/docs/main-street.pdf

Oregon Shakespeare Festival. (n.d.). History of Ashland and the festival. Retrieved from https://www.osfashland.org/about/our-history.aspx

Oregon Shakespeare Festival. (2014). Oregon Shakespeare Festival state and local economic impact. Retrieved from https://www.osfashland.org/~/media/Files/PDF/About%20OSF/Impact2014_logo.ashx

Paradis, T. W. (2000). Main Street transformed: Community sense of place for nonmetropolitan tourism business districts. *Urban Geography, 21*(7), 609–639.

CHAPTER 9

Community Special Events for Tourism

"Opportunities don't happen. You create them."
—Chris Grossner

CHAPTER OBJECTIVES

- To understand the role of community special events in tourism
- To appreciate the range of community special events that communities manage and/or sponsor
- To provide insight into the responsibilities and difficulties of community event management
- To understand that community special events bring benefits to both the resident and visitor population
- To gain an appreciation of the elements that must be considered when organizing events.

Introduction

The role that numerous agencies such as the park and recreation department, chambers of commerce and/or main street programs play in community tourism has expanded over the years. Not only do these agencies provide services for the resident population, they also play a key role coordinating, facilitating, and managing special events and festivals for the community. Often these events are designed to attract tourists for economic reasons. It is important to note that the parks and recreation organization plays both a central role in some communities and a supporting role in others. Holding special events and festivals in a community, depending on the scope, normally does not require special facilities. Therefore, communities of any size can hold these events in existing parks, town squares, pavilions and other public facilities. Many communities rely on the parks and recreation department and their sports complexes to hold tournaments which attract visitors from out of town.

Communities hold special events and festivals for many reasons, which include enhancing the local image of the place and providing economic benefits for businesses and the community. Visitors' motivations to attend a festival or event are among the first considerations to account for organizing a festival. Attendees to festivals and events are motivated by learning about a place, supporting events and community, socialization, and novelty. Businesses engage in the sponsorship of special events and festivals in order to promote their businesses but also to give back to the community and support others. Government involvement supports local businesses, and provides some funding (albeit a minimum at most times) for the ongoing support of these events.

Special events are occasions drawing individuals together to enjoy a recreation or educational experience that is meaningful, significant and relevant to their well-being (Edginton & O'Neill, 1999). Events and festivals are many and varied. Music and art festivals are popular, as well as food and beverage-based events. In fact, the development of food tourism as a generator of income, and enhancement of community pride and identity has emerged as an objective of many communities. For example, a study of small communities and their food-based community festivals in Northeast Iowa found that the total economic impact was $2,638,811, with an additional tourist spending of $1 generating $1.61 of output in the economy of selected counties in Northeast Iowa (Lankford, Cela, & Lankford, 2005).

This chapter provides information on the typologies for special events and festivals. The role of the various organizers play in holding the events is also discussed, as well as the benefits of holding these events. Information on the factors of success for community special events is also described. Examples of park and recreation agency supported or sponsored events are contrasted.

Purpose of Special Events

Park and recreation agencies, as well as main street programs and chambers of commerce are utilizing special events to provide more variety to the programs offered in the community, and to highlight the community and its assets. Special events are targeted for the community, the visitors, or both. Edginton and O'Neill (1999) note that a special event has four characteristics:

- A specifically planned and focused event
- A singular occurrence, an extraordinary activity of some importance, deviating from the routine, an event outside the normal program of activities of the agency, an opportunity for a recreation experience outside the normal range of choices or beyond the everyday experience
- A "crowd" participating, either by specific invitation or open invitation
- A publicized occurrence of finite length

It should be noted that event planning, programming, and management are a function of the recreation programming process. Parks and recreation professionals are well suited to plan, manage, collaborate, and partner with community groups to stage these events. Edginton and O'Neill (1999) further elaborate on the purposes of special events, to include the following three areas: affect of the organization, promotion of community, and economic benefits. Figure 9.1 (adapted from Edginton and O'Neill) delineates how these three purposes impact an organization and community.

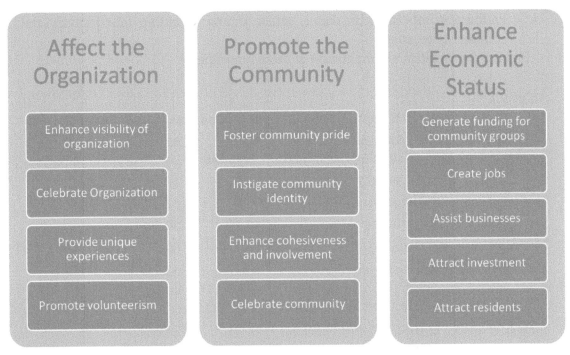

Figure 9.1. Functions and Purposes of Special Events

A study representing city administrators, planners, recreation directors, and tourism and convention professionals sought to identify perceptions of community-based tourism and special events. Respondents represented 48 communities across the U.S. of various sizes, all known to have a tourism industry that was considered community oriented. As one can see in Table 9.1, the improvement of the local economy, employment, and increased quality of recreational attractions were the viewed as the primary benefits (UNI STEP, 2013) of special events, which resulted in tourists visitations. Interestingly, the purpose of festivals as proposed by Edginton and O'Neill (1999) in Figure 9.1 is supported by these perceived benefits in terms of economics, community identity, and recreational opportunities.

Typologies of Special Events

Edginton and O'Neill (1999) details the types of special events, which include the following:

- Fairs, expositions, and shows are considered hall mark events. These include events such as county and state fairs, hobby and craft shows, garden shows, pet shows, art expositions, business and trade events.

- Holiday celebrations, festivals, music festivals, and parades that focus on folk festivals, cultural and heritage events, and carnivals.
- Sports competitions such as golf events, tournaments for youth and adult amateur for soccer, softball, etc., marathons and mini marathons, fishing, hunting and boat races. Included would be spectator events such as college and professional sports, dog and horse racing etc.
- Performing arts such as dance, music drama including folk festivals and community theatre.

Figure 9.2 provides a representation of these typologies.

Table 9.1
Perceived Importance of Benefits of Special Events for Communities

How important are the following benefits to your community as a result of special events?	Very Important	Important	Not Important
Improvement of local economy	84.9%	15.1%	
Increased employment opportunities	66%	32.1%	1.9%
Improvement of quality of life	49.1%	50.9%	
Development of community pride	37.7%	60.4%	1.9%
Promotion of cultural exchange	30.2%	52.8%	17%
Preservation of cultural identity of host population	28.3%	50.9%	20.8%
Increased quality of attractions/recreational opportunities	56.6%	43.4%	

Source: UNI-STEP; 2012-2013 Community-Based Tourism Survey; Nelson (2014)

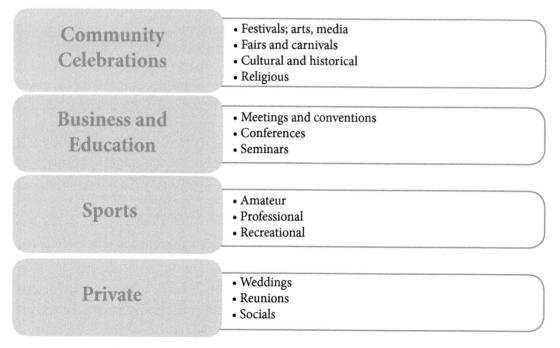

Figure 9.2. Typology of Community Events and Festivals (Adapted from Getz et al., 2007)

An example of one of these events is the Mendocino (California) Music Festival (http://mendocinomusic.org/about/). Partners and organizers include the Mendocino Recreation Association and the Mendocino Chamber of Commerce. The two-week festival in July operates on donations with over 200 volunteers. Community members offer living arrangements for musicians through the "house a musician" program. The event was established in 1986, which is a blend of music consisting of orchestra concerts, Big Bands, chamber music ensembles, dance, blues, jazz, world, folk, bluegrass, and popular contemporary music. Daytime concerts include lecture/recitals at the Piano Series, a performance by participants in the Emerging Artists Program, and small concerts in intimate venues throughout the historic towns of Mendocino and Fort Bragg (http://mendocinomusic.org/about/).

The Mendocino County Chamber of Commerce, in conjunction with the parks and recreation department, California State Parks also collaborate with local communities to offer festivals celebrating the California Coastal National Monument. This celebration involves the North Coast Brewing Company, and various festivals (crab feeds, wine festivals, Mendocino Music Festival, whale festivals, film festivals, beer festivals, art festivals, parades) to raise funding and awareness. Included are also promotion of events including hiking and bike trails, cinemas, water sports, and ocean/beach activities.

It is instructive to understand why visitors are attracted to communities. A study by the Sustainable Tourism and Environment Program (STEP) at the University of Northern Iowa of small, medium, and large tourism-based communities notes a variety of reasons that visitors come to the communities. Communities were purposely selected based on their dependence on tourism as an economic strategy. It is interesting to note the various reasons and then think about amenities and attractions. Scenery, parks, gardens, outdoor recreation, and recreation top the list. Of importance is that sports, museums, shopping, and food are listed, yet they are not the main attractions in the selected communities (See Figure 9.3).

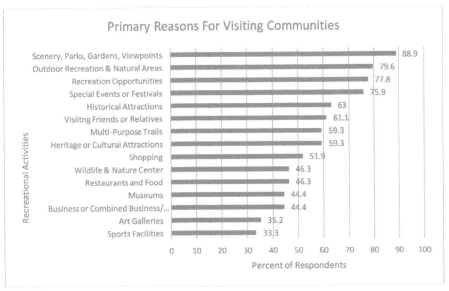

Figure 9.3. Reasons to Visit Community. (Nelson, 2014; UNI-STEP; 2012–2013 Community-Based Tourism Survey)

Table 9.2 compares popular community based special events and festivals and their amenities. Interestingly, a review of the table suggests that each community has identified primary and secondary amenity attractions. For example, Hot Springs Arkansas primary attraction is the hot springs and bathhouses of which now comprise a national park. Of particular interest is the interdependency among the tourism industry, community, businesses, and parks and recreation agencies who work to ensure an improved quality of life for area residents (Hawkins and Cunningham 1996), while enhancing the visitor product. As one can see in Table 9.2, the success of a community special events is a result of public and private partnerships. It is important to note that these events are held in public parks, facilities and spaces.

Table 9.2

Examples of Community-Based Special Events and Festivals

State	City	Example Festivals for Visitors and Community	Website
AR	Hot Springs	Festivals: Hot Springs Music Festival, Hot Springs Fishing Challenge	http://www.hotsprings.org
CA	Mendocino	Festivals: Two-week music festival drawing national and international artists	http://mendocino-music.org/about/
CA	San Francisco	Festival: Outside Lands Music Festival	http://www.sfout-sidelands.com/the-park/attractions
CO	Aspen	Festivals: Winter X Games, JAS Aspen June Snowmass Experience, tribal dances, food and wine festivals, writing festivals	http://www.colorado.com/cities-and-towns/aspen
CO	Glenwood Springs	Festivals: Strawberry Days Festival, ghost walk event	http://www.visit-glenwood.com
IA	Amana Colonies	Festivals: Culinary, Car Clubs, Oktoberfest, Maipole dancers for Maifest (German heritage celebration)	http://www.amana-colonies.com
IA	Decorah	Festivals: Oneota Film Festival, Tractor Days, Nordic Fest, Lawn Chair Nights for concerts, Rendezvous Days	http://www.visitdec-orah.com
IL	Galena	Festivals: hot air balloon race, art festivals, vintage orchestra, Oktoberfest, county fair, pub crawls, parades, pottery tours, ice sculpting festivals, dance festivals, 50s-themed festivals, wine lovers	http://www.visitgale-na.org/index.cfm

Table 9.2 (cont.)

IL	Springfield	Festivals: Historic events, Abraham Lincoln tributes	http://www.visitspringfieldillinois.com
MI	Traverse City	Festivals: music festivals, film festivals, microbrew festivals, wine and art festivals	http://www.traversecity.com/summer/things-to-do/events/festivals/
MN	Wabash	Festivals: SeptOberFest, Riverboat Days, Grumpy Old Men Festival, Watermelon Festival	http://www.exploremississippibluffs.com/wabasha/
MN	Washington County	Festival: Lake Elmo Blue Grass Festival	http://www.co.washington.mn.us/index.aspx?NID=1559
OR	Ashland	Festivals: Shakespeare festival, Crab Fest, holiday festivals, honey festival, multicultural festivals, film, food, wine and brew festivals, walkathons, running relays	https://www.osfashland.org
OR	Champoeg	Festival: Folk Dance Festival at Historic Barn	http://oregonstateparks.org/index.cfm?do=parkPage.dsp_parkPage&parkId=79
WA	Leavenworth	Festivals: International celebrations, music festivals, Kinder Fest (Bavarian Village Celebration, River Salmon Festival, Autumn Leaf Festival, Quilt Festival, Rockfest (climbing)	http://www.leavenworth.org
WA	Walla Walla	Festivals: Sweet Onion Festival, Stopover music festival	http://www.walla-walla.org
WI	Mineral Point	Festivals: Cornish Festival, Book Festival, film festivals, county fair, "city-wide garage sales"	http://mineralpoint.com

An interesting example and profile of a community-based festival that involves a public university, city parks and recreation, and a nonprofit is the College Hill Arts Festival held in Cedar Falls, Iowa. Now celebrating its 37th anniversary, the College Hill Arts Festival was conceived in 1979 and came alive with 30 or so local and northeast

Iowa artists showcasing their original artwork. Today this top-ranked, national arts festival features 75 talented artists who turn the corner of West 23rd & College Street on the campus of the University of Northern Iowa into a living museum. These artists have come to Cedar Falls from all over the United States to give Festival patrons the very best art experience possible. These juried artists exhibit and sell their original artwork in categories including ceramics, fiber, wood, jewelry, metal sculpture, painting, photography, and glass. The Festival, staffed entirely by volunteers, has become a very unique opportunity to connect nationally known artists and the Cedar Valley community in an effort to create a top-quality juried art festival and to make fine art easily accessible to the public.

Nationally recognized artist Gary Kelley became a Festival supporter in 1985 by creating his first College Hill Arts Festival poster. Kelley's annual creations have become "must haves" for Festival supporters and he has won numerous national awards for his Festival designs. Complementing the artists' exhibits is a variety of musical groups performing on stage, hands-on creative activities for children sponsored by the Hearst Center for the Arts, plus balloon sculptures and face painting—all free—and a variety of food vendors to entice Festival attendees. And, unique to festivals, the College Hill Arts Festival features a Young Art Collectors Gallery with original artwork created by the exhibiting artists with prices of $10 or less, which encourages youth ages 14 and under to make independent decisions about art based on their own feelings. The 2014 Festival was ranked in the top 300 events nationwide by Art Fair Source Book. In addition, for nine out of the last 10 years, the College Hill Arts Festival has been named by *Sunshine Artist* magazine on its list of "100 Best Fine Art & Design" Shows in the United States (Bartlett, 2015; and adapted from Lankford, Grybovych & Lankford, 2015).

Factors of Success and Management for Community Special Events

Collaboration and coordination of special events and festivals involves multiple organizations and volunteers. The importance of building and maintaining partnerships in the community cannot be overstated. By communicating goals to partners, a community can gather more support (fiscal, human resources etc.) for the events. See Figure 9.4 for an example of the types of interests that are represented in community-based festivals and events (adapted from Lankford, Grybovych, & Lankford, 2015).

A study recently demonstrated the role that the parks and recreation agency plays in supporting special events in a community (Table 9.3). Various stakeholders collaborate to make a successful event and festival. Not surprisingly, the visitor convention bureau always collaborates followed by the chamber of commerce. Of particular interest is that the parks and recreation department always or sometimes (97.3%) collaborates for community tourism. This finding suggests that the role of the local government is particularly important and supportive of tourism efforts (UNI-STEP, 2013).

In another study (Table 9.4), Saunders (2005) researched the factors that make community festivals successful. Based on the work of Wilson, Fesenmaier, & Fesenmaier (2001), Saunders tested the following factors by examining festivals and events in small, medium, and large communities (27 communities).

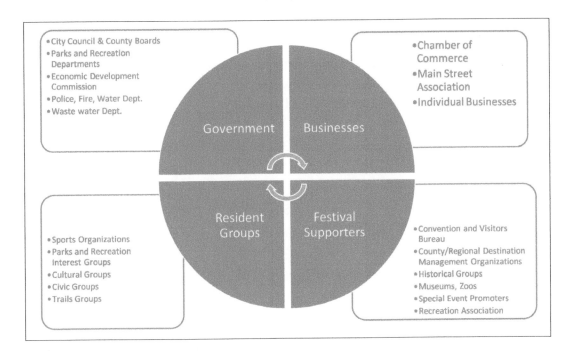

Figure 9.4. Community Stakeholders in Community-Based Events and Festivals (Adapted from Lankford, Grybovych, & Lankford, 2015).

Importantly, one can see that coordination, cooperation, community government, community support are the basis for successful community-based tourism and festivals. This list of factors may be a tool for communities in assessing their current position with regard to developing tourism. Wilson et al. (2001) defined success as "a community tourism attraction that has established an effective infrastructure to support tourism development." The authors also defined unsuccessful communities as "one with substantial natural/cultural resources, but that has not established the economic, political, and community-based infrastructure necessary to support tourism development. Saunders (2005) clearly identified that community support, volunteers, festival management, funding, local government support, and planning were essential elements to successful special events and festivals. Of particular interest are the role and expertise that parks and recreation organizations provide in staging such events.

Managing and Planning Successful Events

Before a park and recreation agency moves forward in the planning stage of an event, they should have clear goals, objectives, and a vision statement. Important questions to consider are as follows:

- Why is the event being held?
- Who will the stakeholders (those who are interested or involved in the event) be?
- When will the event be held?
- Where will the event be staged?
- What is the event content or product/experience sought?
- How will the event be evaluated?

Table 9.3

Stakeholder Collaboration in Promoting Special Events and Festivals

Which stakeholders collaborate toward a successful visitor industry in your community?	Always Collaborate	Sometimes	Never
Parks and recreation	67.3%	30.8%	1.9%
Visitor convention bureau/visitor center/tourism office	90.2%	7.8%	2%
Chamber of commerce	58.5%	34%	7.5%
Economic development authority	50%	37.5%	12.5%
Main street organization	42.2%	31.1%	26.7%
Community festival group	48%	38%	14%

Source: UNI-STEP; 2013 Community-Based Tourism Survey

Table 9.4

Factors of Success for Rural Community Tourism and Festivals
(In Order of Importance)

Wilson et al. (2001) Community Tourism	Saunders (2005) Festivals
A Complete Tourism Package	Widespread Community Support for Tourism and the Festival
Good Leadership	Volunteers
Support and Participation of Local Government	Festival Management
Sufficient Funds for Tourism Development	Coordination and Cooperation with Businesses
Strategic Planning	Sufficient Funding
Coordination and Cooperation between Businesses and Local Leadership	Support and Coordination from Local Government
Coordination and Cooperation between Rural Tourism Entrepreneurs	Choice of Festival Activities
Information and Technical Assistance for Development and Promotion	Strategic Planning
Supportive Convention & Visitors Bureau	Supportive Convention & Visitors Bureau
Widespread Community Support for Tourism	Information and Technical Assistance
	Cooperation with Professionals
	Complete Visitor Package

The City of Maple Ridge Parks and Leisure Department in British Columbia has provided the following checklist (see Table 9.5) for planning a community wide event (City of Maple Ridge, 2015). It is important to remember that events take months and sometimes years to plan and host. This checklist provided by the Parks and Leisure Department begins with considerations that are a least five months out from the event, and concludes with an after action phase. One should note that evaluation of the event is not on this list. It is important that surveys be collected during the event to document satisfaction, visitor characteristics and economic impacts for the community. Volunteers would randomly select individuals to fill out a one page survey for the evaluation. A focus group could also be formed after the event to evaluate the event or aspects of the event. It is important that the survey data be made available to the event manager, planner, volunteers and park and recreation agency as soon as practical.

Table 9.5
Community Event Planning Checklist

At Least 5 Months Before the Event	4 Months Before the Event
Form event planning committee	Decide on a theme and title of event
Establish a regular meeting location and dates (e.g., every two weeks)	Decide on activities (e.g. performers, speakers, displays, food vendors, crafts, parade)
Determine the purpose of the event and brainstorm activities	Hold auditions for entertainers
Choose a tentative date and location	Determine roles and responsibilities for committee members (e.g. promotions, food, speakers, stage, equipment & logistics)
Check availability of event venue and consider restrictions (e.g. seating capacity)	Establish an initial budget
Identify the intended audience	Research insurance requirements
Determine possible event sponsors & grant funders	Apply for special permits, licenses, insurance, etc. (e.g., food vendor and road closure permits)
Create sponsor levels and amounts	Create a fund-raising plan and begin contacting possible funders
	Book the Community Event Kit Trailer

Table 9.5 (cont.)

3 Months Before the Event	2 Months Before the Event
Develop an advertising and publicity plan	Submit a Special Event Application
Request logos from corporate sponsors	Submit a food vendor information to Health Unit
Design a site map of your event. Include power sources, water hookup, activity and stage locations, parking, volunteer & general information booth	Prepare ads, posters, Facebook pages, and other promotions
Plan for first aid, security, electrical, water equipment, recycling, porta-potties	Design a volunteer application form
Contract entertainment and sound production	Contact the Community Volunteer Center with volunteer information
Create a food vendors' application form and post on-line	Begin advertising volunteer positions
Consider accessibility to event (e.g., wheelchair accessible parking)	Design a safety plan. Consider first aid, lost and found center, traffic plan, security, fire lanes
	Develop a green plan (e.g., bike parking, advertise bus routes, recycling plan

1 Month Before the Event	3 Weeks Before the Event
Notify emergency and transit services of any road closures. Advertise road closure in local newspaper	Design a volunteer schedule and list of tasks
Design press releases	Begin to schedule volunteers for 2- or 4-hour shifts
Prepare signage for event (e.g., stage schedule)	Plan volunteer refreshments and appreciation
Finalize entertainment schedule and contracts	Prepare volunteers' IDs (e.g., t-shirts, aprons, or name tags)
Submit safety and site plan for municipal approval	

2 Weeks Before the Event	1 Week Before the Event
Submit press releases to local media, radio stations, public service announcers	Host a volunteer information and training session
Host a site walk-through of event with committee members	Confirm number of volunteers, entertainers, sound production, and other staff
	Schedule pick up/ delivery of any rented or loaned equipment

Table 9.5 (cont.)

Day of Event	Week After the Event
	Write checks for payments to be made on event day
	Prepare speaking notes for emcee
Day of Event	**Week After the Event**
Set up registration and volunteer center area	Send thank-you notes
Register volunteers and assign tasks	Reconcile all invoices
Meet with key organizers for a communication session (pre-event)	Meet with the event planning committee to evaluate the event
Reserve parking for loading zone, VIPs, accessible parking, Event Trailer	
Check entrances to ensure clear, safe and unobstructed access to facility	
Set up equipment (e.g., tents, traffic cones, barricades, signage)	
Set up stage and sound equipment	
Decorate	
Implement traffic and safety plan	
Greet entertainers and vendors, assist with set up	
After event, take down decorations, clean up garbage, tear down stage and other equipment	
Return supplies to source locations	

Table 9.6
City of San Diego, California Event Management Permit System Requirements

Venue Design	Type of Event
Event Components (such as music and other activities)	Setup and Dismantle Plan
VIP/Dignitary Presence	Alcohol Management
Cash Management	Security Responsibilities
Storm Water Management	Recycling/Trash Plans
Insurance Requirements	Traffic Management Plan
Americans with Disabilities (ADA) Compliance	Community Support/Issues
Illegal Vendors	Additional Required Permits/Approvals
Cost-Reduction Strategies	Other

Another example of event management is from the City of San Diego, California. The city has developed an extensive permit system for city special events and festivals. This example demonstrates to event organizers the permits required to conduct the event within the city limits. San Diego prides itself on its special events, from major conventions and international sporting events to community based festivals, parades and athletic events. The city hosts thousands of events each year with a goal to enhance the vitality, quality of life and economic prosperity of San Diego through the support of special events in San Diego (City of San Diego, 2015). Table 9.6 provides the framework set forth in the guide for event promoters and organizers. Of particular interest is that permits are required for many of the items listed below, or detailed plans that would be approved by the city. As one can see, many of the items listed are basically a planning process or guide to event management.

Edginton and O'Neill (1999) note that special events require careful and extensive planning to be successful. The following section will detail these considerations. Specifically, they recommend consideration of the following aspects:

- Staffing
- Scheduling
- Location
- Financing and budget, as well as sponsorships
- Marketing and media relations
- Risk management and legal considerations
- Event production
- Evaluation

Staffing

Three levels of staffing are required for successful events, which include an overall event manager (or director), the planning and management team, and the committees. The event organizers must appoint, designate, or hire a person to provide leadership, supervision, and coordination of the event. It is important to note that cities with larger parks and recreation organizations have a staff member who assumes this role on a full-time basis. Smaller park and recreation organizations utilize staff time as events are scheduled. The manager (director) oversees volunteer coordination, fund-raising and budgeting, communications, marketing and promotion, event production, and evaluation. The role is one of coordination, monitoring, and guidance of the process for these events. The manager ensures the goals and objectives are being met by the event, as well as any community concerns that may arise from hosting large and intrusive events.

The event manager is responsible for the formation of an event management team. Ideally, the team has people with expertise in finance, budgeting, marketing, communications and public relations, permits and vendor compliance, and evaluation. The team members would be responsible for formation of volunteer committees who also have interest in and expertise with these skills. Edginton and O'Neill (1999) suggest committees should be formed to have responsibilities for the following:

- **Finance,** to develop and monitor a budget. This committee works with the park and recreation agency, a treasurer and coordinates with the committees on sponsorship and concessions/vendors.
- **Marketing, promotion and media relations** committee prepares a marketing plan, to include promotion and advertising. Importantly, the community monitors community relations using the media.
- **Crowd control and safety** committee is concerned with behaviors that may arise, such as alcohol use, drugs, traffic, signage and transportation issues, etc. This committee coordinates with the parks and recreation, police, fire, and medical representatives of the community.
- **Production and event management** committee is responsible for the staging of the event or festival. There may be subcommittees representing entertainment, maintenance, food and beverage, volunteers, activities, prizes and awards, judges, or VIP liaisons.

It should be noted that most all community events rely heavily on volunteers. Management of the volunteer process is crucial to the success of any volunteer effort. Fortunately, parks and recreation organizations rely on and are experienced with using volunteers in the delivery of services. An active event is a major community event and will need adequate numbers of volunteers in order to be successful. There should be a safety and information meeting approximately one week before the event so volunteers are informed of their rights and responsibilities, have timelines for the event and emergency contact information. At the safety meeting, include training on incident reporting and traffic issues.

Scheduling

The event manager and the event planning committee, in coordination with the park and recreation agency and other organizations, must schedule the event so that sponsors, community members, and visitors are best served. Scheduling requires a collaborative approach with other agencies, communities, and businesses so that competition is avoided and maximum participation and support is increased. Avoiding holidays, school, and other community functions are also considerations. Thinking about school holidays that may increase family visitations to the event is also important. In addition, if there are competing events, there may be a lack of facilities available to adequately stage the event. Finally, the day and time of week might be a consideration for families and youth.

Location of Event

Consideration of rental fees, maintenance, and supervision costs is important when considering the location of the event. For example, important questions to answer consist of sound systems, parking, access for handicap, crowd control (fencing, barriers, etc.), sanitary facilities, and seating or facility capacity.

Finances

Event planners and organizers must address the question of budget for the event and the source of the funds. The parks and recreation agency would provide a line item for the sponsorship of the event. The organizers, working with a treasurer, would establish and maintain fiscal controls of the budget. Oversight of committee expenditures, supplies, and vendors and services is the responsibility of the event manager. A procedure for expending and reporting the budget must be established.

Revenue sources can come from a variety of public, nonprofit, and private organizations, including individual donations. In addition tickets and fees (entry fee, dinner fee, etc.) are considered revenue sources. Often, ticket sales constitutes the largest portion of revenue. When public park and recreation agencies sponsor events, ticket sales, etc., are usually offered at cost of offering the event or sometimes at a loss, when it is considered a community program. Since the governmental unit does collect taxes for the provision of recreation programs, this is considered standard practice to offer the event at no or reduced costs for the community.

Grants are sometimes available to host an event. Arts councils, private foundations, and individuals will sometimes provide grant funding for an event. Often, event organizers obtain one to three sponsors for the event. These usually are businesses who want to create a positive image of their business and the community. In-kind services are also considered revenue. This may be in the form of the local electricians union doing all the electrical work as a contribution or the local businesses supplying prizes for drawings (again advertising their business and product).

Marketing and Media Relations

Effective marketing and promotion of the event is important for the budget and covering costs of the event. Marketing is especially important in events since they are periodic events. Publicity, advertising and personal contact by staff, volunteers, and others in the community will help promote the event. Often, media outlets will provide services in-kind for the event, thereby helping with the budget but also promoting the event.

Risk Management and Legal Considerations

Not only is a risk management plan essential, it is required by many governmental units. The plan allows the manager of the event to predetermine areas of potential risk. Without a risk management plan, the sponsoring agency places themselves at risk of legal liability, let alone at risk for personal injury of participants. The plan would cover weather (lighting, tornado), power failures, crowd control, unruly patron behavior, fire, traffic, security, public safety (fire safety, emergencies, and evacuations), ADA access, OSHA, health regulations for food and beverages, and documentation of permits as required by the governmental unit. This plan is coordinated with the police, fire, ambulance medical unit, hospitals etc. for implementation. A committee is normally charged with developing this plan and ensuring that it is implemented.

Event Production

Event production consists of a committee or number of committees who address the following components of an event:

- Decorations (banners, signs, plantings)
- Entertainment (assures quality including talent, appearance, and content appropriate to event)
- Operations and maintenance (set up, clean up, seating, removal of equipment, trash, etc.)

- Signage (collects, inventories, and stores all signs for event)
- Transportation (parking, bus shuttles, handicap access, etc.)
- Concessions (food and beverage and supervision of vendors)
- Parking and traffic (coordinates with police a parking and traffic plan)
- Children's activities (as appropriate for entertainment and child care)
- Prizes and awards

Evaluation of Event

Probably the least understood and most often dismissed aspect of event management is the evaluation of the event. There should be a formal, predetermined, one- or two-page survey used to collect responses from participants. Collection of responses would be over the entire event period on random days, times, and locations. The survey would cover items important to the organizers, as well as the economic impacts and the levels of satisfaction with the event. A report would be written and presented to the organizing group, who would then use the findings to improve the next event.

Summary

Many cities and counties are active promoting and holding festivals and community events. Festivals and community events are closely associated with municipal park and recreation agencies. Communities hold special events and festivals for many reasons, which include enhancing the image of the community, providing economic benefits, and celebrating the culture or history. There is documented evidence that events create more social benefits than social costs (Gursoy, Kim, & Uysal, 2002) when properly planned and managed. There is also evidence that when parks and recreation agencies hold smaller scaled events (for example marathons, Senior Games, soccer, softball, etc.), they are considered more sustainable from a social, economic, and environmental perspective (Gibson, Kaplanidou, & Kang, 2012). Often these events are family oriented, attracting moderate numbers of people, yet bringing some benefits to the community.

Events have distinctive characteristics, such as a specific planned event, a singular occurrence outside of normal recreation programs, and a finite length for the event. The function and purpose of the event varies by community, but generally influences and shapes the organization (affect), promotes the community and enhances the economic situation. Studies have shown that benefits of special events support these functions and purposes.

Typologies for community events generally can be categorized as community celebrations (festivals, fairs, parades, music, etc.), business and educational event (conferences and meetings), sports (amateur, recreation, and professional), and private events (weddings and reunions). Studies have noted that attending a community special event is ranked in the top five reasons to visit a community or region.

Community events widely vary, as was demonstrated in Table 9.2. It is important to consider that no matter what the type of event, it usually involves the public parks and recreation areas, facilities and organization at some point. Collaboration and partnerships between government, businesses, resident groups and festival organizers are necessary for successful events. Studies have demonstrated that park and recreation agencies are involved in over 95% of community events in some fashion.

Key Concepts

- Special events
- Role of parks and recreation in special events
- Impact of special events
- Event planning
- Event management

Useful Internet Sites, Exercises, and Resources

Exercise 1

Visit the website of a medium or large city and find where to register for a special event. Compare three cities and how they permit an event. Contrast the differences and discuss in class.

Exercise 2

Find 3 Internet sites for special events that are multi-day in length. Review and contrast the information provided from a "tourist" point of view. Then review and contrast the information from a planner point of view. What can be improved? Why? How?

Questions for Review and Case Problems

1. Why do communities hold special events and festivals?
2. What types of festivals can you name and describe in your community?
3. What are the four characteristics of special events?
4. What are the functions and purposes of special events?
5. What are the benefits of special events and festivals?
6. Describe the typology of special events, list events in your community that fit that typology.
7. Compare and contrast the reasons why people visit a community. How does that compare to your community?
8. List the community stakeholders in your community who are involved in event planning and management.
9. What are the factors for success for special events?
10. What are the essential eight planning considerations for successful special events?

References

Bartlett, M. S. (2015). University of Northern Iowa. Personal Communication, July 10, 2015.

Cela, A., Knowles-Lankford, J., & Lankford, S. (2007). Local food festivals in Northeast Iowa communities: A visitor and economic impact study. *Managing Leisure, 12*(2 & 3), pp. 171–186.

City of Maple Ridge Parks and Leisure. (2015). Planning a special event. Retrieved from http://mrpmparksandleisure.ca/DocumentCenter/View/65

City of San Diego. (2015). Special event planning guide. Retrieved from http://www.sandiego.gov/specialevents/pdf/planningguide.pdf

Edginton, C. R., & O'Neill, J. (1999). Program, services, and event management. In B. van der Smissen, M. Moiseichik, V. Hartenburg, & L. Twardzik (Eds.), *Management of park and recreation agencies* (pp. 175–232).

Getz, D., Andersson, T., & Larson, M. (2007). Managing festival stakeholders: Concepts and case studies. *Event Management, 10,* 103–122.

Getz, D., & Frisby, W. (1991). Developing a municipal policy for festivals and events. *Recreation Canada,* October 1991.

Gibson, H., Kaplanidou, K., & Kang, S. J. (2012). Small-scale event sport tourism: A case study in sustainable tourism. *Sport Management Review, 15*(2), 160–170.

Lankford, S. Cela, A., & Lankford, J. (2005). Place-based food tourism in Northeast Iowa. Sustainable Tourism and Environment Program. University of Northern Iowa. Retrieced from http://www.uni.edu/step/reports/place_based_food.pdf

Lankford, S., Grybovych, O., & Lankford, J. (2017). *An introduction to community-based tourism.* Urbana, IL: Sagamore.

Nelson, M. (2014). *Characteristics of community-based tourism practices: A stakeholder perspective.* AMA Research Paper, University of Northern Iowa.

Saunders, K. (2005). *Factors of success for Northeast Iowa community festivals.* AMA Research Paper, University of Northern Iowa. Retrieved from http://www.uni.edu/step/reports/festivals_success.pdf

UNI STEP (2013). *Characteristics of community-based tourism practices: A stakeholder perspective.* University of Northern Iowa Sustainable Tourism and Environment.

Wilson, S., Fesenmaier, D. R., Fesenmaier, J., & Van Es, J. C. (2001). Factors for success in rural tourism development. *Journal of Travel Research, 40*(2), 132–138.

CHAPTER 10

Economic Impacts of Community-Based Tourism

"The principal motivations for a business or region to serve tourists are generally economic. An individual business is interested primarily in its own revenues and costs, while a community or region is concerned with tourism's overall contribution to the economy, as well as its social, fiscal, and environmental impacts. A good understanding of tourism's economic impacts is therefore important for the tourism industry, government officials, and the community as a whole."

–D. J. Stynes (1997)

CHAPTER OBJECTIVES

- Outline the main types of tourism impacts
- Outline and discuss direct, indirect, and induced economic impacts
- Discuss different approaches to tourism economic impact assessment
- Review the main economic impact analysis approaches
- Outline and review the main input-output analysis models
- Discuss common mistakes in economic impact studies
- Review two case studies examining economic impacts of wine and food tourists in rural Northeast Iowa

Introduction

Travel and tourism industries have long been major contributors to increased economic activity around the world. They have created jobs and are major industries in many regions. In some communities and even countries tourism is the dominant economic activity. This has led many people to think of tourism only in terms of economic impacts, jobs, and taxes. However, the range of impacts from tourism is broad and often influences areas beyond those commonly associated with tourism (Kreag, 2002). The main impacts of tourism can be grouped in four categories: economic, environmental, social, and cultural. Table 10.1 draws on the work of Lankford and Howard (1993) and Ap and Crompton (1998) who summarized positive and negative impacts of tourism that have been reported in the literature. We keep the description of the tourism impacts concise to maintain a focus on the primary focus of this chapter: the economic impacts of community-based tourism.

Table 10.1
Positive and Negative Impacts of Tourism

POSITIVE IMPACTS	NEGATIVE IMPACTS
Positive Economic Impacts • Contributes to income and standard of living • Improves the local economy • Increases employment opportunities • Improves investment, development, and infrastructure spending in the economy • Increases tax revenues • Improves public utilities infrastructure • Improves public transport infrastructure • Increases opportunities for shopping	**Negative Economic Impacts** • Increased price and shortage of goods and services • Increased price of land and housing • Increased cost of living/property taxes
Positive Environmental Impacts • Preservation of the natural environment • Preservation of historic buildings and monuments • Improvement of the area's appearance	**Negative Environmental Impacts** • Increased traffic congestion • Overcrowding • Increased noise pollution and litter
Positive Social Impacts • Improves the quality of life • Increases availability of recreation opportunities • Improves quality of fire and police protection	**Negative Social and Cultural Impacts** • Increased prostitution • Increased alcoholism • Increased smuggling • Heightened tension • Increasingly hectic community and personal life • Creation of a fake folk culture
Positive Cultural Impacts • Improves understanding and image of different communities or cultures • Promotes cultural exchange • Facilitates meeting visitors • Preserves cultural identity of host population • Increases demand for historical and cultural exhibits	

Economic development is a priority in many communities, and tourism is often recognized as an important contributor. To show elected officials that they are central to their communities' economic health, many agencies, individual facilities, and events hire external consultants to conduct economic impact studies to legitimize public support (Crompton & McKay, 1994). As a result, many economic impact studies tend to emphasize the benefits and disregard the costs of tourism (or overinflate economic impacts of tourism), either because of methodological flaws or because many economic costs are intangible and thus difficult to measure. In addition, different studies often produce different results, and while it might be tempting to go with the highest impact numbers, that might not necessarily be the right strategy. Crompton and Lee (2000) remind us that economic impact studies only provide "best guesses" rather than inviolable accuracy, and that if you hire five different consultants, you will get five different results. These discrepancies "are normal and occur because economic impact analyses can be conducted using different assumptions and procedures, thus leading to different impacts being identified" (Crompton & McKay, 1994, p. 33).

Direct, Indirect, and Induced Economic Impacts

Economic impacts are the effects a project or policy has on the economy of a designated area, measured in terms of the change in business sales, jobs, value added, income, or tax revenue. In tourism, economic impacts are commonly defined as the net economic change in the incomes of host residents that results from spending by tourists. The core of economic impact analyses is the multiplier concept, what Archer (1973) likened to the ripples set up in a pool if more water is poured into the system (the pool represents the local economy, and the additional water symbolizes extra spending by the visitors). The diagram of the multiplier process (direct and indirect impacts) is shown in Figure 10.1.

The total economic impacts of visitor spending are a sum of direct, indirect, and induced impacts. Direct impacts (direct consequence of travel activity in the area) represent direct expenditures of the visitors. In Figure 10.1, festival visitors spend money on restaurant meals and drinks, hotel accommodation, retail purchases, and festival tickets and concessions. These are direct injections in the local economy.

Indirect impacts represent subsequent rounds of economic activity resulting from initial expenditures by the visitors. For example, businesses spend part of their receipts on goods and services they need to serve customers, their suppliers then must make additional purchases, and so the chain continues through numerous rounds, with portions leaking out each round. Figure 10.1 showcases five possible ways a hotel can disburse the money it receives from the visitors (the pattern can be replicated for other establishments as well), as well as successive rounds of spending by the three selected sectors (the other two sectors in the diagram represent leakages).

Induced impacts represent proportion of household income (additional wages and salaries) spent locally on goods and services. In other words, as residents' wages and salaries increase, local consumption increases as well. Since tourism-related businesses tend to be labor intensive, they tend to have larger induced rather than indirect impacts. The typology of economic impacts is illustrated in Figure 10.2.

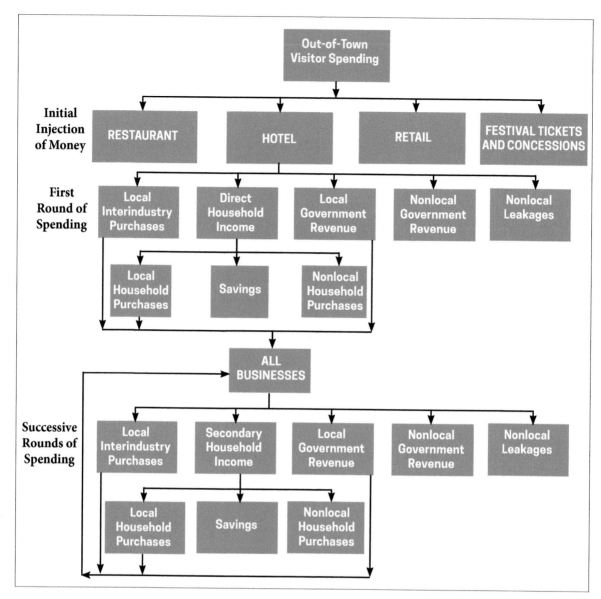

Figure 10.1. The Multiplier Process (Liu & Var, 1982).

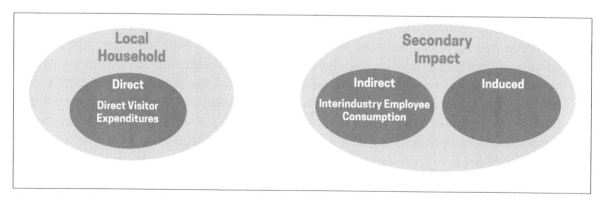

Figure 10.2. Typology of Economic Impacts.

In line with the discussion of primary and secondary benefits of tourism, it is important to note that there also are primary and secondary costs related to tourism. Primary (direct) costs represent public expenditures on services for the visitors and account for environmental damage done by visitors. Secondary costs represent public expenditures on public goods and services required to service those businesses and employees that are impacted at the secondary level.

Multipliers

The ratio of the total to initial change in a local economy is called a multiplier and is rather easy to calculate. Four multipliers are commonly used to assess impacts of initial visitor expenditures:

- **Output (sales) multipliers**–estimate the total change in local sales resulting from $1 spent by the visitors. If a region reports a sales multiplier of 1.4, it means each $1 of direct sales (tourist expenditures) generated an additional $.40 for the local economy.
- **Employment multipliers**–measure the total change in employment (the number of new jobs created in the area).
- **Income multipliers**–measure the total increase in income generated from $1 spent by the visitors.
- **Value added multipliers**–provide an estimate of the additional value added to the products as a result of visitor spending. Value added includes employee compensation, indirect business taxes, proprietary, and other property income.

Unfortunately, tourism multipliers have frequently been misapplied, misused, and misunderstood (for example, many studies do not properly account for visitor purchases of goods that are not locally made). Consequently, it is not uncommon to find reports overestimating secondary effects of tourism spending (multipliers of 2.0 or greater). In reality, tourism spending multipliers are most likely to fall somewhere between 1.0 and 1.5. The value of the multipliers depends on the following main factors: the geographic size of the region, size and economic diversity of the regional economy, the nature of the economic sectors involved, and the study year. Larger areas with diversified economies will have higher multipliers that will need to be adjusted year to year to reflect economic (price) changes.

Another important concept in the economic impact modeling is that of leakages. They represent savings, purchases of imports, and tax leakages—money that is lost from local circulation. The most common causes of leakages include the following: imported food and drink, foreign exchange costs associated with the development of tourist facilities (especially in developing countries), remittances by foreign owned companies, remittances by foreign (extra-regional) workers, management fees to franchisers, payments to airlines, imports, and such. The lower the rate of leakage of spending out of the economy, the greater the recirculation and the greater the multiplier effect.

Economic Impact Analysis: Main Approaches and Common Mistakes

Economic impacts of visitor spending are typically estimated by some variation of the following equation:

*Economic impacts of tourist spending = Number of tourists ** Average spending per visitor * Multiplier*

The four typical approaches researchers can employ to estimate economic impacts of tourism include subjective expert opinion, secondary data in aggregate form, secondary data in disaggregate form, and primary data/formal models. A brief review of these approaches is outlined in Table 10.2.

Table 10.2
Approaches to Tourism Economic Impact Assessment

Level	Tourism activity	Spending	Multipliers
1 – Judgment	Expert judgment to estimate tourism activity	Expert judgment or an "engineering approach"	Expert judgment to estimate multipliers
2 – Secondary data	Existing tourism counts for the area or total estimates from a similar area or facility	Use or adjust spending averages from studies of a similar area/market	Use or adjust aggregate tourism spending multipliers from a similar region/ study
3 – Secondary data	Estimate tourism activity by segment or revise estimates by segment from another area	Adjust spending that is disaggregated within particular spending categories and segments	Use sector-specific multipliers from published sources
4 – Primary data	Visitor survey to estimate number of tourists by segment or a demand model	Survey random sample of visitors to estimate average spending by segment and spending category	Use an input-output model of the region's economy

Source: Stynes (1999)

While primary data approach is usually considered superior to other approaches to tourism economic impact assessment, Stynes (1999) cautions:

As one moves from judgment to secondary data to primary data and formal models, the methods become more complex and the time and expense of the study increases. The added cost is hopefully associated with estimates that are both more accurate and more detailed, although this isn't always the case. In some cases good judgment or existing data may be more accurate than a new visitor survey, particularly if the survey has a low response rate, small sample size, and measurement and sampling procedures that do not guarantee a representative sample or reliable measurements. (p. 1)

In other words, any method, when applied inappropriately, can generate false outcomes. What follows below is a list of the most common mistakes found in economic impact studies (modified from Crompton, 2006; Frechtling, 1994):

- **Inclusion of local residents, time switchers and casuals (especially in case of tourism events):** Economic impacts relate only to new money injected into an economy not to expenditures made by local residents (those expenditures represent recycling of the money that already is in the area), time switchers (visitors who have been planning a visit to the community, but changed the timing of their visit to coincide with the event), or casuals (visitors who were already in the area, and decided to go to the event instead of doing something else).

- **Ignoring displacement costs:** It is plausible to assume that visitors from outside a community who are attracted by a tourism event may displace other visitors who otherwise would have come to the community but did not, due to lack of accommodation or to avoid the crowds.

- **Exaggerating visitor numbers:** Accurate economic impact measures depend on reasonably accurate counts of visitors. As many community events are not gated and/or do not charge admission, attendance estimates are commonly exaggerated.

- **Inappropriate aggregation of the study area:** Magnitude of any economic impact depends on the size of the area under study. When the geographical area of impact is changed, it changes the definition of which participants are visitors and which are locals. Larger area under study will therefore result in higher impact numbers.

- **Misinterpretation of economic impact multipliers:** Many economic impact studies rely on statistical software that typically produces three types of economic impact measures: sales (output), personal income, and employment. A careful and appropriate interpretation of these indicators is needed for a correct interpretation of impact results.

- **Equating economic impacts with travel spending in the area:** Frechtling (1994, p. 2) illustrates the fallacy of this approach with two examples:

  > The extreme case is represented by a hotel in an underdeveloped economy, owned by nonresidents, staffed with nonresident employees who send their earnings home, and serviced by imported goods and services. Travelers may spend millions of dollars in the hotel each year, but the contribution to the wealth or income of the residents is virtually nonexistent.

A similar case can be found in the developed economy. Consider a popular self-service gasoline service station in a resort area. Visitors purchase gasoline and oil provided by non-resident suppliers. The station itself is owned by an oil company headquartered elsewhere. The employees may be residents, but it takes only one to oversee the sale of several hundred thousand dollars of petroleum products a year. The dollars spent are a poor guide to the impact on resident wealth or income.

Ultimately, the results of any economic impact analysis greatly depend on the structure and assumptions of the model applied. For example, a properly designed economic impact study of a tourism event would require data regarding the sources of the expenditures, the geographic starting point of expenditures, the destination or end point of expenditures, as well as the reason for expenditures, among others. Without these, the resulting estimate will likely misstate true net economic impacts (Tyrrell & Johnston, 2006).

Economic Impact Modeling

Economic impacts of any industry can be measured in a number of different ways, included among them are industry output, gross domestic product (value added), household or labor income, employment, and tax revenues (The Outspan Group, 2007). Further, economic impact models can be designed to report only one or multiple types of impacts, but generally reflect the economy in a specific geographic area (therefore generate estimates of economic impacts within that area) at a certain time. The most common models for estimating economic impacts include the following:

- **Cost-Benefit Analysis (CBA)**–estimates and totals up the equivalent money value of the benefits and costs to the community of projects to establish whether they are worthwhile.
- **Keynesian multiplier models**–estimate the proportion of tourist expenditures that remains in the economy once imports and savings have been filtered.
- **Ad hoc multiplier models**–include only selected economic sectors to estimate economic impacts, and so are particularly useful in the context of regional analysis.
- **Input-Output (I-O) models**–calculate multipliers to show the benefits of tourism which include increased output, earnings and employment. Multipliers are derived from input-output tables representing the structure of an economy.
- **Tourism Satellite Accounts (TSA)**–measure importance of the tourism industry in terms of macroeconomic variables, using information from national accounts.
- **Computable General Equilibrium (CGE) models**–incorporate the whole economy and treat it as an integrated system. They include an industry input-output model but also the other nonindustrial sectors of the economy.

Among these, input-output analysis appears to be a relatively reliable method to trace the effects of initial tourism spending in an economy (Fletcher, 1989, 1994). The theoretical framework for the analysis was developed by Wassily Leontief, for which he received the Nobel Prize in 1973. The main advantages of I-O models are their flexibility, attention to sectorial interdependencies, comprehensive view of the economy, and policy neutrality. On the downside, they have been criticized for the partial approach in allowing for the positive impacts on the economy only while ignoring the negative impacts which are likely to be of a comparable magnitude (Dwyer, Forsyth, & Spurr, 2006). In addition, it should be noted that this analysis is a valid measure of short term economic impacts only, rather than of the overall efficiency of resource allocation (Archer & Fletcher, 1990). Despite the criticism, it appears that the benefits of I-O modeling outweigh costs, and so it continues to be the most common method for estimating economic impacts. In fact, the compilation of input-output tables for national and regional economies is now a routine practice governed by a United Nations standard.

The most popular input-output models that are used today include the following:

- **The National Park Service's "Money generation model" (MGM)**–a simple model that relies largely on judgment and available secondary data in a highly aggregate form
- **The Bureau of Economic Analysis's (BEA) RIMS II user handbook**–uses published multipliers to estimate economic impacts
- **The MI-REC/IMPLAN model**–uses county level data to estimate input-output models for regions down to a county level

Among these, an inexpensive and quite accessible economic impact analysis model for use in tourism is the MI-REC/IMPLAN system, developed in 1993 as a collaboration of two researchers from the University of Minnesota with the US Forest Service Land Use Planning Unit in Colorado. The software combines a spreadsheet program for estimating tourist spending with the IMPLAN input-output modeling system. The first steps are to define the study area, enter the number of visitors, and categorize tourist expenditures by IMPLAN sector. Several spending data sets from recent surveys are available, as well as an option to customize spending obtained from a local survey. Regional multipliers are then calculated for the sectors that received expenditures, representing the value of the total economic activity generated in a region per $1 of initial expenditures in a particular sector. The model provides comprehensive measures of direct, indirect, and induced effects of changes in the regional economy.

In addition to the above mentioned models, there exist a variety of commercial economic impact calculators, some of better quality than others. The DMAI Event Impact Calculator, for example, measures the economic value of an event and calculates its return on investment to local taxes. The calculator was developed by Tourism Economics (an Oxford Economics Company), and includes three distinct modules: meetings (including business meetings, conventions, and trade shows), sports (including amateur, college, and professional events), and festivals and cultural events. It is mainly used by Destination Marketing Organizations to quantify the economic benefits generated by their marketing and sales efforts (or show local policymakers the economic value of meetings, conventions, and trade shows). The calculator requires minimal user inputs but can be customized to a specific destination; the outputs include direct impacts of events on businesses, employment, income, and taxes (Destination

Marketing Association International, 2017). While much more simplistic as compared to the IMPLAN system, the DMAI calculator provides the basic information regarding the economic impact of local events.

Practical Implications

Today, changing economic structures force many communities to look for ways to diversify their local economies through tourism and other service industries. Economic impact studies can help predict the "ripple effects" of new and expanding (or old and declining) industries. Used wisely, economic impact assessment can provide planners and communities with estimates of employment, gross sales, and income that will result from tourism. Comparison of the alternatives can help communities decide where to invest resources for the greatest benefit (Miller, 1996). However, while it is tempting to use existing data sets to estimate economic impacts of tourism, these will only provide a picture of what the economic impacts might look like someplace else at some other time. As noted, multipliers (the core of economic impact analyses) are highly variable and must be adjusted to a specific geographic region with a unique economy at a particular time. It is highly recommended to rely on primary data (usually visitor surveys) to determine economic impacts of tourism in a specific community. While time consuming, these are relatively inexpensive and provide the most accurate depiction of economic impacts in a community. To illustrate an example of economic impact analysis, we share two case studies that were conducted in rural Northeastern Iowa examining economic impacts of food and wine travelers.

Case Studies: Economic Impacts of Wine and Food Tourism in Rural Northeast Iowa (to view full reports, visit http://www.uni.edu/step)

Purpose of the studies: To estimate economic impacts of wine and food tourism in rural Northeast Iowa.

Methodology: (1) Wine tourism study–a questionnaire survey was administered in 2005 at three wineries on the Iowa Wine Trail, (2) food tourism study–a questionnaire survey was administered in 2005 at 11 local food festivals. Both studies sought to examine visitor profile, visitor motivations, and economic impacts of these niche tourism markets on the Northeastern Iowa economy.

Results: Tables 10.3–10.5 illustrate economic impacts of food and wine tourism in the region.

Table 10.3
Economic Impacts of Wine Visitors in Rural Northeast Iowa

Multiplier	Direct Impact	Indirect Impact	Induced Impact	Total Impact
Economic impacts ($ Sales/output)	1,823,472	404,013	418,145	2,645,627
Economic impacts ($ Value added/income)	921,223	198,605	227,942	1,347,771
Economic impacts (Employment/jobs)	42.6	4.3	4.6	52.6

Source: STEP-UNI (2006). Development of a regional wine culture in Iowa.

An interpretation of Table 10.3 reveals the following picture of the economic impacts of wine tourists in the region: initial wine visitors' expenditures of $1.82 million generated $2.65 million in terms of sales, $1.35 million in terms of personal income, and created 53 full-time-equivalent jobs. For those wishing to examine the table closer, two indicators are most noteworthy: total impact on resident income and the number of jobs created. While sales impacts estimate an increase in sales, they may represent purchases of products outside the region, and are therefore of most interest to business owners rather than tourism planners and developers. The impacts on resident income, on the other hand, measure effects of visitor expenditures on the changes in household incomes. These impacts are usually lower than those of sales but provide a more accurate depiction of how tourism can impact resident incomes/standard of living. Secondly, the number of jobs created—a very important indicator—needs to be interpreted with caution. Fifty-two new jobs attributed to wine tourism do not necessarily represent new full-time positions, since business owners often release existing employees from other duties to accommodate temporary peak demand, or request existing employees to work overtime (Crompton & McKay, 1994). New hires will most likely be temporary, part time and/or seasonal.

Results of the food tourism study in Table 10.4 can be interpreted similarly.

Table 10.4

Economic Impacts of Food Visitors in Rural Northeast Iowa

Multiplier	Direct Impact	Indirect Impact	Induced Impact	Total Impact
Economic impacts ($ Sales/ output)	1,642,394	464,932	531,480	2,638,811
Economic impacts ($ Value added/ income)	857,234	262,165	293,907	1,413,309
Economic impacts (Employment/ jobs)	39.6	4.9	6.1	51.1

Source: STEP-UNI (2005). A study of place-based food tourism in Northeast Iowa communities.

Finally, Table 10.5 compares tourism multipliers for local food tourism and wine tourism with tourism multipliers from the previous study that examined economic impacts of visitors to the Iowa's Silos and Smokestacks National Heritage Area (SSNHA), one of 49 federally designated heritage areas in the nation that is an Affiliated Area of the National Park Service.

Table 10.5

Tourism Multipliers for Food Tourism, Wine Tourism, and Agritourism/Heritage Tourism in Rural Northeast Iowa

Multiplier	Wine Tourism	Food Tourism	SSNHA Visitors
Sales/output	1.45	1.61	1.66
Value added/ income	1.46	1.64	1.72
Employment/jobs	1.23	1.29	1.34

Sources: STEP-UNI (2006). Development of a regional wine culture in Iowa.
STEP-UNI (2005). A study of place-based food tourism in Northeast Iowa communities.
STEP-UNI (2004). Silos & Smokestacks National Heritage Area tourism study.

Higher multipliers generated by food tourism and visitors to Silos and Smokestacks National Heritage Area can be explained in part by the larger area under examination. As it was noted earlier, larger areas with diversified economies will inadvertently produce higher economic impacts and higher multipliers. In this example, the food tourism study area comprised of the 30 counties, while the wine tourism study included only 10 counties. These contextual differences are important to accurate interpretation of economic impacts and multipliers in both studies.

Summary

This chapter sought to examine economic impacts of community-based tourism. There are a number of reasons why understanding tourism impacts is important for communities:

- Economic significance of tourism gives the industry greater respect among the business community, public officials, and the public in general (Stynes, 1997). This often translates into decisions or public policies that are favorable to tourism.
- Economic impact assessment provides a better understanding of the role and importance of tourism in a regional economy. Comparison of the alternatives can help communities decide where to invest time and resources to get the greatest benefit (Miller, 1996).
- Tourism enterprises depend on each other, other sectors of the economy, local government, as well as local residents. In other words, tourism impacts the entire community one way or another. For tourism to succeed, community support is extremely important, and this support can be acquired by showcasing the positive impacts of tourism on the local economy.

In order to obtain an accurate depiction of economic impacts of tourism on the local economy, communities can choose to use existing data sets, or run their own economic impact analyses using primary data (usually visitor surveys). At the same time, it is extremely important to remember that economic impacts of tourism are only one type of tourism impacts (others being environmental, social, and cultural impacts), and that besides the positive impacts, there are also costs involved. With that in mind, touting the great benefits of tourism will not mean anything to the residents unless there are visible positive changes in the quality of life.

Key Concepts

- Economic, environmental, social, and cultural impacts of tourism
- Direct, indirect, and induced economic impacts
- Economic impact analysis
- Input-output analysis
- Tourism multipliers

Useful Internet Sites, Exercises, and Resources

1. Visit World Travel & Tourism Council website at https://www.wttc.org. Go to "Research" tab, then select "Economic research," "Economic impact analysis." Review several country/ regional/ benchmark reports.
2. Browse website of Tourism Economics at http://www.tourismeconomics.com.
3. Visit U.S. Travel Association website at https://www.ustravel.org. Go to "Research" tab, then select "Economic impact map." Review economic impact of tourism in different states.
4. Browse over a decade of economic impact studies of tourism in the state of New Jersey at http://www.visitnj.org/new-jersey-tourism-research-and-information.

Questions for Review and Case Problems

1. What are the main approaches to tourism economic impact assessment?
2. What is economic impact analysis, and how is it usually done?
3. What are the most common mistakes in economic impact studies?

References

Ap, J., & Crompton, J. (1998). Developing and testing a tourism impact scale. *Journal of Travel Research, 37*(2), 120–130.

Archer, B. H. (1973). *The impact of domestic tourism.* Bangor, UK: University of Wales Press.

Archer, B., & Fletcher, J. (1990). *Multiplier analysis in tourism, cahiers du tourisme.* Série C, No. 103. Centre des Hautes Etudes Touristiques, Aix-en-Provence.

Crompton, J. L. (2006). Economic impact studies: Instruments for political shenanigans? *Journal of Travel Research, 45*(1), 67–82.

Crompton, J. L., & Lee, S. (2000). Programs that work: The economic impact of 30 sports tournaments, festivals, and spectator events in seven U.S. cities. *Journal of Park and Recreation Administration, 18*(2), 107–126.

Crompton, J. L., & McKay, S. L. (1994). Measuring the economic impact of festivals and events: Some myths, misapplications, and ethical dilemmas. *Festival Management and Event Tourism, 2*(1), 33–43.

Destination Marketing Association International. (2017). The DMAI Event Impact Calculator. Retrieved from http://www.destinationmarketing.org/topics/event-impact-calculator

Dwyer, L., Forsyth, P., & Spurr, R. (2006). Assessing the economic impacts of events: A Computable General Equilibrium approach. *Journal of Travel Research, 45*(1), 59–66.

Fletcher, J. E. (1989). Input-output analysis and tourism impact studies. *Annals of Tourism Research, 16*(4), 514–529.

Fletcher, J. E. (1994). Input-output analysis. In S. F. Witt & L. Moutinho (Eds.), *Tourism marketing and management handbook* (2nd ed., pp. 480–484). New York, NY: Prentice Hall.

Frechtling, D. C. (1994). Assessing the economic impacts of travel and tourism: Introduction to travel economic impact estimation. In J. R. Brent Ritchie & C. R. Goeldner (Eds.), *Travel, tourism, and hospitality research: A handbook for managers and researchers* (2nd ed.). New York, NY: John Wiley & Sons.

Kreag, G. (2002). *The impacts of tourism.* Minneapolis, MN: University of Minnesota.

Lankford, S., & Howard, D. (1993). Developing a Tourism Impact Attitude Scale. *Annals of Tourism Research, 21*(1), 121–139.

Liu, J., & Var, T. (1982). Differential multipliers for the accommodation sector. *Tourism Management.* September: 177–187.

Miller, W. P. (1992). *Economic multipliers: how communities can use them for planning.* Cooperative Extension Service, University of Arkansas.

STEP-UNI (2004). Silos & Smokestacks National Heritage Area tourism study. Retrieved from http://www.uni.edu/step

STEP-UNI (2005). A study of place-based food tourism in Northeast Iowa communities. Retrieved from http://www.uni.edu/step

STEP-UNI. (2006). Development of a regional wine culture in Iowa. Retrieved from http://www.uni.edu/step

Stynes, D. J. (1997). *Economic impacts of tourism*. Illinois Bureau of Tourism, Department of Commerce and Community Affairs.

Stynes, D. J. (1999). *Approaches to estimating the economic impacts of tourism: Some examples*. East Lansing, MI: Department of Park, Recreation and Tourism Resources, Michigan State University.

The Outspan Group Inc. (2007). *Economic impact models: an assessment of selected models for British Columbia tourism events, festivals and attractions*. Amherst Island, Ontario.

Tyrrell, T. J., & Johnston, R. J. (2006). The economic impacts of tourism: A special issue. *Journal of Travel Research, 45*(1), 3–7.

CHAPTER 11

Futures of Community-Based Tourism

"Change is the law of life. And those who look only to the past or present are certain to miss the future."

—John F. Kennedy

CHAPTER OBJECTIVES

- To build an awareness of trends and future issues in tourism
- To understand the factors that influence tourism and travel
- To gain specific knowledge of the challenges for labor in tourism and travel

Introduction

Solnit (2011) likens tourism to an invasion where visitors transform a culture. They seek the exotic, the different, or the ancient. But in their wake, "the culture they left behind appears again, or that limbo which is tourist culture springs up, or the place they come to see becomes its own impersonation" (p. 18). Regardless of the impacts, the travel and tourism industry is an important source of revenue and jobs to many economies, families and persons. From the initial planning stages to the trip home, the number of jobs for workers in travel and tourism are on the rise. According to the World Travel and Tourism Council (WTTC), the latest annual research shows the contribution of travel and tourism to world GDP grew for the fifth consecutive year in 2014, rising to a total of 9.8% of world GDP (US$7.6 trillion). The sector now supports nearly 277 million people in employment; that's 1 in 11 jobs on the planet (WTTC, 2015).

This chapter presents selected trends in tourism that may influence community-based tourism. It is important to know that any predictions on the future of tourism should be cautiously considered. For example, many of the studies on future trends are national, regional, and/or global in perspective. Determining local impacts on community-based tourism is relatively risky and problematic from a North American perspective. For example, a study by Dwyer et al. (2008) reports on "Megatrends Underpinning Tourism to 2020." This study focuses on international travel trends and does not necessarily apply to local tourism trends. However, in this chapter we highlight pertinent trends which influence the tourism sector.

Trends in Travel and Tourism

The WTTC (World Travel and Tourism Council), identified four drivers of transformation, listed in Table 11.1, which will affect travel and tourism and the businesses which provide visitor services.

Table 11.1
Transformations in a Rapidly Changing World

Four Drivers of Transformation
1) Global Connectivity • Technological advances are connecting the most remote places and communities. • An increase in trade of goods and services as well as cross-culture understanding. • Negative impact: cultures and natural resources become eroded. Financial crises can jump market to market
2) The Rise of the Rest • Emerging and developing countries are growing and the purchasing power of the global middle class is projected to double by 2030. • An increase in consumer demand and a shift in patterns of demand (geographically and in preferences) • Growing populations put pressure on resources
3) Eco-Limits • We consume more than 50% of the natural resources than the Earth can replenish. It is estimated that we will need two planets by 2030 and three planets by 2050 to sustain us. • Travel and tourism are affected by resource constraints and climate changes, as the industry's growth is expected to take place in regions prone to climate change and resource scarcity
4) Socioeconomic Development and Well-Being • Governments, businesses, and consumers are increasingly focusing on the importance of well-being and sense of empowerment of societies. • Travel and tourism's power to create jobs and bolster whole economies is increasingly recognized as what sets it apart from other industries. • Demographic change, increasingly complex patterns of labor migration, high unemployment, and implications of growing income are aspects of a bigger picture that no industry can ignore • If ignored, risks to short- and long-term business investment strategy will be high. • Travel and tourism businesses will be potentially be forced to delay or cancel their investment and seek opportunities elsewhere.

Travel and tourism expansion in 2017 is forecasted to continue at a stronger rate than ever before and travel and tourism forecasts over the next 10 years look extremely favorable with predicted growth rates of 3.9% annually (WTTC, n.d.). In response, the WTTC has developed "Tourism for Tomorrow" to address the challenges posed by such growth. The WTTC notes that more people have the means to travel, which impacts natural resources. In addition, economic inequality will result if host communities' and employees' needs are not taken into account.

It is WTTC's vision for tourism to respond to the demands of increasing numbers of consumers in the face of shrinking natural resources; to reflect the needs of employees and destination communities; to look beyond competitive boundaries to strike new alliances; and to recognize the need to start addressing these challenges. They are calling on businesses in travel and tourism to be accountable, show leadership, invest in sustainable solutions, and work together to drive real change. For example, WTTC members are spearheading environmental programs such as the Hotel Carbon Measurement Initiative and the Human Capital Initiative. Table 11.2 identifies the ways in which businesses in travel and tourism can respond to lead in a changing world.

Table 11.2
Potential Travel and Tourism Business Response to Changing World Conditions

- **Be Accountable**
  - Take responsibility: understand, identify, measure and publish range of impacts (both positive and negative)
  - Measure: measure, monitor, and evaluate impacts on a regular basis.
  - Report Openly: in a transparent way with clear indicators of progress made and areas to improve

- **Show Leadership**
  - Communicate: public commitment at CEO and board level that is reflected throughout the organization and communicated widely
  - Deliver: actionable projects delivered on the ground so commitments are backed up with real change
  - Encourage: high standards as part of everyday business through educating and empowering consumers, suppliers and employees to make sustainable decisions and publicly recognize best practice

- **Invest**
  - Integrate: sustainable solutions into long-term investment strategies
  - Commit: their own resources through investment programs and strategies with built-in systems which monitor return on investment and value creation according to their impact on "people, planet, and profit."
  - Leverage: investment opportunities available through government and other sources, seeking out joint-funding programs and incentive schemes where they exist, working together to develop them where they do not, and using leadership positions to encourage others to contribute

Table 11.2 (cont.)

• Collaborate
–Identify: new partners and ways of collaborating
–Develop: new networks either within the company or externally with other companies and groups with similar interests
–Unite: together with "one voice."

Francis (2015) provides a summary of future trends and issues in tourism that relates to community tourism. Importantly, one can see a continued trend related to traveling by car close to home and using alternative transportation, while seeking more meaningful experiences. The community-based tourism industry can deliver these experiences to enrich travelers' perspective of the places they visit.

Table 11.3
Travel Trends and Predictions in Community Tourism

Travel with a Purpose	The "why" and "how" of travel will become more important than the "where."
Keeping it Local	People will start traveling to places closer to home.
Alternative Transport	People will use alternative methods for travel (i.e., train, boat, and bike) because of increased costs and carbon footprint awareness.
Changing Climates and Future Planning	Due to climate change, we will see a change in the way destinations are presented and marketed to travelers.

Source: Francis, (2015)

The Center for Responsible Tourism (2015) provided a list of trends and statistics that relate to the future of tourism. Tables 11.4 to 11.6 provide a summary of what the experts say, quotes from surveys and statistics for consumer demand for responsible travel, the business case for responsible tourism, and the destination case for responsible tourism. Throughout the tables, one can see the themes of community, sustainability, and concern for the environment on the part of businesses. Importantly, the greening of the tourism industry globally and locally continues to offer business opportunities and attract tourists. For example, a 2013 study by TripAdvisor found that 85% of U.S. hoteliers indicate that they currently have green practices in place. The Center for Responsible Travel (2015) notes about half of the states in the U.S. have voluntary "green" lodging certification programs, most focused on environmental efficiencies. In several states, including Florida and California, state employers are encouraged to use certified hotels when on state business.

Table 11.4

Future Trends for Consumer Demand for Responsible Travel

Experts Say	Example of Surveys and Statistics
"Responsible travel is moving beyond the confines of ecotravel, ecolodges, and other overtly green offerings. Increasingly, it is about the 'how' as much as the 'what' of travel." —American Society of Travel Writers (ASTA)	Some 43% of respondents said they would be considering the ethical or environmental footprint of their main holiday in 2014, with nearly 10% more saying they would be doing so partially, according to *Blue & Green Tomorrow's Sustainable Tourism 2014*.
	In April 2014, U.S. travelers stated that they turned off lights (96%) and air conditioning (72%) when not in their hotel room, participated in their hotels' towel/linen reuse program (90%), and used their hotels' recycling facilities (81%) in order to travel "green." That said, only 12.7% were willing to pay US$10–$25 extra, while over 30% of global tourists were only willing to pay only US$ 1–$5 extra per night for an environmentally friendly hotel.
	One in five consumers (21%) say they are prepared to pay more for a holiday with a company that has a better environmental and social record; this has increased from 14% in 2012 and 17% in 2010. There is also growing support for holidays to have an environmental and social rating, similar to star ratings for hotels, with over one-third (36%) of consumers in favor of this, up from 25% in 2012 and 29% in 2010.
"The encouraging thing is that sustainable tourism is becoming more widely accepted—so much so that UNESCO, the United Nations Educational, Scientific and Cultural Organization, now believes it will go from 'alternative' to 'mainstream' within a decade." —Alex Blackburne, Editor, *Blue & Green Tomorrow*	A 2013 TripAdvisor.com survey of 1,300 U.S. travelers shows that nearly two-thirds "often" or "always" consider the environment when choosing hotels, transportation and meals.

Table 11.4 (cont.)

	This 2012 National Travel & Tourism Strategy found similar trends among Americans traveling abroad: "Nature-based, culture-based, heritage and outdoor adventure travel represent a significant segment of the outbound tourism market as well."
	In 2014, domestic and international travelers made over 292 million recreation visits to the 370 recreation areas administered by the U.S. National Park Service.
	U.S. consumers who are focused on health and fitness, the environment, personal development, sustainable living and social justice (known as conscientious consumers), number 41 million people, or 19% of U.S. adults, according to a 2012 study by the non-profit organization LOHAS (Lifestyles Of Health And Sustainability). Conscientious travelers are part of this "LOHAS pool."

Table 11.5

Future Trends for the Business Case for Responsible Tourism

Experts Say	Example of Surveys and Statistics
"There are a growing number of consumers, particularly the young, who are prepared to pay a premium for a holiday that is more sustainable.... So, it makes clear economic sense for companies to have a well thought out sustainability plan that sells the positive benefits of sustainability to consumers and taps into this growing market." —Nikki White, Head of Destinations & Sustainability, ABTA	85% of U.S. hoteliers indicate that they currently have "green" practices in place, according to a 2013 study by TripAdvisor.
	A 2013 Conference Board survey of over 120 multinational corporations in Europe and the U.S. found that 73% identified "integrating sustainability into their corporate strategy" as a top priority for their executive leadership team.

Table 11.5 (cont.)

"Being a Responsible Business is part of IHG's DNA. As one of the world's leading hotel companies, with a broad portfolio of brands, we have an unrivalled opportunity to bring about positive change in the environment and community both at a local and global level." —Richard Solomons, Chief Executive Officer, InterContinental Hotel Group	A 2012 report by The Travel Foundation and Forum for the Future identifies six key benefits travel businesses will gain by adopting responsible practices: <ul><li>Reduce costs and improve efficiencies.</li><li>Manage risks and meet emerging legal and regulatory requirements.</li><li>Engage staff in CSR, which has proven to be a key driver of employee satisfaction.</li><li>Gain competitive advantage by offering differentiating experiences to customers.</li><li>Meet emerging consumer trends.</li><li>Protect your business by protecting the environment on which it depends.</li></ul>
	Some specific examples of businesses demonstrating the economic and strategic benefits of sustainability include: <ul><li>Many leading hoteliers have created senior management positions in sustainability, recognizing its importance to their business. Examples include: Marriott, Hilton, IHG, Fairmont, Wyndham, Accor and Kimpton, among hoteliers, as well as Royal Caribbean Cruise Lines, TUI Travel, and Vail Resorts.</li><li>Marriott International has developed a "green" hotel prototype pre-certified by the U.S. Green Building Council as part of its LEED Volume Program. This prototype saves Marriott's hotel owners an average of $100,000 in development costs, six months in design time, and up to 25% in terms of energy and water consumption.</li></ul>

Table 11.6

Future Trends for the Destination Case for Responsible Tourism

Experts Say	Example of Surveys and Statistics
"In a growing number of destinations, the business leaders, citizens, and government authorities are realizing that safeguarding their distinctive sense of place—cultural assets, natural habitats, historic feature, scenic appeal —are essential for reaping the benefits of responsible tourism. A trend to encourage." —Jonathan Tourtellot, Geotourism Editor, *National Geographic Traveler*	The UNWTO predicts that ecotourism, nature, heritage, cultural, and "soft adventure" tourism will grow rapidly over the next two decades and global spending on ecotourism is expected to increase at a higher rate than the tourism industry as a whole.
"Tourism—done right—can be a powerful tool for conserving wilderness and heritage areas. For both traveler and local, it increases appreciation of the spiritual and environmental importance of conserving biodiversity." —Kerry Lorimer, *Code Green: Experiences of a Lifetime*	Ecotourism has made its mark worldwide as a popular way to see the sights without leaving a trace. Such tourism could grow to 25% of the global travel market within six years and account for US\$ 470 billion per year in revenues, according to The International Ecotourism Society (TIES).
"In the end it's all about protecting our product. If the product—our destinations—aren't protected in environmental and social terms then people won't want to visit them; it is as simple as that." —John De Vial, Head of Financial Protection, ABTA	The 2012 Trip Advisor survey found that travelers rank the "top three eco-friendly" U.S. cities as Portland, Oregon; San Francisco, California; and Seattle, Washington.
"Destinations are threatened by climate change impacts, extreme weather, water scarcity, unprecedented rates of biodiversity loss, disease and growing poverty and inequality… Sustainable tourism addresses the challenges head on, by protecting destinations at the same time as enhancing brand value, increasing profits, saving costs, and improving competitive positioning, both for attracting and retaining customers and recruiting the best talent," according to the 2012 study by The Travel Foundation and Forum for the Future.	In 2011, *Condé Nast Traveler* ranked Charleston, South Carolina, as the "Top U.S. City" based on its annual Readers' Choice survey. In the previous 14 Readers' Choice surveys (1997–2010), Charleston was ranked in the top five cities. The city's well-regulated, overnight tourism centered on its historic homes, buildings, and culture attracts four million annual visitors and generates more than US\$ 3 billion in annual revenue.

The United States Travel Association provides ongoing travel facts and statistics for the travel industry. The following information is retrieved from the USTA, 2015 Travel Facts and Statistics. Travel facts and statistics include the following:

1. Fewer adults are traveling with children. In 2012, 26% of domestic leisure travelers traveled with children under the age of 18 (408.5 million trips) compared with 2008, when 31% of adults traveled with children (466.2 million trips).

2. Driving versus flying. In 2012, 33% of domestic business trips included air travel compared to just 11% of leisure trips. Nearly eight in 10 (79%) leisure trips were by car, compared to less than half (48%) of business trips.

3. Leisure travelers are older than business travelers.
   - The average age of leisure travelers is 47.5 years old. Mature travelers comprise 36% of leisure travel volume (18% are 65+, 18% are 55–64). Nearly two in 10 (19%) are 45–55, 17% are 35–44, 20% are 25–34; and 8% are 18–24 years old.
   - The average age for business travelers is 45.9 years old. The majority (26%) are aged 45–54; 20% are 55–64; nearly one quarter (24%) are 35–44; 19% 25–34; and 4% are 18–24 years of age. Only 7% are 65+.

4. Trip planning sources have shifted over the last several years, with social media and mobile devices being used more often. In 2012, nearly one-quarter (23%) of domestic leisure travelers relied on friends and relatives to plan their trips, while three in ten (31%) utilized their own past experiences. One in 10 used destination websites, 9% used traveler provider websites (airline, hotel, rental car, cruise, tours, etc.), 5% used social networking, and 4% used a mobile device to help plan their trip.

- Compared to 2009, only 2% used social networking sources, and 1% used their mobile device to assist in trip planning. Direct experiences and destination websites were relied on slightly more in 2009 than in 2012.

Leisure Travel
- Direct spending on leisure travel by domestic and international travelers totaled $644.9 billion in 2014.
- Spending on leisure travel generated $96.6 billion in tax revenue.
- More than three out of four domestic trips taken are for leisure purposes (78%).
- Leisure travel for U.S. residents in 2014 generated $1.7 billion.
- Top leisure travel activities for U.S. domestic travelers are (1) visiting relatives, (2) shopping, (3) visiting friends, (4) fine dining, and (5) beaches.

Business Travel
- Direct spending on business travel by domestic and international travelers, including expenditures on meetings, events, and incentive programs (ME&I), totaled $230 billion in 2014.
- ME&I travel accounted for $114.2 billion of all business travel spending.
- U.S. residents logged 452 billion person-trips* for business purposes in 2014, with 36.7% for meetings and events.
- For every dollar invested in business travel, businesses benefit from an average of $9.50 in increased revenue and $2.90 in new profits (2012).

*Person-trip defined as one person on a trip away from home overnight in paid accommodations or on a day or overnight trip places 50 miles or more (one-way) away from home.

An interesting assessment demonstrating the power of travel in the United States was presented by the U.S. Travel Association. The project "Time Off" is a research-driven initiative to prove the personal, business, social, and economic benefits of taking earned time off. The aim of the project is to shift business culture so that the perception of using personal time off (PTO) is not considered frivolous, but essential to strengthening relationships and improving personal health, a business investment with proven returns, and an economic necessity. As the conveners of a national movement to change how Americans view time off, U.S. Travel had to lead by example. But a review of the numbers revealed that the association's staff included some of the worst offenders of passing on PTO. For example, the U.S. Travel President and CEO Roger Dow examined days off with his employees, at the end of 2013. He realized his 55-person trade association was carrying a $353,000 vacation liability—more than $6,400 per staffer. It was a number that has steadily climbed; in just 10 years, it had grown 126%.

Among the findings of the study, it was found that using the 429 million days of time off (to which workers have access) would deliver a $160 billion increase to the U.S. economy, create 1.2 million new American jobs, and generate $21 billion in federal, state, and local revenues. Recommendations include the following:

- Encouraging workers to use just one more day each year would generate $73 billion annually for our economy.
- It's not just the $54 billion in earned benefits that employees forfeit each year by skipping on vacation to serve as veritable volunteers at work. And it's not just the $224 billion vacation liability sitting on the balance sheets of the U.S. private sector, accrued over years of paid time off (PTO) rollover. Those big numbers matter, but foregoing vacation hits employees' health, happiness, and performance at work—something that can be just as harmful to a business as a balance sheet liability. Each year, Americans fail to use 429 million vacation days, and with those days, $160 billion in economic opportunity is lost.

A review of the trends exposes the inter-relationship between social, cultural, and environmental conditions. The travel and tourism industry will have to adjust to changing social, cultural, and environmental conditions in order to stay economically viable. Regardless, the desire to travel is long-standing and will likely continue in the future no matter the means available to travel. Figure 11.1 summarizes the future trends travel and tourism must embrace. Successful community initiatives will address resident as well as visitor needs and in doing so will support the quality of community life.

Figure 11.1 and 11.2 display future trends that affect tourism in international and local markets. Many of these trends have been identified by the WTTC, USTA, the Center for Responsible Tourism, and other organizations tracking travel and tourism trends. There are a number of additional trends displayed including the "sharing economy," regional airports, cost factors, epidemics/pandemics and terrorism.

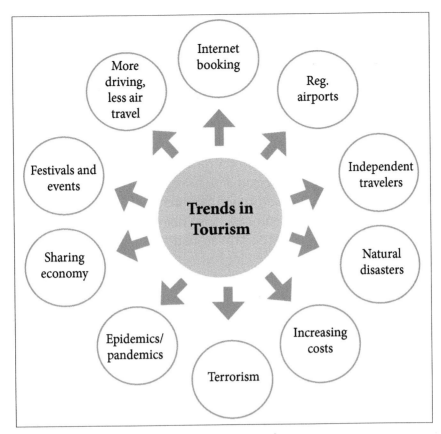

Figure 11.1. Broad Future Trends that Affect Tourism

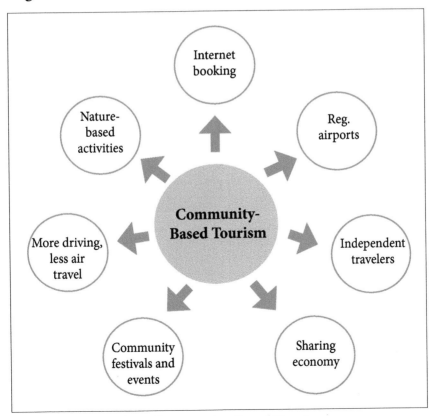

Figure 11.2. Trends in Community-Based Tourism

The "sharing economy" or "collaborative consumption" describes the shift in economic activity that uses information and social technologies to "share" goods or services typically with a monetary value. Mobile technologies, GPS-enabled smartphones, and an increasing trust of the Internet and online payments have enable a shift toward the "sharing economy." The term "sharing economy" appeared after 2000 and has become widely used in the travel and tourism industry. Craigslist is an example of a common platform used in the sharing economy. Although corporations, nonprofits, and government use information technology to share resources, the opportunity is available for peer-to-peer sharing. A person who has an extra bedroom, house, or even couch is now able to share that resource through the Internet using a variety of platforms. Airbnb (http://www.airbnb.com/) is an example of this type of platform. Airbnb is an online marketplace for people to list, discover, and book unique accommodations around the world. It has over 600,000 listings across 160 countries. Table 11.7 lists a number of platforms available in the travel and tourism industry that offer a range of services in the lodging, transportation, dining, and entertainment industries. Whether it is a monetary or social paradigm shift, the sharing economy has influenced the travel and tourism industry.

Table 11.7
Examples of Sharing Economy Services in Travel and Tourism Industry

Lodging	Transportation	Dining	Entertainment
Airbnb	Uber	Eatwith	Vayable
HomeAway	Lyft	Feastly	Sidetour
VRBO	Sidecar	Cookening	Incrediblue
Flipkey	Carpooling	Cookisto	Getyourguide
Roomorama	Blablacar	Kitchensurfing	Boatbound
Wimdu	Zimride		GetmyBoat
9Flats	Relayrides		Dopios
OneFineStay	Getaround		
Housetrip	Flightcar		
Homestay			
Couchsurfing			
Homeexchange			
Lovehomeswap			
Guesttoguest			
Knok			

Summary

It is WTTC's vision for tourism to respond to the demands of increasing numbers of consumers in the face of shrinking natural resources; to reflect the needs of employees and destination communities; to look beyond competitive boundaries to strike new alliances; and to recognize the need to start addressing these challenges. They are calling on businesses in travel and tourism to be accountable, show leadership, invest in sustainable solutions, and work together to drive real change. The themes of community, sustainability and concern for the environment on the part of businesses are central to future trends. Importantly, the greening of the tourism industry globally and locally continues to offer business opportunities and attract tourists.

A review of the trends exposes the inter-relationship between social, cultural, and environmental conditions. The travel and tourism industry will have to adjust to changing social, cultural, and environmental conditions in order to stay economically viable. Regardless, the desire to travel is long-standing and will likely continue in the future no matter the means available to travel.

The "sharing economy" or "collaborative consumption" describes the shift in economic activity which uses information and social technologies to "share" goods or services typically with a monetary value. Mobile technologies, GPS-enabled smartphones, and an increasing trust of the Internet and online payments have enable a shift toward the "sharing economy."

Key Concepts

- Futures of tourism
- Trends affecting tourism
- Labor and employment in tourism
- Employment types and opportunities
- Training opportunities

Useful Internet Sites, Exercises, and Resources

http://crctourism.com.au/wms/upload/resources/bookshop/FactSheets/80046_Dwyer_SUMMARY_SHEET.pdf

http://www.responsibletravel.com/resources/future-of-tourism/travel-trends.htm

http://www.projecttimeoff.com/resources/fact-sheets/project-time-research-overview

http://en-corporate.canada.travel/resources-industry/tools
http://www.ustravel.org/

http://tiac.travel/_Library/TIAC_Publications/TIAC_Annual_Report_EN_FINAL.pdf

http://www.wttc.org/mission/tourism-for-tomorrow/

http://www.wttc.org/mission/tourism-for-tomorrow/

Exercise 1

1. Visit the Canada and U.S. Travel website and compare, contrast and discuss the future trends for both countries.

Questions for Review

1. Identify the trends of tourism development in your home town or area.
2. What factors or trends impact the success for tourism is prevalent in your home town or area?
3. Can you identify the key trends in tourism for the future?
4. What trends do you think will help local tourism?
5. What trends do you think will hinder local tourism?

References

Center for Responsible Travel. (2015). The case for responsible travel. Retrieved from http://www.responsibletravel.org/resources/documents/2015%20Trends%20&%20Statistics_Final.pdf

Dwyer, L., Edwards, D., Mistilis, N., Roman, C., Scott, N., & Cooper, C. (2008). Mega-trends underpinning tourism 2020. Retrieved from http://crctourism.com.au/wms/upload/resources/bookshop/FactSheets/80046_Dwyer_SUMMARY_SHEET.pdf, September 13, 2015.

Forum for the Future. (2012). Tourism 2023. Retrieved from https://www.forumfor-thefuture.org/sites/default/files/project/downloads/tourism-2023execsummary.pdf

Francis, J. (2015). Travel trends and predictions. Responsible Travel.com. Retrieved from http://www.responsibletravel.com/resources/future-of-tourism/travel-trends.htm

Solnit, R. (2011). *A book of migrations*. London, UK, New York, NY: Verso.

Trip Advisor. (2013). TripA dvisor green leaders program highlights eco-friendly hotels to help travelers plan greener trips. Retrieved from http://www.tripadvisor.com/PressCenter-i5903-c1-Press_Releases.html.

United Nations World Tourism Organization. (2010). Basic concepts and definitions: Travel and tourism. Retrieved from http://unstats.un.org/unsd/tradeserv/Workshops/Chisinau/docs/05%20a%20-%20UNWTO-Basis%20concepts.pdf

U.S. Travel Association. (2014). U.S. travel answer sheet. Retrieved from https://www.ustravel.org/sites/default/files/page/2009/09/US_Travel_AnswerSheet_June_2014.pdf, June 7, 2015.

U.S. Travel Association. (2015). Travel facts and statistics. Retrieved from https://www.ustravel.org/about-us-travel

World Travel and Tourism Council. (n.d.). Economic impact analysis. Retrieved from https://www.wttc.org/research/economic-research/economic-impact-analysis

CHAPTER 12

Careers in Community-Based Tourism

"This diversified, highly lucrative field offers jobs involving a host of specialized functions and includes such elements as travel agencies, cruise ship and tour-group companies, airlines, hotels and resorts, theme parks, and numerous other attractions and services."

–R. Kraus (2002)

CHAPTER OBJECTIVES

- To gain knowledge of the types of careers in tourism
- To understand the requirements for careers in tourism and travel
- To appreciate the training opportunities for tourism careers

Introduction

This chapter presents various statistics on training, employment opportunities, and careers for community tourism. A job in travel and tourism can be an exciting career path, whether you enjoy traveling or providing educational and entertainment services to visitors and community residents. Positions in this field range from travel agents to marketing roles in international tourism departments, to local visitor and guide services. These jobs do tend to fluctuate with the economy, since people tend to travel less during periods of recession or unemployment. However, it is expected that the travel and tourism industry will continue to experience continued growth, so careers in this field are promising.

Tourism is a diverse industry that offers long-term career opportunities for individuals who want to put their education and skills to work in various environments. People in tourism may work indoors or outdoors, standard hours or on a flexible schedule, seasonal jobs or year-round. The opportunities are unlimited.

Tourism Training and Education

There is a long-standing debate as to whether tourism is in fact an industry on its own or rather a field of study (Tribe, 1997). Edgell (1990), for example, argues that "there is no other industry in the economy that is linked to so many diverse and different kinds of products and services" (p. 7), and labels tourism the most "wide-ranging industry." As a consequence, there appears to be no consensus on what tourism as an industry entails. As Youell (1998) explains:

> If we consider that the study of tourism impinges on such disciplines as geography, psychology, sociology, economics, anthropology, planning, business studies, politics, and economics, to name but a few, it is easy to understand the difficulty in agreeing on a workable definition. Sectors as diverse as hotels, leisure centres, local government planning departments, airlines, conservation bodies, travel agencies, museums, transport providers, and entertainment complexes all lay claim to inclusion in any definition of tourism (p. 9).

One can easily locate a broad range of tourism degrees offered, as there is no common agreement about the nature of tourism skills. Originating from technical training schools in Europe, tourism curriculum has been dominated by a focus on specific occupational skills (Inui, Wheeler, & Lankford, 2006). Until recently, much of tourism training has been very specialized (i.e., ticketing agents, hotel chefs, etc.), and has mostly taken place within hotel and hospitality management. These inconsistencies have led Tribe (1997) as far as to speak of the "indiscipline" of tourism.

This is important for a number of reasons. Employing highly skilled staff is critical to the success of any destination, and competitiveness of the entire tourism industry greatly depends on the availability of good quality personnel to deliver, operate, and manage the tourism product (Amoah & Baum, 1997). However, since different sectors of the industry require different sets of skills, it does not seem feasible to design a "one-size-fits-all" education or training tourism program (Airey & Johnson, 1999; Wattanacharoensil, 2014). It is important to note that the nature of tourism education is driven by business and economic considerations (Inui, Wheeler, & Lankford, 2006).

The interdisciplinary nature of tourism calls for a number of disciplines to study the field, and Tribe (1997) argues that all of them could be grouped into business and nonbusiness elements. Maintaining a precise distinction between the two is difficult, but it has been suggested that an industrial placements may provide a guide to the business orientation of individual courses. Most often this is done through internships, apprenticeships, student work experiences, practicums, and sandwich placement programs (Busby, 2003; Tribe, 2001).

The purpose of practical student experiences is to increase student employability, but even more so to close the gap between tourism education and real or perceived needs of the tourism industry. As Amoah and Baum (1997) argue, contents of higher education curriculum have often focused on providing broad-based, generic knowledge, while "the industry seeks personal skills such as communication, adaptability, leadership, and numeracy... it has even been said that small-firm employers especially tend to prefer job experience to qualifications in recruitment" (p. 7). In support, Churchward and

Riley (2002) observe that traditional emphasis of higher education curriculum on the fundamental theories and principles of the operations and management originated from the assumption that the industry will teach specific application. However, recent focus on increasing employability of graduates has shifted this emphasis to preparing students ready to be placed in positions of responsibility with minimal need for additional training (Chen & Gursoy, 2009). Programs that incorporate internships seem to be successful in this regard, and graduate employability is becoming more important for purposes of benchmarking, rankings, as well as a criterion in prospective student decision making.

There is no common agreement about the nature of skills needed for positions in tourism, but there appears to be a set of skills applicable across different sectors—so-called transferable skills—that are becoming central in many tourism education and training programs. In the early 1990s, a number of governments suggested that educational institutions adapt their program offerings to develop transferable skills in their graduates. These skills are often viewed as key to ensuring that the labor force is flexible and able to adapt to the rapidly changing market (DfEE, 1998). Two sets of checklists of transferable skills are outlined below. Among many studies examining transferable skills two are worth noting: a study by Gibbs, Rust, Jenkins, & Jaques (1994) and a government-commissioned study by Coopers & Lybrand (1998) (see Table 12.1).

Table 12.1

Checklist of Transferable Skills/Skills to Improve Employability

Gibbs, Rust, Jenkins, & Jaques (1994)
- Communication skills (writing reports, giving presentations, using media)
- Group work skills (leadership, sharing, co-operation, teamwork)
- Personal skills (independence, autonomy, self-assessment, self-confidence)
- Interpersonal skills (influencing, counseling, listening, interviewing, assertiveness, negotiation)
- Organizational skills (time management, project management, objective-setting, project evaluation)
- Teaching and training skills (identifying learning needs, designing and running workshops, coaching, peer tutoring)
- Information gathering skills (locating information sources, evaluating sources and data, extracting relevant information, interpretation of data, presentation of data)
- Problem-solving skills (problem analysis, creative problem solving, decision-making)
- Language skills (oral skills, use of a foreign language)
- Information technology skills (using work processing, databases, spread-sheets, graphics)
- Entrepreneurship skills (taking initiatives, seizing opportunities, creativity)

Coopers & Lybrand (1998)
- Traditional intellectual skills (i.e. critical thinking)
- The "new" core skills (communication skills, technology skills, and numeracy skills)
- Personal attributes such as self-reliance, adaptability, flexibility, creativity, drive, etc.
- Personal attributes such as self-reliance, adaptability, flexibility, creativity, drive, etc.

In addition to developing transferable skills in graduates, it has also been suggested that tourism programs should constantly monitor the field and stay in touch with industry professionals to identify any gaps that may exist between their perceptions and the current curriculum (Chen & Gursoy, 2009). Ideally, the programs would be able to close the gap between what is taught to students and what the industry expects of the students being hired.

But tourism is a rapidly changing industry, meaning that existing job descriptions and requirements keep changing, and new jobs are being created all the time. As a result, more than just a degree in tourism is needed to be successful in the industry. As Petrova and Mason (2004) point out, the value of a degree in tourism may be less about the knowledge gained in studying and more about the evidence of interest and commitment to the tourism industry. They quote a tour operator:

> A degree in tourism does not mean that you are going to be successful in the industry. It means you have got good background, a good understanding, but it is all about the individual and how they choose to use that. (Petrova & Mason, 2004, p. 160)

In the end, students who graduate with unrealistic career expectations fail to secure their dream jobs because they are unprepared for the ever-changing job market (Chen & Gursoy, 2009). Several research studies suggest the following strategies to prepare and succeed in the tourism industry:

- Develop transferable skills to increase employability (see the list above)
- Focus on academic subjects closely related to specific needs in the field, such as programming, marketing, finance, management, and human resources (Busby, 2003; Kraus, 2002)
- Seek experiences to develop leadership, managerial, communication, planning and technical skills (Ehlers, 2005; Mayo & Thomas-Haysbert, 2005)
- Get an industry experience through an internship
- Remember, flexibility is one of the most important success factors in the tourism field (Clark & Schukar, 2003)
- Be proactive and prepared for the changes, continue to learn and improve new professional skills, and develop a lifelong learning attitude long after graduation (Chen & Gursoy, 2009)

Tourism Careers

Tourism is highly labor intensive and a significant source of employment around the world. It accounts for almost 10% of the world's GDP and 6% of global trade. According to the World Travel & Tourism Council (WTTC), the industry will account for 1 in 10 jobs on the planet by 2023). Data from the International Labor Organization shows that accommodation and restaurants, together with other private sector services, are expected to create jobs at the fastest rate of any sector in the economy for the next five years (UNWTO, 2015). Indeed, over the period of 2009–2013, employment in hotels and restaurants in OECD countries grew on average by 1.4% per year, as compared with growth of 0.7% in the economy as a whole (Stacey, 2015).

Tourism industry is rather unique in that it accounts for a higher share of women's employment and entrepreneurship as compared to the broader economy, and creates employment opportunities for young people (G20, 2015). At a 2015 G20 series of meetings of leaders and ministers of the world's 20 major economies, tourism ministers of G20 members specifically focused on the capacity of tourism to promote more and better jobs, in particular for women and youth as a means to reduce inequalities at national and international level and promote inclusive and robust growth.

Tourism industry as an employer faces many challenges, among them seasonality, high share of SMEs, working conditions, recruitment and retention difficulties, high turnover and vacancy rates, poor image, and weak training culture. At the same time, tourism creates jobs for people of all ages and skill levels, and provides opportunities to enter the labor market, gain experience, develop skills and move up the value chain into higher level, better paid positions (Stacey, 2015). Careers in tourism have always been popular since they provide the opportunity to join an exciting industry that is an important part of the world economy.

Tourism provides a broad range of career opportunities in industries that include the following (Williams, n.d.):

- Hotels and resorts
- Restaurants and commercial food service
- Meeting and event planning
- Tourism destinations and attractions
- Leisure, recreation and sports management
- Airlines, cruises and other transportation
- Environmentally sustainable and cultural tourism development
- Spa and wellness management

Travel and tourism is comprised of three predominate industries: transportation, tourism, and hospitality. While you're traveling, you will realized the types of jobs people are working: there is someone accountable for the mode of transportation, someone responsible for booking your tickets, someone in charge of the activities in which you take part in, someone taking care of your entertainment in the evening, serving your drinks, and showing you the sights. Figure 12.1 lists the types of jobs in each industry. Table 12.2 suggests possible career paths in several selected sectors of the tourism industry.

Among different sectors of the industry, the entertainment and commercial recreation are projected to grow 31% over the period of 2006–2016. As a result, employment in the meeting, convention, and event planning sector is expected to grow 33% over the period of 2012–2022, much faster than the average for all occupations (Bureau of Labor Statistics, 2014). Those employed in this field work in a wide variety of outdoor and indoor settings ranging from huge events like the Olympics, small corporate incentive travel programs, ecotourism companies in national/state parks, professional sports teams, convention and visitors' bureaus, to theme parks. A closer look at some of the possible careers in hospitality and event management is provided in Tables 12.3 and 12.4.

Transportation	Tourism	Hospitality
• Airlines • Bus companies • Cruise companies • Railroads • Rental car companies • Bicycle rentals	• Tourism technology • Travel agencies • Tour companies • Attractions • Festivals and events • Sports tourism • Tourist offices and administration centers • Convention and visitor bureaus and destination management organizations	• Hotels, motels, and resorts • Food service • Bars/pubs

Figure 12.1. Career opportunities in transportation, tourism, and hospitality industries.

Table 12.2
Career Paths in Selected Sectors of Tourism

Tourism operations	Office assistant Site guide Museum attendant Sales executive
Attractions and theme parks	Attractions attendant Ticket sales officer Guest service coordinator Marketing/sales supervisor
Guiding	Ranger Tour leader/manager Tour guide
Tour wholesaling	Sales reservation agent Group tour coordinator
Retail travel sales	Travel sales assistant Travel consultant
Visitor information services	Booking agent Travel advisor Area tourism manager
Meetings and events	Conference assistant Meetings manager Event manager

Source: Tourism Training Australia (2002)

Table 12.3
Careers in Hospitality Management

Hotel management	Hotels, resorts and clubs Food and beverage Spas and private clinics Catering and banquets Facilities
Tourism management	Travel Transport and logistics Ecotourism and sustainable tourism Cruises
Hospitality real estate and finance	Investment banking Asset management Finance and revenue Real estate investment portfolio manager Property management
Hospitality marketing	Digital marketing Brand management Communications Public relations Media
Human resources management	Training and development Talent acquisition Incentives and reward programs
Hospitality event management	Hotel event and conference planning Project management Catering and event entrepreneur Promotion, sponsorship and media for events

Source: Glion Institute of Higher Education, 2015.

Table 12.4
Careers in Event, Sport, and Entertainment Management

Event management	Event team account manager Event logistics manager Project manager at an event agency Marketing events manager Communications and marketing Conference manager

Table 12.4 (cont.)

Sport management	VIP guest and visitor services Events and competition prize manager Tour manager Sponsorship and media coordinator Venue manager
Entertainment management	Production manager Exhibition organizer Sponsorship and digital sales manager Creative production manager Content manager/producer Fund-raising and marketing manager

Source: Glion Institute of Higher Education (2015)

It is relatively easy to find job opportunities in the industry, since it is so large and there are so many types of visitor establishments and attractions. We suggest the following strategies to help one further increase employability and chances for a successful career:

- Take classes in business, marketing, public relations, and human resources
- Consider study abroad for a semester
- Gain experience in decision-making, planning, budgeting, and human resources through internships, student co-op opportunities, and summer jobs
- Seek leadership roles in student organizations and professional associations. Attend their meetings and conferences
- Gain relevant experience at related organizations such as restaurants, campus dining facilities, hotels, conference centers, recreational venues, and attractions. Prepare to work "from the bottom up" to gain industry experience
- Gain experience through planning activities and events on and off campus
- Develop excellent interpersonal and public speaking skills
- Study the industry leaders and trends by reading professional publications
- Learn to pay attention to details, working well in teams, handling stress, and meeting deadlines

Summary

In summary, the tourism industry is incredibly diverse, and is already responsible for more than 10% of global employment. A great benefit of working in the travel and tourism industry is the fact that the field is international and changes along with global trends (Segal, 2015). Among trends impacting jobs in tourism, the following are worth noting here:

1. **As the number of emerging tourism destinations continues to grow, the number of available careers in travel and tourism will continue to increase as well.** According to the World Tourism Organization, the number of international tourists is projected to reach 1.2 billion by 2020. The top three tourism regions are expected to be Europe (717 million tourists), East Asia, and the Pacific (397

million), and the Americas (282 million), followed by Africa, the Middle East, and South Asia. We can safely assume that a great number of new jobs will be available in these destinations (Envisage International Corporation, 2015).

2. **While tourism has traditionally been an industry that emphasized hands-on experience, the competitive nature of the business now requires a combination of experience and higher education to build a successful career.** Tourism is changing and becoming increasingly complex, requiring higher level skills and opening up new career opportunities, while still offering a core pool of low skilled jobs. Higher education credentials greatly increase employability prospects; research shows that around three-quarters of travel and tourism graduates are in employment six months after finishing their studies. However, there is more than one pathway to a successful career, and it may not always be in a straight line.

3. **The travel and tourism industry appears to be in consolidation mode (according to industry analysis by Hoover's Inc.).** This means that smaller companies are merging or being acquired by big players like American Express, Marriott, and Carlson Wagonlit. It might make sense to begin one's career with one of the larger corporations in order to gain exposure to many facets of the business while having relative job security (Segal, 2015).

4. **Emphasis on transferable skills.** Tourism professionals are not bound by traditional career paths or narrow definition of a profession; this gives them a great freedom to pursue careers across boundaries. Tourism is known to offer a huge range and diversity of career paths and potentially a very rewarding future, and individual success is often determined by one's ability to demonstrate transferable skills. In particular, employers feel that there is a need for better team-working skills, customer service skills, communication skills, planning and organizing, and problem-solving skills.

Key Concepts

- Employment types and opportunities
- Training opportunities

Useful Internet Sites, Exercises, and Resources

1. Visit a job search website, such as https://www.monster.com, search for travel and tourism jobs. Browse the results of your search.

2. Visit All About Careers website at https://www.allaboutcareers.com, search for "tourism." Browse career requirements for a broad range of sectors that comprise the tourism industry.

3. Visit Tourism HR Canada website at http://www.discovertourism.ca. Take one of the tourism career quizzes.

Exercise I

Visit the Canada Travel website and the U.S. Travel website to examine the similarities and differences in the labor markets for the future.

Questions for Review

1. Identify the types of tourism jobs in your home town or area.
2. What jobs do you find most appealing?
3. What training is needed for the jobs you have identified in question 2?

References

Airey, D., & Johnson, S. (1999). The content of tourism degree courses in the UK. *Tourism Management, 20*(2), 229–235.

Amoah, V. A., & Baum, T. (1997). Tourism education: Policy versus practice. *International Journal of Contemporary Hospitality Management, 9*(1), 5–12.

Bureau of Labor Statistics, U.S. Department of Labor. (2014). *Occupational outlook handbook, 2014-15 edition*. Meeting, convention, and event planners. Retrieved from http://www.bls.gov/ooh

Busby, G. (2003). Tourism degree internships: a longitudinal study. *Journal of Vocational Education and Training, 55*(3), 319–334.

Chen, B. T., & Gursoy, D. (2007). Preparing students for careers in the leisure, recreation, and tourism field. *Journal of Teaching in Travel & Tourism, 7*(3), 21–41.

Churchward, J., & Riley, M. (2002). Tourism occupations and education: an exploratory study. *International Journal of Tourism Research, 4*(2), 77–86.

Clark, S., & Schukar, C. (2003). The wide world of parks and recreation. *Parks & Recreation, 38*(10), 56–63.

Coopers & Lybrand. (1998). *Skills development in higher education*. Report for CVCP/ DfEE/HEQE, November, London: Committee of Vice-Chancellors and Principals of the universities of the UK (CVCP).

DfEE. (1998). Toward a national skills agenda. National Skills Taskforce, DfEE SKTI, 15.

Edgell, D. L. (1990). *International tourism policy*. New York, NY: Van Nostrand Reinhold.

Ehlers, A. (2005). A study of recruitment competency indicators for potential hospitality employees. *Consortium Journal of Hospitality and Tourism, 9*(2), 59–68.

Envisage International Corporation. (2015). Careers in tourism. Retrieved from http://www.internationalstudent.com/study-tourism/careers-in-tourism

G20. (2015). G20 Ministers of Tourism discuss how tourism can create more and better jobs. Retrieved from https://g20.org/

Gibbs, G., Rust, C., Jenkins, A. & Jaques, D. (1994). *Developing students' transferable skills*. Oxford Brookes, UK: Oxford Centre for Staff Development.

Glion Institute of Higher Education. (2015). Hospitality and event management careers. Retrieved from http://www.glion.edu/your-future-career

Inui, Y., Wheeler, D., & Lankford, S. (2006). Rethinking tourism education: What should schools teach? *Journal of Hospitality, Leisure, Sport and Tourism Education, 5*(2), 25–35.

Kraus, R. (2002). Careers in recreation: expanding horizons. *Journal of Physical Education, Recreation and Dance, 73*(5), 46–49.

Mayo, C., & Thomas-Haysbert, C. (2005). Core competencies needed by hospitality graduates. *Consortium Journal of Hospitality and Tourism Management, 9*(2), 5–18.

Petrova, P., & Mason, P. (2004). The value of tourism degrees: A Luton-based case study. *Education + Training, 46*(3), 153–161.

Segal, N. (2015). Careers in travel and tourism. Retrieved from http://career-advice.monster.com

Stacey, J. (2015). Supporting quality jobs in tourism. *OECD Tourism Papers*. Paris: OECD Publishing.

Tribe, J. (1997). The indiscipline of tourism. *Annals of Tourism Research, 24*(3), 638–657.

Tribe J. (2001). Research paradigms and the tourism curriculum. *Journal of Travel Research, 39*(4), 442–448.

Tourism Training Australia. (2002). Tourism industry sector career paths. Retrieved from http://www.tourismtraining.com.au

UNWTO. (2015, 01 October). Press release: UNWTO welcomes the G20 Tourism Ministers' commitment to promote more and better jobs. Retrieved from http://media.unwto.org

Wattanacharoensil, W. (2014). Tourism curriculum in a global perspective: past, present, and future. *International Education Studies, 7*(1), 9–20.

Williams, L. L. (n.d.). Is a career in hospitality and tourism in your future? Retrieved from http://www.internationalstudentguidetotheusa.com

Youell, R. (1998). *Tourism: An introduction*. Harlow, UK: Longman.

Index

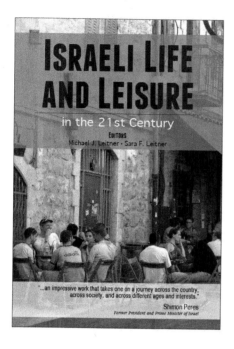

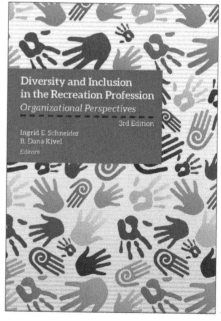